I0058176

# BANKING AND THE BUSINESS CYCLE

## A Study of the Great Depression in the United States

C. A. PHILLIPS, Ph.D.

*Dean, the College of Commerce,*
*State University of Iowa*

T. F. McMANUS, Ph.D.
*College of New Rochelle, New York*

R. W. NELSON, Ph.D.
*State University of Iowa*

The Ludwig von Mises Institute
2014
ISBN: 978-1-610160-37-7

*"* * * reckless inflations of credit—the chief cause of all economic malaise * * *"*
Alfred Marshall


*"* * * the recent world-wide fall of prices is best described as a monetary phenomenon which has occurred as the result of the monetary system failing to solve successfully a problem of unprecedented difficulty and complexity set it by a conjunction of highly intractable non-monetary phenomena."*
The Macmillan Committee Report

# PREFACE

The task that is attempted in this book is a contribution
to an understanding of the banking and financial events of
the War and post-War period as the underlying causes of
the Great Depression in the United States.   There were
many causes which contributed to this collapse; among
others, mention might be made of misguided tariff policy,
war debts, monopolistic practices.   Our failure to accord
certain non-monetary phenomena special treatment is not
to be construed as disregarding their influence; we have pre-
ferred to focus attention upon those causes which we believe
to be predominantly basic.

There is good reason for this belief.   In no previous depression have all of the same non-monetary phenomena
been present; in no previous depression have the monetary
phenomena been absent.   The financial mistakes of the past
two decades are not dissimilar to those of England during
and following the Napoleonic Wars, and the inflation of the
Civil War and the depression of the 'seventies bear striking
resemblance to the recent upheaval; the follies of the ages
are repeated again and again.   It is a melancholy fact that
each generation must relearn the fundamental principles of
money in the bitter school of experience.   The inflationists, it
would seem, we always have with us.   It is nevertheless a
duty of economists to devote attention to periodic reiteration
of the ancient truths of monetary science; it is necessary to
make as familiar as possible the workings of the financial
machinery if further errors are to be avoided in the future.
It is to the mismanagement of the monetary mechanism
that most of our recent troubles are chiefly ascribable.   And
with the juggernaut of another inflationary boom already
upon us, emphasis upon the monetary causes of the last
depression, to the neglect of others, is not only warranted

but needful if progress toward an understanding of business cycles is to be expected.

The scope of this study we have endeavored to explain fully in the introductory chapter. It remains for us here to indicate our obligations to those who have aided in one way or another in the constructive part of the work. Theorists in the field of business cycle causation owe a permanent debt of gratitude to the work of Robertson, Hayek, and Keynes; ours will be sufficiently obvious in the pages which follow, but we would emphasize it at this point. Our purpose has been in large part that of developing the underlying theoretical portion of their works into an explanation of the depression in this country. Of American economists writing before the event, Dr. B. M. Anderson, Jr. and Professor H. Parker Willis were perhaps most conversant with the nature of the post-War banking developments leading up to the 1929 panic, and our own knowledge has been enriched by their analyses. Professor Ralph A. Young's study for the National Industrial Conference Board, *The Banking Situation in the United States*, proved an invaluable guide. Finally, Professor T. E. Gregory has unknowingly aided in smoothing several knotty points.

We are indebted to Professor James Washington Bell of Northwestern University and to Dr. Howard Bowen of the State University of Iowa for direct and personal interest while the work was in preparation. Professor Bell read the manuscript in entirety, and made suggestions as to organization and placement of emphasis which have been incorporated. Dr. Bowen was an interested and friendly critic during the earliest stages, and aided in clarifying several theoretical questions, especially in Chapter V. But no amount of acknowledgment to others can shift responsibility for any faults which may inhere in the volume.

C. A. P.
T. F. M.
R. W. N.

February 28, 1937

# TABLE OF CONTENTS

CHAPTER                                                PAGE

I. INTRODUCTION . . . . . . . . . .   1

II. GENERATING THE GREAT DEPRESSION   .   11

    Points of Departure . . . . . . . . .   11
    Inflation and Its Causes . . . . . . .   13
    Banking in Relation to War Finance . . . .   14
    Utilization of Surplus Reserves Through Government Borrowing Productive of Manifold Deposit
    Expansion . . . . . . . . . . . .   15
    Extent of Inflation . . . . . . . . . .   19
    Forces Underlying Inflation . . . . . . .   20
    Credit "Slack" in the United States . . . .   22
    Reduction of Reserve Requirements an Inflationistic Step . . . . . . . . . . . .   23
    Reserve Banking Inherently Inflationistic . . .   24
    Issue of Federal Reserve Notes Favored Inflation .   28
    The Federal Reserve Act and Time Deposits . .   29
    Unequal Credit Expansion of Member and Non-Member Banks . . . . . . . . . .   29
    Banks' Purchase of Government Securities a Potent Cause of Credit Expansion . . . . .   33
    Post-War Price Levels Abnormal . . . . .   34
    Post-War Depression Inevitable . . . . . .   35
    Proximate Versus Ultimate Causes of the Great Depression . . . . . . . . . . . .   35

III. THE RÔLE OF GOLD . . . . . . . .   37

    "Popular" Explanations . . . . . . . .   37
    Erroneous Explanations of Depression Indict Gold   38
    Critical Examination of Warren-Pearson Contentions . . . . . . . . . . . . .   40
        Importance of Location of Gold Is Pivotal .   44
        Bearing of Gold Exchange Standard . . .   48
        Significance of Gold Bullion Standard . . .   49
        Increasing Use of Checks Effects Gold Economy   49
        Cessation of Gold Production Would Have
        Resulted in No Shortage . . . . . .   50

CHAPTER                                                    PAGE
The Question of Maldistribution of Gold . . . .    51
    Maldistribution Merely Symptomatic   . . .     51
    Conditions Requisite to Satisfactory Operation of
        Gold Standard   .   .   .   .   .   .   .   .   .    53
    Toppling of Prices Was Last Stage of Decline from
        Heights of War Inflation   .   .   .   .   .   .   .    55

IV. OVERPRODUCTION, UNDERCONSUMPTION,
    AND MALDISTRIBUTION OF INCOME AS
    CYCLICAL FORCES   .   .   .   .   .   .   .   .    57

    The Underconsumption Theory   .   .   .   .   .    57
    Variants of the Underconsumption Theory      . .    58
    Overproduction Contrasted with Ill-Assorted Pro-
        duction   .   .   .   .   .   .   .   .   .   .   .    59
        Price, the Key-Log   .   .   .   .   .   .   .    61
        Enlarged Production Constitutes Enhanced
            Demand .   .   .   .   .   .   .   .   .   .   .    62
        Overproduction Apparent, Not Real     .   .   .    63
        Technological Unemployment   .   .   .   .   .    64
        Excessive Credit Expansion Leads to Misap-
            plication of Capital   .   .   .   .   .   .    67
    The Underconsumption Contention   .   .   .   .   .    69
        Underconsumption Idea May Have Partial
            Validity Temporarily   .   .   .   .   .   .    69
        Refutation of Underconsumption Theory   . .    70
    Maldistribution of Income as a Possible Cyclical
        Force  .   .   .   .   .   .   .   .   .   .   .   .    73
        Banking Policy a Disturbing Factor   .   .   .    76

V. POST-WAR DEVELOPMENTS IN AMERICAN
    BANKING .   .   .   .   .   .   .   .   .   .   .   .    78

    Unprecedented Expansion and Contraction of
        Capital Credit   .   .   .   .   .   .   .   .   .    79
    Factors Underlying Credit Expansion   .   .   .   .    79
    Effects of Investment Credit Inflation   .   .   .   .    81
    The Extent of Inflation   .   .   .   .   .   .   .   .    82
    The Initiating Source of the Inflation   .   .   .   .    85
    Open-Market Purchases Significant .   .   .   .   .    88
    Facilitating Factors in the Inflation .   .   .   .   .    91
    Disproportionate Growth of Time Deposits Re-
        sulted in Progressive Decline in Average Reserve-
        Deposit Ratio   .   .   .   .   .   .   .   .   .   .    95

CHAPTER                                                                PAGE

Bank Credit Expansion Versus Direct Saving as
Affecting Growth of Time Deposits . . . .    98
Payment of Interest on Time Deposits a Factor in
Their Expansion . . . . . . . . . . .    100
Federal Reserve Board Cognizant of Time-Deposit
Developments . . . . . . . . . .    100
The Paradox of Increasing Member Bank Credit
Combined with Rising Reserve Ratio of Federal
Reserve Banks . . . . . . . . . . .    101
The Nature of the Inflation . . . . . . .    103
Commercial Loans Strikingly Stable . . .    105
Effects of the Inflation . . . . . . .    106
Liquidity of Banks Impaired . . . . .    107
Two Aspects of Liquidity . . . . . .    108
Decline in Ratio of Gold to Deposits Suggests
Declining Liquidity . . . . . . .    110
Credit Extension by Indirection . . . . .    111
An Inherently Instable Boom . . . . .    112

VI. THE FUNDAMENTAL CAUSES OF THE GREAT
DEPRESSION . . . . . . . . . . . . .    115

Developments in Business Cycle and Monetary
Theory . . . . . . . . . . . . .    115
An Integrated Explanation . . . . . .    116
Dominating Explanatory Considerations . . .    118
Complexity of Present-Day Competitive Economic
Order . . . . . . . . . . . . . .    119
Inherent Disequilibrating Forces . . . . .    119
Oscillation Greatest in Capital Goods Indus-
tries . . . . . . . . . . . . .    120
Production of Iron and Steel as "Trade"
Barometers . . . . . . . .    122
Constructional Activity in United States
during Pre-Depression Period Pro-
digious . . . . . . . . . .    124
Production of Machine Tools an Indicator
of Variations in Production of Capital
Goods . . . . . . . . . .    126
Production of Consumption Goods Relatively
Stable . . . . . . . . . . . .    126
Disparity Between Investment and Saving Causes
Cyclical Swings in Business Activity . . . .    128
Genesis of Saving and Investment Disparities . .    129

CHAPTER                                                        PAGE

Oscillation of Market Rate of Interest About
Natural Rate Supplies Condition for Divergence
Between Rate of Investment and Rate of Saving    129
Manufacture of "Bank Money" Creates Disparity
Between Market and Natural Rates of Interest
and Alters Structure of Production    .    .    .    .    132
Pivotal Importance of Degree of Stability in Rate of
Increase of Investment .    .    .    .    .    .    .    135
Bank Credit Expansion Accelerates Rate of In-
vestment Increase    .    .    .    .    .    .    .    135
"Created" Purchasing Power Enhances Profits in
Circular Fashion .    .    .    .    .    .    .    .    137
Exaggerated Character of Recent Cycle Attributable
to Central Banking Operation    .    .    .    .    .    139
Foregoing Analysis Compatible with Explanation
of Earlier Cycles .    .    .    .    .    .    .    .    140
The Immediate, Inciting Cause of Decline    .    .    .    142
Both Market Rate and Natural or Productivity
Rate of Interest Vary Toward Convergence    .    .    143
That Natural Rate of Interest Varies Is Peculiarly
Important    .    .    .    .    .    .    .    .    .    144
Sound Theory Essential to Accurate Forecasting    .    146
Recent Cycle Theories Diversely Deficient    .    .    .    147

VII. THE FUNDAMENTAL CAUSES OF THE GREAT
DEPRESSION (Continued)    .    .    .    .    .    .    149

Forecasters Led into Error by Previous Cycle Pat-
terns    .    .    .    .    .    .    .    .    .    .    149
Neglected Factors .    .    .    .    .    .    .    .    .    150
Percussive Character of Stock Market Crash.    .    .    151
Stock Market Boom, with Its Fleeting Profits,
Sustained Consumer Demand, Delayed and
Intensified Disaster    .    .    .    .    .    .    153
Stock Market Boom Stimulated by Rapid Re-
tirement of Federal Debt and Mushroom
Growth of Investment Trusts    .    .    .    .    153
Stock Prices in Relation to Corporate Earnings    155
Bank Credit Directly Underlay Stock Market
Advance .    .    .    .    .    .    .    .    .    .    158
Chronological Aspects of Production Decline in
Relation to Stock Market Collapse    .    .    .    .    160
Prolonged Process of Investment Deflation    .    .    .    160

CHAPTER                                                    PAGE

How Shrinkage in Security Values Repressed Pro-
  duction Activity . . . . . . . . .   161
Shaken Confidence Reflected in Drastically Cur-
  tailed Construction Notably in Capital Goods
  Industries   . . . . . . . . . .   162
Impact on Income . . . . . . . . .   164
Entanglement of Banks with Depression . . . .   167
  Bank Failures Dealt Disruption . . . . .   168
The Equilibrium Theory of the Business Cycle . .   170
Equilibrium View Essential   . . . . . . .   172

VIII. BANKING POLICY AND THE PRICE LEVEL .   175

Misleading Behavior of Post-War Price Level   . .   175
Unjustified Criticism of Federal Reserve Board .  .   176
Stable Price Level and—Ensuing Depression!  .  .   177
Did Federal Reserve Board Deliberately Attempt
  Price Stabilization? . . . . . . . .   178
Currency Management Difficult—But Not New   .   181
Rediscount Rate Changes and Open-Market Opera-
  tions as Instruments of Control   . . . . .   182
Motivation of Adoption of Price-Stabilization
  Policy . . . . . . . . . . . . .   184
Historical Analogy Prompts Skepticism as to
  Fullness of Post-War Price Recession  . . . .   184
Unprecedented Technical Progress Indicated Falling
  Prices Normal   . . . . . . . . .   186
Parallelism Between Growth of Bank Credit and
  Productivity . . . . . . . . . .   188
Absence of Inventory Inflation   . . . . .   189
Effects of Inflation Best Measured Where Use of
  Credit Most Active . . . . . . . .   190
Why Stabilization of Price Level Is an Improper
  Objective of Banking Policy and an Inadequate
  Guide . . . . . . . . . . . .   191
Artificial Support of Price Level Resulted in
  "Relative" Inflation . . . . . . . .   193
Bearing of Cycle Theory upon Control Policy  . .   195
Theoretical Foundations of Federal Reserve Policy   196
Some International Consequences of "Easy Money"
  Policy of the United States . . . . . .   197
Currency Management the Offspring of War Finance   199
Policy of Stabilization of Price Level Tends Toward
  Its Own Collapse . . . . . . . . .   200

CHAPTER                                                          PAGE

Suggested Guide for Credit Control . . . . . 202
Objectives of Policy of Stabilizing Rate of Credit
Growth . . . . . . . . . . . . 203
Objections to Falling Price Level Examined . 204
Falling Prices Place Premium on Industrial
Efficiency . . . . . . . . . . 206
Stabilization of Rate of Credit Growth Would Tend
Toward Equilibration of Investment and Saving . 207
Velocity Changes as a Factor Affecting Bank
Credit or Management . . . . . . . . 208

IX. THE ECONOMIC IMPLICATIONS OF RE-
COVERY . . . . . . . . . . . . 211
No Easy Road to Recovery from Depression . . 216
Saving Versus Spending Our Way to Prosperity . 218
Equilibrium Begets Purchasing Power . . . . 219
Cost Reduction, Earnings on Capital, and the
Standard of Living . . . . . . . . . 220
The Common and Current Misunderstanding
of Relations Between Monetary Wage Rates
and "Real" Purchasing Power . . . . 222
Reducing Wage Rates Would Lead to Increased
Wages—An Illustration . . . . . . . . 226
The Fallaciousness of the Doctrine That High Wage
Rates Are Synonymous with Full Purchasing
Power . . . . . . . . . . . . . 229
Wage Rates, Depression and Recovery—1920–1921
and 1929–1936 . . . . . . . . . 229
Restoration of Equilibrium Between Natural and
Market Rates of Interest . . . . . . . 232
Accelerated Activity in Production of Durable
Goods a Key to Employment and Recovery . . 234
Desirability of Lower Prices in Capital-Goods In-
dustries Dictates Lowered Wage Rates Therein . 236
Expansion of Bank Credit, Expansion of Business—
A Question of Order . . . . . . . . 240
A "Natural," as Opposed to a Forced, Rise in Prices 241
The Price Level and the Debt Level . . . . . 244
Conclusion . . . . . . . . . . . 245

BIBLIOGRAPHY . . . . . . . . . . 249

INDEX . . . . . . . . . . . . . 271

# BANKING AND THE BUSINESS CYCLE

## CHAPTER I

## INTRODUCTION

In 1921, following the upheaval of prices which accompanied the primary post-War deflation, Professor T. E. Gregory, in writing on the situation then prevailing in the foreign exchanges, was moved to lament that: [1]

> Ours is a weary and disillusioned generation, dealing with a world which is nearer collapse than it has been at any time since the downfall of the Roman Empire.   The problem which is discussed in this little book is an integral part of the general problem of reconstruction after the ravages of war.   It will be shown in detail in the course of the subsequent chapters that the main cause of the dislocation of the exchanges has been the almost universal disregard of the rules of common sense in the treatment of the money supply of the world, or, as it is usually put, the dislocation of the exchanges is an inevitable effect of inflation.

Thirteen years later, near the nadir of the Great Depression, Professor J. M. Clark wrote in like vein: [2]

> The peculiarly grave and threatening character of the present emergency needs no proof. As to how close it has brought us to a complete collapse of our economic system economists, like others, can only conjecture.

Certainly ours is a weary and disillusioned generation. The tragedies of the War and the sufferings and disappointments of subsequent years have left the occidental world

[1] *Foreign Exchange Before, During, and After the War* (London: Oxford University Press, 3rd ed., 1925), p. 9.
[2] *Strategic Factors in Business Cycles* (New York: National Bureau of Economic Research, 1934), p. 4.

cynical and despairing. Old ideals, old values, old institutions, old faiths—all have crumbled, leaving stretches of barren waste all too receptive to the seeds scattered so freely by economic charlatans and political medicine-men. Partial economic disintegration has been accompanied by the collapse of democratic governments. With the remaining ruins as foundations, with a frantic energy born of despair, no inconsiderable fraction of mankind has set about attempting to construct new shelters in the form of totalitarian states, to be entrusted to the custodianship of authoritarian dictators. Certainly the forces of economic liberalism have suffered severe reverses; whether or not those reverses terminate in a complete rout appears to depend upon the course of events during the remainder of the present decade.

During recent years a number of pseudo-economists have indulged in much glibness about the passing of the "economy of scarcity" and the arrival of the "economy of abundance." Sophistry of this sort has claimed the public ear far too long; it is high time that the speciousness of such fantastic views be clearly and definitely exposed. Attention needs to be focused on the hard elementary fact that man's darkest curse has ever been his poverty, and that it yet is and promises to continue so for numberless generations. No economist worthy of the name, moreover, should need to be reminded that in the absence of "scarcity" there would be no system of "economy" and no "science of economics."

Professor Gustav Cassel has said that [1] "Our attention must now for a long time onwards be devoted towards a complete analysis of the upheaval now in progress." The present study is directed to an inquiry into certain of the more fundamental aspects of major industrial fluctuations, and to the relationship of banking operations thereto, special reference being had throughout to the causes and relevant phases of the cycle beginning in the United States in 1922 and ending with the Great Depression. It is at the same time

---

[1] "The Problem of Business Cycles," in the Skandinaviska Kreditaktiebolaget *Quarterly Report*, January, 1933, p. 3.

devoted to the formulation of a theory of business cycles—
for "the present crisis is, in fact, a crisis also for the entire
theory of business cycles." [1] The theory of business cycles
here set forth, it is believed, is not only one which is applicable as a general explanation of depressions, but also one
whose validity is particularly well illustrated by setting it
against the background of the experience of the recent crisis.
Accordingly, this theory of the cycle is correlated with the
banking and financial situation in the United States during
the post-War years into an explanation of the causes of the
Great Depression.

"Causes" is used advisedly, it being "at once evident that
no general or single theory is valid for so varying and varied
a phenomenon as crisis." [2] And, as Professor Clark states,[3]
most "theoretical studies give us causes that are too few and
too simple, such as over-production, under-consumption,
over-saving, or failure to distribute to laborers their whole
product or enough of the whole product of industry to enable
them to buy the things they have produced." The present
apparent need is not for the propagating of novel theories,
but rather for the orienting and synthesizing of extant
knowledge.

The special objective of this volume is an integration of
views of the business cycle frequently considered as conflicting—the monetary, the structural, and the equilibrium
theories. Hence the theoretical portion may be denoted an
eclectic theory of the business cycle. The views of those who
argue that the cycle is a "purely monetary phenomenon," of
those who hold that those "real" phenomena connected
with the alterations in the structure of production are the
root causes, and of those who are devotees of the equilibrium
theory of business cycles, have been drawn upon to effect a
synthesis or combination of these three main theories. The
monetary or bank credit theory occupies first rank in the

[1] *Ibid.*, p. 3.
[2] Cassel, G., *The Theory of Social Economy* (New York: Harcourt, Brace & Co., 1932), p. 538.
[3] *Strategic Factors in Business Cycles*, p. 6.

chain of causation and explains the origin of the boom; the structural view, with its emphasis upon the changes in the structure of production and the disequilibrium between saving and investment, explains the underlying character of the boom; and the equilibrium theory is necessary to describe the depression proper and to explain its severity and persistence. All three theories in combination give a more nearly complete understanding of the whole cycle than can any single or more particularistic view.

The central thesis of the volume is that the Great Depression and the feverish activity of the immediately preceding years were notably bank credit phenomena. The markedly oscillatory movements of the economic pendulum in the United States during the 'twenties and early 'thirties are attributable to forces resident in central banking. But for the superimposition of the Federal Reserve Banks upon our commercial banking structure, the amplitude of the cycle in question would have been greatly restricted.

However, if it be regarded from a point of observation that focuses attention on the continuity of historical processes, the recent depression will be seen to have been directly connected with the efforts at reconstruction that followed after the dislocations caused by war. The ultimate causes of the depression are traceable to the War; just as the late war was the Great War, the recent depression was the Great Depression. But the more immediate causes of the depression grew out of the post-War inflation of bank credit in this country. It is sought to show that the main cause of the dislocation in trade and industry was, in Gregory's language, the "disregard of the rules of common sense in the treatment of the money supply" of the United States; the depression is proximately an effect of inflation. The post-War inflation in the United States was an investment credit inflation, however, as distinguished from the commodity credit inflation of War-time. An explanation of the nature of this investment inflation and its relation to the subsequent depression will be essayed in the ensuing chapters.

It therefore becomes necessary to inquire rather fully into the character and nature of post-War developments within the banking system of the United States prior to 1929, particularly from 1922 onwards. The striking and far-reaching changes which were developing in the structure and operation of the American banking system were intimately connected in a causal fashion with the development of the investment boom and with the origins of the depression itself. The historical complex of factors and circumstances that leads up to any crisis usually ferments long before the actual occurrence of the crisis; therefore the causes of a particular crisis must be traced farther back than is commonly supposed. An understanding of what was taking place in American banking during the post-War years is therefore essential to a thorough analysis of the causes of the depression. The reader should be warned, however, that this is not a history, either of the entire post-War banking situation in this country, or of post-War American economic life, or of the depression itself in its entirety: rather, the emphasis is upon an analysis of those factors in banking and economic development which were basically causal to the Great Depression.

As the depression has been denominated primarily a central banking phenomenon, it will also be desirable to attempt to unravel some of the changes caused in the structure, organization, and operation of the American banking system by the establishment of the central banking system represented by the Federal Reserve System. The special character of the depression is traced to the hyper-elasticity of the Federal Reserve System, and to the operation of that system as exemplified in the "managed currency" experiment of the Federal Reserve Board, working in opposition to what D. H. Robertson labels "the over-mastering tendency of prices to fall" [1] after a war financed by inflationary measures. By virtue of that experiment, the Board succeeded in holding up the price level for a surprising length

---

[1] *Journal of the Institute of Bankers* (June, 1931), Vol. LII, Part VI, p. 236.

of time, but in so doing unwittingly aided in producing the boom and its consequent depression. The depression, in other words, was the price paid for the experimentation with currency management by the Federal Reserve Board during the period when the dislocations caused by war had not as yet been corrected and when the post-War deflation of prices had not been completed. Nor were the effects of this Federal Reserve Board action confined solely to the United States; the banking and industrial systems of leading commercial nations are interrelated so closely that the mistaken policy of one large central banking organization may be highly conducive to the precipitation of a world-wide depression.

Furthermore, some of the causes of the depression are to be found in the provisions of the Reserve Act itself, the nature of which and their effects upon the banking system did not become noticeable or fully operative until after 1922. The first of these is simply the establishment of a system of central banking, without sufficient appreciation on the part of its sponsors of the fact that central banking is inherently inflationistic in nature, in consequence of the play between gold inflows, bank reserves, and prices which central banking makes possible. Other provisions having like significance were the permission of payment of interest upon time deposits by National and other member banks, the fixing of a lower reserve ratio against time than against demand deposits, and the general reduction of reserve requirements contained in the original Act as well as the further reductions effected as an aid to war financing by the Amendment of June 21, 1917.

Through the purchase of investments commercial banks impart a positive upward impulsion to the business cycle. Coming in as a marginal determining factor in the price of bonds, purchases of investments by banks force down the long-term market rate of interest so that it becomes profitable, in view of the existing realized rate of return to capital at important new investment margins, to float new bond issues and to embark upon new capital development; this results in an investment boom which effects a change in the structure of production in favor of a more rapid growth of capital goods relative to the production of consumption goods. But the purchase of bonds by the banks has another influence which is directly connected with, and which helps make possible, the investment boom: the purchase of investments by banks creates new deposits in the banking system in much the same fashion as does the granting of loans. The banks thus place in the hands of entrepreneurs a volume of purchasing power in excess of the volume of real savings being effected voluntarily by the public, producing a disequilibrium between saving and investment that constitutes the heart of the boom. This enlargement of the stream of credit issuing from the banks permits and encourages the making of new investment commitments, without restraining consideration of the effect of such action upon the productive structures, and the resulting boom represents a movement of the economic system away from equilibrium, rather than toward it. When the rate of increase of current investment declines, or when the volume of investment actually decreases, depression ensues: the cessation of credit creation, or even a diminution in the rate of growth of credit, brings about the causally significant decline in the rate of investment.

But the ability of the banks to buy bonds as investment assets is conditioned by their reserve position. If the banks are possessed of a surplusage of reserves, they may buy bonds or otherwise expand credit; if they have no excess reserves, they may not do so. The volume of reserves in the member banks, however, is subject to enlargement or diminution by the action of the Federal Reserve Banks; that is to say, the Reserve Banks may "create" excess reserves for the member banks much as the member banks "create" credit. The adoption of such a policy by the Reserve System on three separate occasions during the 'twenties was the significant action leading to an expansion of total bank credit during that period.

The boom is brought to an end, not only because of the restriction upon the supply of credit and purchasing power, but also because of the rise in the market rate of interest on new bond issues and other instruments of borrowing resulting from that restriction. Moreover, the realized rate of return on new capital development tends to fall in the later stages of a boom because of the fact that increases in wage rates gradually pare down the share going to capital. There ensues a general disequilibrium throughout the system, not only between wage rates and the cost of living, between costs and prices, and between production and consumption, but also a disequilibrium between investment and saving the reverse of that which prevails during the boom. As long as these general disequilibria persist, and as long as new investment in the sense of the production of new durable goods continues at a low ebb, depression continues.[1]

Recovery from depression can proceed only when the disequilibria produced by the preceding investment boom are overcome. When the anticipated productivity of capital at new investment margins exceeds the price paid currently for the use of loanable funds, conditions again obtain in which there is prospect of profit in new investment activity. This can be brought about most effectively by correcting the disparity between costs and the value of current new investment, that is, by bringing costs into line with prices, particularly in the capital goods industries. And, since the major portion of the costs of industry represents payments to labor, it is particularly desirable that wage scales be genuinely flexible. Widespread wage-rate reductions would cause, temporarily, some diversion of the income stream away from employed laborers in favor of the capitalist-entrepreneurs. This procedure will alter the share going to

---

[1] "Depression has continued because there is no prospect of profitable investment. And why is there no prospect of profitable investment? Because costs, which by reason of the inflationary boom have become too high in relation to prices, have not been reduced." Lionel Robbins, in Lloyds Bank *Monthly Review* (October, 1932), Vol. III (NS), No. 32, p. 432.

capital by converting losses into profits; but it is upon profits, or the prospect of profits, that all expansive activities of modern industry depend. Laborers, considered collectively, would be richly compensated for accepting the temporary shrinkage of money income that would be entailed by the initial reductions in wage rates; the increased volume of employment and the reduced prices that would follow from such a policy would shortly raise the aggregate real income of labor far above any level at which it could be maintained in the face of depression conditions.

No less important than the problem of explaining the causes of the depression is that of explaining its severity and duration. Here again, Federal Reserve policy has occupied an important rôle. The expansionist policy of 1927 served the Board's purpose in checking the decline in business which began in that year, but it also operated to sustain the boom for an additional two years and to force it to unprecedented heights. In particular, the stock market proved the beneficiary of the Reserve Board's action in 1927. Yet when the stock boom eventually collapsed, it loosed business activity from its false and insecure moorings and the descent into the maelstrom of disaster began. The very height to which the investment and stock market booms attained was enough to indicate that the reaction would be severe; this statement has kinship with no "action and reaction" theory, but simply means that overcapitalization and misdirection of capital became so exaggerated during the last two years of boom that deflation and liquidation were likely to be protracted. Once business activity began to decline, every effort was made to avert or delay the necessary liquidation, both by Federal Reserve action aimed at sustaining the market situation, and by the widespread advocacy of a policy of maintaining wage rates on the part of government, trade unions, and employers. Furthermore, the enormity of the stock market crash itself, involving such a large percentage of the population in its ruins, contributed to the severity of the depression. Lastly, the fact that in no previous depression had there been such a wholesale destruction of bank credit, attributable in large part in this instance to the entanglement of the banking system with the preceding investment and stock market frenzies, aids in explaining the unprecedented duration of the Great Depression.

## CHAPTER II

# GENERATING THE GREAT DEPRESSION

Two events occurred in 1914 that were to have profound influence upon subsequent economic developments in the United States. The first of these was external, the outbreak in Europe of the World War; the second was internal, the formal inauguration of the Federal Reserve System. Both were events propagative of an unprecedented orgy of inflation. The two, inextricably intertwined, brought about a great inflation of bank credit in connection with war finance, and both were productive of striking changes in the economic structure of the world during and after the War.

## POINTS OF DEPARTURE

No attempt is made here to develop a full and considered estimate of the dislocations caused by the War upon all subsequent economic development. It is enough to indicate that the maladjustments and disturbances directly and indirectly chargeable to it have been enormous, not only in this country but all over the world. The War broke in upon the relatively smooth development of pre-War industry with the force of a revolution. It diverted industry and commerce into new, transient, war-time channels, from which it was necessary to withdraw resources in the following decade. It imposed upon the post-War economy the necessity of restoring the capital destroyed by the War and the task of satisfying the pent-up demand for certain types of goods whose production was restricted during the period of conflict. But the most serious economic dislocations that appeared after 1918 were those caused by the inflation which resulted from the methods by which the War was financed— an inflation which affected the whole structure of production, prices, wages, and debts. The inflated price level was a war heritage that was to prove largely determinative of subsequent banking and economic developments. To the effects of credit inflation based upon gold in this country were added those of the paper money inflations abroad, every belligerent nation (with the exception of the United States) having suspended the gold standard and having inflated its note currency at one time or another after 1914.

Closely connected with the process of war inflation in this country was the inauguration of the Federal Reserve System. The superimposition of this system of central banking (or bankers' banking, as it is sometimes called) upon the banking system operative in the United States prior to 1914 served both to shape and to accelerate the course of inflation. It made possible the method of financing the War that was adopted in this country (without the necessity of suspending the gold standard), and it also assisted in making possible the financial assistance lent the Allied Powers after the United States entered the War.

The present study is concerned with banking operations and finance in relation to the Great Depression; its logical starting point is war finance and the inflation of bank credit and currency associated with the financing of the World War. For the roots of this depression, it is believed, are to be found principally in changes in the world economic system which developed during and after the World War as a result of the excesses of inflation engaged in during the struggle, an inflation which continued, in varying degrees in different countries, until the onset of the depression in 1929.[1] The Great Depression, in other words, is viewed as the inevitable aftermath of the uncontrolled currency and

---

[1] *Vide* Sir Josiah Stamp, *The Financial Aftermath of War* (New York: Charles Scribner's Sons, 1932), pp. 13–14: "If most political events today are economic, then we can also say that most economic questions are also financial. * * * If then most economic questions are financial, we can quite truly say today that most financial questions are affected by what happened during the war, and what has happened in consequence since." And *cf.* Clark, J. M., *Strategic Factors in Business Cycles*, p. 116: "The current depression is * * * not unrelated to * * * the process of post-War reconstruction and the dislocated conditions of international finance and trade, which the War left behind it."

bank credit inflation incident to the financing of the War, and the ill-considered efforts to counteract the normal tendency toward post-war deflation by the palliative of even more inflation. The economic system has a surprising capacity for overcoming the devastation caused by war, but if the dislocations wrought by war and war inflation are not promptly corrected, the inevitable consequence of those dislocations is disaster.

It is in order, therefore, to inquire briefly in the present chapter into the process of inflation as conditioned by war finance, and in this country by the introduction of the Federal Reserve System with its extraordinary capacity for credit expansion. The discussion is confined principally to the situation in the United States, as a discussion of war finance and the course of inflation in the other countries involved would extend beyond the scope of this volume.

## INFLATION AND ITS CAUSES

The term "inflation" has long been the subject of interminable and diverse definition.[1] In the view of the writers, inflation applies to a state of money, credit, and prices arising not only from excessive issues of paper money, but also from any increase in the effective supply of circulating media that outruns the rate of increase of the physical volume of production and trade, thus forcing a rise of prices. Inflation may be caused by an increasing supply of metallic money as well as by excessive supplies of paper money. In the modern world of finance, however, the most important single cause of inflation is the multiplication of bank credit by the banking machinery, resulting in an increase in the volume of purchasing power subject to check at a rate faster than the rate of increase in the volume of available goods.[2] It is the latter

---

[1] So much so that one economist of note has been moved to remark that "there is obviously much to be said for abandoning the term inflation altogether, and so dispensing with the need for any definition." Pigou, A. C., "Inflation," *Economic Journal* (December, 1917), Vol. XXVII, No. 108, p. 490.

[2] See the definition by Professor E. W. Kemmerer in the *American Economic Review* (June, 1918), Vol. VIII, No. 2, p. 247: "Without attempting to harmonize the various conflicting views, nor to give a precise and formal definition of inflation,

form of inflation which will be discussed in the main here, as it was resorted to on an extensive scale by all countries participating in the War, and it was the predominant type of inflation in the case of the United States.

## BANKING IN RELATION TO WAR FINANCE

The World War was probably the worst-financed war in history from the viewpoint of sound fiscal policy. Less of the monetary costs of the War was financed by taxation and more by inflation of one form or another than any of the wars of the nineteenth century. Mr. Hartley Withers estimates that 17½ per cent of the cost of the War to England was covered by taxation,[1] and Sir Josiah Stamp states that England's showing in this respect was better than that of any other European belligerent.[2] Elsewhere Stamp estimates that 63 per cent of the cost of the Napoleonic Wars to England was raised by taxation.[3] The Report of the Committee on War Finance of the American Economic Association estimates the portion of World War costs covered by taxation in the United States at 25 per cent.[4] As previously stated, all of the countries involved in the World War, with the exception of the United States, resorted to the age-old expedient of inflation of the note currency. But the United States, along with virtually all of the other nations, made use of that form of war financing which Mr. Withers denominates "quite the worst way of raising money for war or any other purpose"[5] and which Professor O. M. W. Sprague says is "the most potent single cause of the general advance in

we may note that there is one idea common to most uses of the word, namely the idea of a supply of circulating media in excess of trade needs. It is the idea of re-dundancy of money or circulating credit or both, a redundancy that results in rising prices * * * . More specifically, inflation occurs when *at a given price level*, a country's circulating media—cash and deposit currency—increase *relatively* to trade needs."

[1] *Bankers and Credit* (London: Eveleigh Nash & Grayson, Ltd., 1924), p. 59.
[2] *Taxation During the War* (London: Humphrey Milford, 1932), p. 133.
[3] *The Financial Aftermath of War*, p. 41.
[4] *American Economic Review, Supplement No. 2* (March, 1919), Vol. IX, No. 1, p. 119.
[5] *Bankers and Credit*, p. 42.

prices during periods of war," [1] namely, that of securing money from the banks either by issuing bonds directly to them for which they pay by creating new credits in favor of the Government, or by selling bonds to individuals who cover their subscriptions by borrowing from banks the credits that are newly created for this purpose. Such was the means by which the major portion of the monetary costs of the War was raised by all countries involved, and it is probably a safe assertion that it was employed on a more extensive scale than during any previous war. It is therefore desirable to inquire more fully into how the banking machinery was utilized to serve that end. In order to do so, however, it is necessary to set forth in some detail a particular point of banking theory which was neither understood nor recognized by writers on the subject until the period of War finance brought it into sharp relief.

## UTILIZATION OF SURPLUS RESERVES THROUGH GOVERNMENT BORROWING PRODUCTIVE OF MANIFOLD DEPOSIT EXPANSION

This is the theory that by purchasing investments (bonds), banks create credit within the banking system quite as effectively as by granting loans to their customers. Not only because this process was used extensively in financing the War, but also because the theory of business cycles elaborated in Chapters VI and VII rests directly upon it, it is essential that it be understood at this point in order that there may be a clear grasp of much that follows.

That banks "create" credit by granting loans has long been known and recognized. The precise nature of the process of creation of credit was not generally realized nor adequately analyzed, however, until after the termination of the World War.[2] The correlative process of creation of bank credit, by means of purchases of investments on the part of

[1] "Loans and Taxes in War Finance," *American Economic Review Supplement* (March, 1917), Vol. VII, No. 1, p. 200.
[2] Phillips, C. A., *Bank Credit* (New York: The Macmillan Company, 1920).

the banks, is far from having universal recognition even today. It seems quite certain that some of those responsible for the way in which the War was financed in this country were not cognizant of the procedure by which it was done[1]— they were, as Withers puts it, "making reckless use of a delicate machine which they did not understand and producing consequences which they neither foresaw nor recognized."[2]

So far as is known to the writers, this process of the manufacture of credit on the part of the banks by purchasing investments was first discerned by Withers.[3] In several books published during the War period he indicates an increasing understanding of it in connection with war finance.[4] In his *Bankers and Credit*, however, published in 1924, he elaborates the theory most clearly, and it is appropriate to quote at some length from that work:[5]

> * * * If a bank makes an investment by sending a broker into the Stock Exchange and buying, for example, £100,000 worth of Consols, it pays the seller £100,000 by a draft on its balance at the Bank of England. Its holding in cash is thus reduced by £100,000, its holding of investments is increased by the same amount, but the seller of the Consols pays into his own bank £100,000 of new credit, which has been created by the purchasing bank. The same thing happens when a bank, instead of buying securities on the Stock Exchange, invests by subscribing directly to a new issue made by the Government or any other borrower. * * * If the final receiver of the money borrowed or invested is a customer of the lending bank, then the lending bank will have increased its own deposits; its cash at the Bank of England will be unchanged, and its advances (or investments) and deposits will both be increased by the sum of the loan. It is

---

[1] "The view that bank deposits are potential currency is inapplicable to the deposits created in the Government's War loan account." Leffingwell, R. C. (Assistant Secretary of the Treasury during the War), "Treasury Methods of Financing the War in Relation to Inflation," *Proceedings of the Academy of Political Science* (June, 1920), Vol. IX, No. 1, p. 32.

[2] *Bankers and Credit*, p. 48.

[3] Professor Jacob Hollander attributes priority to Professor A. C. Pigou (1915) and to Professor O. M. W. Sprague (1916); see his *War Borrowing* (New York: The Macmillan Company, 1919), pp. 157–158.

[4] *War and Lombard Street* (1914); *Our Money and the State* (1917); *The Business of Finance* (1918); *War-Time Financial Problems* (1919).

[5] *Bankers and Credit*, pp. 24–25.

thus of the utmost importance to remember * * * that whenever a bank makes an investment or a loan or discounts a bill it is increasing the deposits, either of itself or of some other bank. * * * By this process the banks create buying power or what may be called potential currency.

It will be observed that, although Withers refers in this discussion to the Bank of England (which is a central, or bankers' bank) he is really describing a simple type of credit creation process that does not in any way involve central banking, as such. He is simply making the point that, if newly issued government bonds are purchased by (individual) banks, the immediate outcome of the process is the creation of new credit. His analysis is irrefragable, as far as it goes, but Withers here does not take account of the nature and significance of central banking in relation to the War-time inflation.

The operation of the machinery of bankers' banking made possible the creation of the greater portion of the credit by means of which both the United States and England financed the War. It was not the effect of such transactions as Withers describes that had the most significant influence upon prices in this country; rather, it was the superimposition of bankers' banking upon the commercial banking structure that led to the compound creation of bank credit. For whenever bankers' banking becomes operative, the inflationistic nature of commercial banking is greatly reinforced and accentuated.[1]  In the simplest possible illustration, in a banking system requiring a 10 per cent reserve against deposits, a bank having a reserve of one million dollars in excess of the required ratio may use that reserve to buy one million dollars worth of bonds, giving the Government deposit credit for that amount. As the Government draws checks against this deposit credit and pays them to government contractors, munitions makers, etc., and as they in turn deposit the checks in their (other) banks, the

---

[1] See Phillips, op. cit., Ch. III; and see Hayek, F. A., *Monetary Theory and the Trade Cycle* (New York: Harcourt, Brace & Co., 1932), Ch. IV.

bank which originally bought the bonds tends to part company with cash—but that cash reappears as new, excess, reserve for some other bank (or group of banks) in the system. The second bank in turn may now use 90 per cent of its new reserve to buy, let us say, $900,000 worth of bonds (it being required to set aside $100,000 to satisfy the requirement for a 10 per cent reserve against the deposit of the government contractors), and as the Government checks against the $900,000 deposit created in its favor in exchange for the bonds, the second bank (or group of banks) in turn tends to lose cash to a third bank (or group of banks) in the system. The third bank (or group of banks) may now use its new reserve of cash to buy $810,000 worth of bonds (90 per cent of $900,000 deposited with it) and to create $810,000 of Government deposits, and so the process is repeated again and again.

As this is done, each bank in subscribing for bonds to the extent of 90 per cent of the amount deposited with it creates an equivalent increase in deposits either for itself or for other banks in the system, and it becomes clear that the original creation of credit ultimately makes possible manifold new deposits in the banking system. That is to say, the total credit created on the basis of the excess reserve originally utilized to buy bonds is not simply equal to the amount of that reserve, but is (for a system with a 10 per cent legal reserve ratio against deposits) roughly ten times that amount. The original one million dollars of excess reserve permits the creation of ten million dollars new deposits in the banking system.[1] And to the extent that all banks in the system are possessed of excess reserves and use them simultaneously to buy bonds issued by the Government the expansion is more widespread and proceeds more rapidly. Thus it is

[1] This is true as long as the amounts pass from bank to bank and are not withdrawn in cash and hoarded, or so long as they do not represent larger cash balances circulating in the hands of the public. But the above is intended to illustrate a principle rather than to arrive at a mathematical result. It seems hardly necessary to add that the process just described is the same as obtains when banks utilize excess reserves to grant loans to customers, instead of buying bonds, and as when banks buy bonds on the stock exchange, instead of subscribing to a new Government bond issue.

seen that deposits are basically the offspring of loans and investments for the banking system as a whole.[1]

The machinery of central banking was exploited indirectly to create credit with which to finance the War, moreover, when individuals subscribed to the bond issues and secured the funds with which to pay for the bonds by borrowing from the banks, pledging the bonds as collateral for the loans, provided the central banks were able and willing to make such advances to the local banks as would enable them to maintain adequate legal reserves. This process increased the deposits in the banking system as effectively as when the banks subscribed to the bond issues directly. It was encouraged and facilitated in the United States by the policies of the Treasury Department and the Federal Reserve Board, acting in cooperation under the leadership of Mr. William G. McAdoo in his dual rôle of Secretary of the Treasury and member of the Board. From this procedure, as in that first described, there ensued a great increase in purchasing power that was unaccompanied by an equal increase in production, and hence resulted in inflation.[2]

## EXTENT OF INFLATION

Such were the processes by which the major portion of the War inflation of bank credit took place; it remains to inquire into the extent of the inflation and this is set forth briefly in the following table:

---

[1] "Since the outbreak of War it is the second procedure in the main which has been followed, the surplus cash having been used to subscribe for Treasury Bills and other Government securities. The money so subscribed has again been spent by the Government and returned in the manner above described to the bankers' cash balances, the process being repeated again and again until each £10,000,000 originally advanced by the Bank of England has created new deposits representing new purchasing power to several times that amount." *First Interim Report of the Committee on Currency and Foreign Exchanges After the War* (The Cunliffe Committee Report), Cmd. 9182 (1918), Paragraph 10, *note.*

[2] " * * * the fourth Liberty loan has been placed in a very large degree by the use of bank credit. Precisely how much such credit * * * is not yet certain * * *. In addition to this large use of direct bank credit is to be reckoned the fact that the bonds * * * have been taken by the banks as collateral to secure notes running for long periods * * *. These factors make not only for a serious condition of inflation but also for the maintenance and continuance of the inflation much longer than would otherwise be probable." "Washington Notes" (unsigned), *The Journal of Political Economy* (December, 1918), Vol. XXVI, No. 10, pp. 977–978.

TABLE I

LOANS, INVESTMENTS, AND DEPOSITS, ALL BANKS IN THE UNITED STATES,
AND WHOLESALE COMMODITY PRICES, 1914–1920
(June figures)

| YEAR | LOANS AND INVESTMENTS (Millions) | DEPOSITS (Millions) | WHOLESALE PRICES (U.S.B.L. STAT.) 1913—100 |
|------|------|------|------|
| 1914 | $20,789 | $18,566 | 97 |
| 1915 | 21,466 | 19,131 | 99 |
| 1916 | 24,587 | 22,759 | 123 |
| 1917 | 28,287 | 26,352 | 185 |
| 1918 | 31,813 | 28,765 | 191 |
| 1919 | 36,570 | 33,603 | 203 |
| 1920 | 41,685 | 37,721 | 243 |

Sources: Banking figures, Tables 44 and 45, p. 111, Fifteenth *Annual Report* of the Federal Reserve Board; Wholesale Prices, U. S. Bureau of Labor Statistics.

Thus it will be seen that loans and investments more than doubled in the six-year period from 1914 to 1920. With that doubling went a like increase in deposits for the entire banking system in the United States, since deposits, as just pointed out, are created principally by loans and investments. The increase in deposits for this short period, in other words, was greater than the total increase in deposits during all the long preceding history of banking in the United States. The result was an enormous increase in the price level, as shown by the accompanying figures.

## FORCES UNDERLYING INFLATION

Dr. David Friday, in his book *Profits, Wages, and Prices*, professes not to understand this remarkable rise in the price level during the War period. Speaking of the American situation he says: [1]

> Those of us who opposed Mr. Bryan in 1896 in the belief that the maintenance of the gold standard would insure a stable price level are baffled by this unprecedented phenomenon. If we had abandoned the gold standard and gone to irredeemable paper, or even to a silver standard, the thing could be explained according to the respectable and time-honored laws of economic

[1] Friday, David A., *Profits, Wages, and Prices* (New York: Harcourt, Brace and Howe, Inc., 1920), p. 133.

theory.  But how the price level of a country can multiply by two and one-half while it remains on the gold standard is not easily explained.

Nevertheless, the thing *is* explainable according to the time-honored laws of economic theory; all that is necessary is to substitute bank credit for irredeemable paper.  Bank credit in this day and age is more potent in determining the price level than are circulating notes, or irredeemable paper currency.  As Mr. R. G. Hawtrey rightly points out,[1] "It is not gold that controls money, but money that controls the value of gold. * * * Gold necessarily follows money; the idea that money follows gold is a fallacy."  Bank credit, as is generally known, now does 90 per cent or more of the money work of the country, and is the most important influence affecting the price level, and hence the value of money.

Dr. Friday explains the rise in prices in this country as due to enlarged European demand for American goods for war purposes.[2]  Professor W. C. Mitchell states the same idea.[3]  It will be conceded that enhanced European demand had an appreciable tendency to raise prices in this country, but this alone is far from sufficient to explain the whole of the phenomenal increase.  For it is significant that as late as September, 1915, after a year of European demand and after the influx of over three hundred million dollars in gold from abroad, the price level in this country still stood at 100 (with 1913 as the base year).

The primary explanation of how the price level could multiply two and one-half times during a five-year period while the United States remained on the gold standard is to be found, it is believed, in the superimposition of a system of central banking in the form of the Federal Reserve System upon the commercial banking organization of the United States.  It was in the last third of the year 1915 that the

[1] See the *Journal of the Royal Statistical Society* (1931), Vol. XCIV, Part IV, p. 549.
[2] "Thus Europe raised our prices * * * ." *Profits, Wages, and Prices*, p. 139.
[3] "Unquestionably it was the impetus from Europe that started American prices on their upward course." *American Economic Review, Supplement* (March, 1920), Vol. X, No. 1, p. 131.

sharp increase in Federal Reserve credit outstanding began, and it was with the increase in deposits in the latter part of the year that the real rise in prices started. It is not denied that a contributing cause of this price inflation was found in the huge quantities of gold that flowed into this country from Europe during the early years of the War. But in spite of these imports of gold, without the superimposition of this system of central banking, or bankers' banking, upon the American banking system almost coincident with the outbreak of war, the inflation during the War could not have progressed to the heights it did, or at least would not have done so without suspension of the gold standard and resort to irredeemable paper money.

It is in the operations of the Federal Reserve System, then, that the major explanation of the War-time rise in prices lies. It has already been stated that the Federal Reserve Act wrought many important changes in the American banking system. So far-reaching were these changes in their effects, both during and after the War, that it is desirable at this point to consider certain of the more important ones in some detail. For these changes, together with the general operation of the Federal Reserve System during the War and post-War periods, point the way to the explanation of the Great Depression. What follows is by no means intended as a criticism of central banking or of the Federal Reserve System as such; rather, it is intended to be explanatory of the way in which setting up a system of central banking where one did not exist before made possible vast potentialities of credit expansion.

### CREDIT "SLACK" IN THE UNITED STATES

The principal and immediate effect of the institution of this new system was to economize reserves—that is, to enable a given foundation of gold to support a much larger superstructure of credit than was previously possible. These new credit-creating possibilities were put to use rather promptly in financing the War. Instead of a long period of gradual growth before attaining the maximum expansion, the potentialities of the new system were utilized to the fullest extent by June, 1920, or within a period of five years. The European nations possessed of long-established central banking systems were forced to resort to irredeemable paper because of the fact that their systems had attained virtually maximum credit expansion during the period preceding the War; there was but little "slack" in the European central banking systems at the outbreak of hostilities. Under the spur of the policy of War finance pursued in this country, a comparable degree of expansion for the American system was compressed within half a decade. The result was a forcing process impinging upon a relatively stable pre-War price level, with the prompt and rapid rise in prices already indicated.

Had it not been for the creation of the Federal Reserve System, there would have been a limit to the expansion of bank credit during the War that would speedily have been reached—the ratio of reserves to deposit liabilities would have fallen to the legal minimum and prevented the further expansion of deposit credit, unless new reserves were acquired in some manner. The establishment of the Federal Reserve System, with its pooling and economizing of reserves, thus permitting a greater credit expansion on a given reserve base, had the practical effect of an acquisition of new reserves for the banking system. The credit-expansion powers of the available reserves were magnified several times by the provisions of the Federal Reserve Act.

### REDUCTION OF RESERVE REQUIREMENTS AN INFLATIONISTIC STEP

In the first place, by the terms of the original Act the minimum average legal reserve requirements of member banks were reduced approximately 50 per cent [1] from those

---

[1] The average reserve requirements of all banks prior to the Federal Reserve Act are estimated to have been 21.09%; under the provisions of the original Act, 11.61%; and under the terms of the Amendment of June 21, 1917, 9.76%. See *The Practical Operations of the Federal Reserve System*, issued by the Federal Reserve Bank of Richmond, p. 243.

prevailing under the old National Bank Act, thereby doubling possible credit in the banking system. A billion dollars in reserves which would support about five billion dollars of deposit credit under the terms of the National Bank Act could support about ten billion dollars of credit under the new reserve provisions of the Federal Reserve Act. Yet reserve requirements were further reduced after our entrance into the War by the Amendment of June 21, 1917, which also contained the highly important provision that from then on all lawful reserves of member banks should consist only of deposit credits on the books of the Federal Reserve Banks. The effect of this amendment, as well as the reduction of reserve requirements contained in the original Act, was to enhance the effective reserve base of the banking system, just as effectively as though gold reserves had been increased.[1]

## Reserve Banking Inherently Inflationistic

Quite apart from the reduction in reserve requirements, however, a magnification of the reserve base came about simply as a result of the creation of a central banking system. This is because of the fact that a system of central banking operates to dilute cash, so that reserves in effect go further. In a system devoid of bankers' banking, reserves consist of lawful money in the vaults of individual banks; in a system incorporating central banking, legal reserves for the member banks of the system exist simply as deposit liabilities of the bankers' banks. When the Federal Reserve

[1] Cf. the Report of the Committee on War Finance of the American Economic Association, The American Economic Review, Supplement No. 2 (March, 1919), Vol. IX, No. 1, pp. 96–97: "Recent improvements in our banking system, growing out of the establishment of the Federal Reserve System and its subsequent development, have made our reserve money * * * more efficient than it formerly was; in other words, have enabled a dollar in reserve to do more money work than before. This in effect is equivalent to increasing the supply of reserve money." It has been calculated that if the requirements of the National Bank Act were in vogue December 31, 1924, member banks would have required $3,200,000,000 more in reserves than they held to support the credit then outstanding (The Practical Operations of the Federal System, p. 238); and the Committee on Bank Reserves of the Federal Reserve System estimated that on the same basis in 1931 member banks would have needed $4,400,000,000 of reserves instead of the $2,900,000,000 actually held.

Act, and the amendment thereto of June 21, 1917, required the member banks to transfer their reserves to the Federal Reserve Banks they became reserves for the Reserve Banks, and the transfer gave rise to deposits to the credit of the member banks. These deposit liabilities owed the member banks by the Reserve Banks likewise assumed the rôle of *reserves for the member banks.* Against such deposits the Federal Reserve Banks were required to hold only a fractional reserve, amounting to but 35 per cent of the deposit liabilities. The difference of 65 per cent constituted free or excess reserves for the Reserve Banks, on the basis of which they could grant loans to the member banks, increasing the deposits of the latter with the Federal Reserve Banks. And as these increased deposits with the Federal Reserve Banks represented increased reserves for the member banks, the latter were able to increase their deposits by granting additional loans to their customers.[1] Hence it is apparent that central banking is inherently inflationistic, at least during the period following its introduction, on account of the greater expansion of credit it makes possible on a given amount of reserves.

Thus, if the commercial banks prior to the inauguration of a system of bankers' banking are required to hold an average reserve, say, of 10 per cent against deposit liabilities, their deposits may be ten times that reserve, or, they may expand credit roughly on a ten-fold basis. With the reserves of the commercial banks transferred to the Federal Reserve Banks, and with the latter required to maintain a reserve of only 35 per cent against the deposit liabilities due to the member banks, credit expansion may, at its utmost, proceed to approximately thirty times the amount of the reserves. Thus it is seen that the establishment of a central banking system magnified the former expansive power

[1] Under the old system, when a bank's reserve fell below the legal minimum it was prohibited by law from making additional loans; and if its reserve was exhausted it was declared insolvent. Under the new system, borrowing from the bankers' bank is the equivalent of going into the reserve under the old system, but without any penalty; indeed, the process of borrowing serves to replenish, or add to, the borrowing bank's reserve.

virtually three-fold, in addition to the doubled expansibility brought about by the reduction in reserve requirements contained in the Federal Reserve Act.

Let us analyze a concrete example. Suppose the total cash reserves of all commercial banks prior to the introduction of central banking amounted to one billion dollars; on the basis of these reserves, and with an assumed minimum reserve-deposit ratio of 10 per cent, the banking system could expand credit to the extent of 10 billion dollars. Now, suppose that the Federal Reserve System is established, and all reserves are transferred to the vaults of the new Reserve Banks, where they become deposits to the credit of (and at the same time are counted as the reserves for) the member banks. Against this billion dollars of deposits the Reserve Banks must maintain a minimum cash reserve of 35 per cent, or 350 million dollars. The remainder of the billion dollars of cash, 650 million dollars, becomes excess reserve for the Reserve Banks. On the basis of such excess reserve the Reserve Banks are able to increase their deposits, and hence the new reserves of the member banks, by the maximum amount of about 1.9 billion dollars. This they may do at the request of the member banks, by rediscounting for them eligible commercial paper, or by granting them direct loans, properly collateralled. The Reserve Banks may also expand deposits on their own initiative, through what are known as "open market operations"—the purchase of Government bonds and other specified securities in the "open market." The purchase of these securities increases the reserves of the member banks by increasing their deposits with the Federal Reserve Banks, in much the same manner as that by which the member banks increase their own deposits to the credit of their customers when they buy bonds, described above.

If the entire proceeds of such loans (or such bond purchases) are left on deposit with the Reserve Banks by the member banks, the legal reserves of the latter are increased by that amount, 1.9 billion dollars. In other words, the

Federal Reserve Banks now have 2.9 billion dollars in deposits to the credit of the member institutions (against which they have the one billion dollars as reserve, or a reserve ratio of 35 per cent), or, conversely, the member banks now have 2.9 billion dollars in legal reserves, on the basis of which it is possible for them to expand credit to a total amount of 29 billion dollars. By virtue of the possession of this new, added, reserve of 1.9 billion dollars—the existence of which is attributable directly and wholly to the establishment and operation of a system of bankers' banks—the member banks can now add 19 billion dollars new credit to the antecedently existing 10 billion dollars.

Thus it is seen that, whereas the billion dollars in the vaults of the commercial banks supported a credit structure of 10 billion dollars (on the assumption of a 10 per cent reserve-deposit ratio), the same billion dollars may, as a result of the creation of the central banking system, support a credit structure of 29 billion dollars when transferred to the vaults of the Federal Reserve Banks. The superimposition of the system of central banking by and of itself thus virtually triples the possible expansive power of the banking system.[1]

This illustration assumes the existence of a 10 per cent reserve-deposit ratio for the commercial banking system. But it was not until the Federal Reserve Act came into effect that such an average reserve ratio legally obtained. The Federal Reserve Act increased the credit-creating possibilities of the commercial banking system in two distinct ways: it reduced average reserve requirements from about 20 per cent to about 10 per cent, thereby doubling the power of credit expansion, and it set up a system of central banking, which tripled this power. The real effect of the Federal Reserve Act, therefore, was to increase the credit expansion potentialities of the banking system not

[1] It is also to be observed that henceforth the same twenty-nine-fold expansion is made possible in connection with each new influx of gold from abroad, whether the gold is deposited directly in the Federal Reserve Banks, or in commercial banks and by them redeposited in the Federal Reserve Banks.

merely three-fold, but virtually six-fold. A billion dollars in reserves, which under the old system would support total deposits of five billion dollars, could under the new system theoretically support nearly six times that amount, or thirty billions.[1] The full effect of the Federal Reserve Act was thus the same as though five billion dollars in new reserves had been acquired by the banking system.

ISSUE OF FEDERAL RESERVE NOTES FAVORED INFLATION

Not all of the gold which was transferred to the Federal Reserve Banks, however, was employed as reserve against the deposits of these banks. A portion of it was made to serve as security for the new Federal Reserve notes provided for by the Act, which required a legal minimum gold backing of 40 per cent. But the restraint on inflation that this procedure implies was offset in part by a related development.

In 1913 the most important single item of paper money in circulation was the gold certificate that was backed dollar for dollar by gold, and of which the circulation amounted to almost exactly one billion dollars. Even before the entrance of the United States into the War, the Federal Reserve Banks had adopted the policy of withholding gold certificates from circulation and issuing in their place Federal Reserve notes. This policy operated to increase further the "free" gold reserves of the Federal Reserve Banks, since for each dollar in gold notes there was released 60 cents in gold backing; that is to say, it put into circulation a form of

---

[1] It should be stressed, once again, that this example demonstrates the possible maximum expansive power; that is, it is assumed that the entire excess reserve of the Federal Reserve Banks is employed for the purpose of supporting additional Federal Reserve Bank deposits, and hence creating additional reserve for the member banks. To the extent that this excess of 650 million dollars (assumed to be gold) is used to support issues of Federal Reserve *notes*, which cannot be counted as legal reserve by member banks, this expansive power is diminished. As a matter of fact, a substantial portion of the gold reserve of the Federal Reserve Banks has been used for this latter purpose.

One other, and minor, qualification or limiting factor should be noted. If the process of credit expansion induces an increase in prices, more cash will be needed for hand-to-hand circulation; provided such additional "pocket money" is obtained by drawing on banks' reserves, to that extent the expansive power of the banking system is decreased.

paper money requiring a 40 per cent gold reserve in place of one requiring 100 per cent reserve. Obviously, such a policy was favorable to the cause of inflation, because it released from required reserve against monetary circulation gold which could serve as reserve against a much larger amount of paper money, or against deposits (reserves) to the credit of the member banks.

## The Federal Reserve Act and Time Deposits

Two important changes with respect to time deposits which accompanied the introduction of the Federal Reserve System remain for comment. In the first place, the Reserve Act sanctioned the acceptance of, and payment of interest on, time deposits by National Banks (and other member banks), thus placing them in a position to compete with state banks and mutual savings banks for such deposits. Secondly, under the National Bank Act the same per cent of reserve had been required against *all* net deposits of a given bank; no distinction had been made between the reserve required against demand and against time deposits. Under the original Federal Reserve Act only 5 per cent reserve was required to be held against time deposits, and by the Amendment of June 21, 1917, this reserve was further reduced to the very modest figure of 3 per cent. The second of these measures was a further factor which operated to release reserves, or which permitted a reduction in "average reserve" requirements. These two changes in banking legislation assisted materially in producing significant changes in American banking during the post-War period (as will be shown in following chapters), and both are important among the causal factors producing the Great Depression.

## Unequal Credit Expansion of Member and Non-Member Banks

It is of interest to examine the effects of this greater expansive power brought about by the Federal Reserve System during the six years immediately following its introduction. This may be done by comparing the relative credit extension of the member banks of the Federal Reserve System and of the banks outside the system, as shown in the following table.

TABLE II

ALL BANKS IN THE UNITED STATES—DEPOSITS OF MEMBER AND NON-
MEMBER BANKS (EXCLUSIVE OF INTERBANK DEPOSITS), 1914–1920
(June figures—in Millions of Dollars)

| YEAR | ALL BANKS | MEMBER BANKS | NON-MEMBER BANKS |
|------|-----------|--------------|------------------|
| 1914 | 18,566 | 6,374* | 12,192 |
| 1915 | 19,131 | 6,678 | 12,453 |
| 1916 | 22,759 | 8,395 | 14,364 |
| 1917 | 26,352 | 10,301 | 16,052 |
| 1918 | 28,765 | 15,670 | 13,095 |
| 1919 | 33,603 | 19,171 | 14,433 |
| 1920 | 37,721 | 21,915 | 15,805 |

Source: Fifteenth *Annual Report* of the Federal Reserve Board (1928), Table 45, p. 111.
* National Banks only.

It is seen that the deposits of all banks increased 100 per cent from 1914 to 1920, but that the deposits of the non-member banks increased by only 30 per cent, whereas the deposits of the member banks increased by almost 250 per cent. The deposits of the member banks constituted about one-third of all deposits in 1914, but in 1920 they represented almost 60 per cent. Of the total increase of over 19 billion dollars in deposits during this period, 80 per cent was accounted for by the member banks. It is to be recognized, of course, that the 1914 figure for the member banks is for National Banks only, the Federal Reserve System not starting operations until November of that year, yet virtually the same results are obtained if computations are made beginning with the figures for June, 1915. Also it is to be noted that some state banks entered the Federal Reserve System after 1914, resulting in a shift of deposits from the non-member banks to the member banks; the number of banks transferred at that time was comparatively small, however, and by no means adequate to account for the disparity in the rates of increase of deposits for the two classes of banks. Further, it is true that a few state banks with large deposits joined the ranks of the member banks after our entrance into the War, accounting in part for the absolute decrease in non-member bank deposits from 1917 to 1918, but this fact alone does not account for the relatively greater increase of member bank deposits as compared with the non-member totals.

The basic explanation of this disparity lies in the creation and operation of the Federal Reserve System. As the member banks reduced their reserve-deposit ratio by purchasing Government bonds or by financing the purchase of such bonds on the part of their customers, the banks could go to the Federal Reserve Banks and improve that ratio by replenishing their reserves. This they could do by rediscounting the notes of those customers whose bond purchases they were financing, or by direct loans collateralled by the Government bonds which they had themselves acquired. Again possessed of excess reserves, they could again purchase bonds for their own account or finance the purchase of them for their customers' accounts. This process was repeated over and over, each time creating new deposits representing new purchasing power. These new reserves taking the form largely of deposits (*credit*) on the books of the Reserve Banks, rather than *cash*, there was not a widespread diffusion of reserves among *all* of the banks of the system as might have occurred during a period of pronounced credit expansion before 1914. The non-member banks, being denied the privilege of replenishing their reserves by borrowing from the Federal Reserve Banks, naturally were unable to increase their deposits so rapidly or so much as the member banks. The non-member banks could, it is true, increase their reserves by borrowing from the member banks in much the same fashion that the latter borrowed from the Reserve Banks, and thus expand credit; but non-member banks did not avail themselves of this privilege on any extensive scale.

The table on page 32 summarizes the growth of loans and

investments in the banking system, 1914–1920, and also reveals the dominant part played by the member banks in that growth.  Considered in conjunction with Table II, it also indicates the fact that increases in deposits in the banking system as a whole follow upon (*i.e.*, are the result of) increases in loans and investments.

Here again, it is to be observed that the greater part of the credit expansion during these years was contributed

TABLE III

ALL BANKS IN THE UNITED STATES—LOANS AND INVESTMENTS OF
MEMBER AND NON-MEMBER BANKS, 1914–1920
(June figures—in Millions of Dollars)

| YEAR | LOANS AND INVESTMENTS | | | INVESTMENTS | | |
|------|-----------|-----------------|-------------------|-----------|-----------------|------------------|
| | All Banks | Member Banks | Non-Member Banks | All Banks | Member Banks | Non-Member Banks |
| 1914 | 20,789 | 8,313 | 12,475 | 5,541 | 1,870 | 3,671 |
| 1915 | 21,466 | 8,764 | 12,702 | 5,823 | 2,044 | 3,779 |
| 1916 | 24,587 | 10,315 | 14,271 | 6,626 | 2,351 | 4,274 |
| 1917 | 28,287 | 12,453 | 15,833 | 7,777 | 3,083 | 4,693 |
| 1918 | 31,813 | 18,507 | 13,306 | 9,421 | 5,274 | 4,147 |
| 1919 | 36,570 | 22,242 | 14,330 | 11,860 | 6,827 | 5,033 |
| 1920 | 41,685 | 25,559 | 16,125 | 10,861 | 6,026 | 4,835 |

Source: Fifteenth *Annual Report* of Federal Reserve Board (1928), Table 44, p. 111.

by the member banks.  Although loans and investments of all banks increased by 100 per cent, those of the non-member banks show a growth of only 33 per cent, whereas the increase for the member banks was more than 200 per cent.  The same is true with respect to investments, considered separately.

One point of particular interest in this table is that the greater part of the increase in total bank credit was represented by loans, rather than by investments, the latter constituting only about one-fourth of the total increase between 1914 and 1920.  Yet the expansion of loans, apparently, was initiated by the growth of investments; investments increased first, to be followed by increases in loans.  A spiral of developments began with the huge issues of Government bonds, proceeded on rapidly to higher prices and an accelerated tempo of general business, and eventuated in the expansion of loans to provide the increased working capital for commerce and industry that was necessitated by the higher level of prices.   What percentage of the increase in loans consisted initially of advances on Government securities for the purpose of covering individuals' subscriptions for Liberty Bonds is not known, but loans of both types—those for the purposes just mentioned and loans to business men for the carrying of inventories at higher prices—together with the bond purchases, provided new credit which found its outlet in an enlarged money demand for commodities, resulting in forcing up the level of wholesale commodity prices.   Hence the rise in the price level is ascribable primarily to the Government's policy of war financing.

### Banks' Purchase of Government Securities a Potent Cause of Credit Expansion

Table IV indicates strikingly the use to which the member banks were put in absorbing issues of Government bonds, thus creating more credit which circulated throughout the entire system.

### TABLE IV

ALL MEMBER BANKS—LOANS AND INVESTMENTS, 1914–1920
(June figures, except as indicated—in Millions of Dollars)

| Year | Loans and Investments | | | | |
|---|---|---|---|---|---|
| | Total | Loans | Investments | | |
| | | | Total | U. S. Securities | Other Securities |
| 1914 (Dec. 31) | 8,498 | 6,419 | 2,079 | 760 | 1,319 |
| 1915 | 8,764 | 6,720 | 2,044 | 799 | 1,295 |
| 1916 | 10,315 | 7,964 | 2,351 | 703 | 1,648 |
| 1917 (Mar. 5) | 11,701 | 9,096 | 2,605 | 687 | 1,918 |
| 1918 | 18,507 | 13,233 | 5,274 | 2,465 | 2,809 |
| 1919 | 22,242 | 15,414 | 6,827 | 3,803 | 3,024 |
| 1920 | 25,559 | 19,533 | 6,026 | 2,811 | 3,215 |

Source: Fifteenth *Annual Report* of the Federal Reserve Board (1928), Table 48, p. 114.

While total investments were increasing 130 per cent from March, 1917 (just prior to the declaration of war in April), to June, 1920, investments in Government securities increased over 300 per cent, and investments in other securities increased but 67 per cent. While loans increased 70 per cent between March, 1917, and June, 1919, investments in Government securities increased 450 per cent during the same period. The growth of member banks' holdings of Government securities during the year of the entrance of the United States into the War is strikingly apparent. The increase of almost seven billion dollars in total loans and investments in virtually the first War year indicates how the creation of credit by the purchase of Government securities led to a multiple expansion of loans and investments in the entire banking system.

### Post-War Price Levels Abnormal

"Lenin is said to have declared that the best way to destroy the Capitalist System was to debauch the currency." [1] How close the capitalist system in America has come to destruction in consequence of the inflationary debauch of the currency indulged in during and since the War by the manufacture of deposit currency is as yet uncertain. For "it is a process that engages," in the vivid language of Mr. J. M. Keynes, "all the hidden forces of economic law on the side of destruction, and does it in a manner which not one man in a million is able to diagnose." [2] The European countries achieved but little liquidation of credit during the 1920–1921 debacle, and several of them went on to further note currency inflation that reached astronomical heights. In the drastic, but brief, deflation of prices in 1920–1921 the United States did not complete the liquidation of inflated bank credit created during the War period: neither prices nor the structure of production and finance arrived at complete equilibrium relationships. The result was that the recovery following the immediate post-War depression rested on a foundation of prior inflation and

---

[1] Keynes, J. M., *Essays in Persuasion* (London: Macmillan & Company, 1931), p. 77.
[2] *Ibid.*, p. 78.

upon a price level which could by no means be considered "normal."

## POST-WAR DEPRESSION INEVITABLE

In a small volume published in 1916 entitled *The Economy and Finance of the War*, by Professor A. C. Pigou of Cambridge University, appears a significant passage: [1]

> * * * after the first few months of transition [after the end of the War], * * * it is practically certain that, to make good the havoc and the waste of war, there will be a strong industrial boom. This boom, if history is any guide, will generate in many minds an unreasoning sense of optimism leading to much wild investment. The result, some years afterwards, will be failures, crisis, and depression. If this danger is to be obviated or mitigated, it is imperative that the Government and the banks should so act as to restrain and keep within limits the initial peace boom.

The depression being dealt with here is that predicted by Professor Pigou in 1916. The only flaw in his remarkable prevision is that the "few years" extended to a decade; but he could not have foreseen, of course, that governments and banks, instead of restraining the investment boom and keeping it within limits, would aid and abet that boom by providing it with even more credit on which to feed.

## PROXIMATE VERSUS ULTIMATE CAUSES OF THE GREAT DEPRESSION

The origins of the Great Depression, then, go back to the War and the inflation produced by war financing, assisted in this country by the operations of the Federal Reserve System. Had the War not intervened, a depression of the character, severity, and duration of the recent one would not have ensued; once the War was undertaken, the depression became to a certain degree inevitable.[2]    At the same time, the pattern of the depression was shaped by

---

[1] London: J. M. Dent and Sons, Ltd., pp. 87–88.

[2] "Great wars are accompanied by prosperity and followed by depression. This is an ancient truth * * * but one which each new generation tends to forget." Leonard P. Ayres, *The Economics of Recovery* (New York: The Macmillan Company, 1933), p. 15.

Federal Reserve credit policy in the post-War years and by the secondary inflation of bank credit engendered by that policy. Federal Reserve policy, however, was undoubtedly conditioned by the disordered state of finance, production, and prices which the War left behind it—for as Stamp says, "most financial questions are affected by what has happened during the war, and what has happened in consequence since." The chief evil legacy of the period of War finance was the inflated price level produced by the War inflation—for it was this inflated price level which was to influence all post-War banking and credit developments, and hence post-War economic events.[1]  During the years beginning with 1922 the Federal Reserve banking authorities embarked on a misguided attempt to prop up that price level artificially by a further inflation of bank credit, in consequence of which the War inflation was carried over to the depression which began in 1929. Hence the proximate cause of the depression was Federal Reserve banking policy following 1921 and the inflation of bank credit induced by that policy; the ultimate controlling influence was the War and the War-time inflation. Later chapters will deal with the way in which this post-War inflation, and the boom which resulted from that inflation, developed, and with the parts the banking system and banking policy played therein.

[1] "It is not the event of war * * * but rather the fact that great wars cause sudden and extreme advances in commodity prices. It is this sudden price advance which largely determines the nature and sequence of the business cycles of the following twenty years or so." *Ibid.*, p. 18.

## CHAPTER III

# THE RÔLE OF GOLD

One of the necessary evils of a depression, it would seem, is the crop of erroneous explanations of it. Unfortunately, there is as yet no universally accepted explanation of the cause, or causes, of depression. It is common practice, therefore, for all sorts of persons, whether with or without qualifications, to try their hands at theorizing upon the origins of the depression. Unfortunately, too, it is the more erroneous ideas of the less properly qualified theorists which seem to gain the largest measure of popular credence, as against the more nearly "correct" views of the trained economists.

## "POPULAR" EXPLANATIONS

The recent depression did not differ in this respect from previous ones. Rather, it was marked by the veritable flood of false economic theories and "popular" explanations which has poured forth since 1929, all tending to obscure and confuse the main issues so that calm and reasoned analysis was at a discount and progress toward a proper explanation retarded.

Such diagnoses, of course, are thoroughly misleading. And they are all the more so in that they commonly possess a certain degree of plausibility which seems to fit with what the public apparently feels is the cause of the trouble. They have in too many cases been appeals to emotion rather than reason. Unfortunately, too, they have been uttered in some instances by authorities whose *dicta* are frequently accepted as determinative of controversial questions; but, as Professor Lionel Robbins of the London School of Economics remarks of one of them, "the authority is weighty, but the argument is slender."

One of the duties devolving upon economists is that of pointing out the errors in fallacious economic contentions, quite as much as the constructive task of formulating sound doctrine and setting forth correct exposition.  In order to clear the ground before proceeding to a discussion of what are considered the major forces accounting for the Great Depression it is appropriate, therefore, to examine briefly a certain few of those theories which have succeeded in influencing popular belief as well as political action.  This chapter and the succeeding one will be concerned with that inquiry.  No attempt will be made to examine the validity of all of the many explanations of the depression which have been put forward: only those will be considered which are demonstrably erroneous yet have had an influence almost inversely proportional to their accuracy.

These theories tend to fall into two groups, or categories. On the one hand are those which hold that gold, according to one or another explanatory version of its causative character, is at the root of our difficulties.  On the other hand are several theories which have as their central feature the contention that it is the maladjustments in income which produce depression, usually known as the underconsumption theory of the business cycle.  This chapter will treat of those views which are inclined to blame the recent disaster upon gold or upon the gold standard; the next will deal with various forms of the underconsumption theory.

ERRONEOUS EXPLANATIONS OF DEPRESSION INDICT GOLD

Gold as the villain of the piece usually occupies a prominent rôle during depression.  The same is true when a damaging decline in prices is in progress, whether or not accompanied by severe depression.  As Professor Gregory points out,[1] " * * * the popularity of the gold standard from time to time is closely correlated to the tendency of the price level.  Thus the movement of prices furnishes the most convenient guide to the movement of opinion."  It

---

[1] The "Gold Supplement" of the London *Times*, June 20, 1933, p. vii.

has frequently been asserted in certain quarters that the recent disaster was brought about by an insufficiency of gold to support the price level, or that it was the result of an inadequate rate of increase of the world's monetary stock of gold. Otherwise stated, it is insisted that prices have necessarily fallen either because the gold supplies of the world at large are insufficient in the absolute sense, or because the per annum rate of increase in the world's monetary gold stock has failed to keep pace with the rate of increase in the physical volume of production. Or, it is argued that maldistribution of the available supply of gold is responsible for the trouble. It is also asserted that the inherent nature of the gold standard itself is a necessary and sufficient explanation.

When the rise in prices began following 1896 with the fresh inflow of Alaskan gold, the increasing use of checks, and the growth of bank credit, it was hoped by many at the time that "the gold question" had been disposed of permanently. The Gold Standard Act of 1900 seemed to lend legislative sanction to that hope. Subsequent events, however, have proved this to be an illusion. The old arguments against the gold standard have been revived and embellished in the light of the remarkable transformation in banking and credit usages since 1896. Among those who have been prominent as latter-day critics of the gold standard may be mentioned, among others, Professor Cassel, Professor J. M. Keynes, and the late Joseph Kitchin abroad; and in this country, Professors Fisher and Rogers of Yale University, and Professors Warren and Pearson of the New York State College of Agriculture at Cornell University. In view of the extraordinary display of popular interest in and enthusiasm for Warren and Pearson's recent treatises, *Prices* and *Gold and Prices*, Professor Warren's erstwhile position of influence as President Roosevelt's so-called monetary adviser, and the devaluation of the gold dollar (seemingly predicated upon a shortage-of-gold theory), it is especially appropriate to accord the Warren-Pearson

theories critical consideration. This should not be construed as in any way minimizing the misleading influence
of the work of others whose views are in part harmonious
with and in part divergent from those of Warren and Pearson. The latter are selected simply because of their recent
prominence and the political significance of the views they
advocate: a comprehensive analysis of all related theories
is too large a task to be essayed here.

CRITICAL EXAMINATION OF WARREN-PEARSON
CONTENTIONS

One of the principal arguments of Professors Warren and
Pearson is to the effect that, in order to insure stability of
the price level, gold production should proceed at a compound rate of 3.15 per cent per annum.[1] They argue that
monetary gold stocks have not increased at this rate since
1915 and *therefore* prices have fallen. Thus, they state: [2]

> From 1845–1849 to 1914, * * * the production of * * *
> commodities increased at a compound rate of 3.15 per cent per
> year. * * * When monetary stocks also increase at this same
> rate, the value of gold is stable. * * * In recent years, the
> world stocks of monetary gold have not been increasing as much
> as 3.15 per cent per year. * * * Some economists have been
> misled by making calculations on the rate of increase in gold
> production since 1922. This is doubly fallacious. It begins
> measurement from an abnormally low point, and would be
> incorrect in any event, for it is world monetary stocks of gold
> and not gold production that must increase at the same rate as
> other things in order to maintain stable prices. * * * Since 1915,

[1] Their theory that the explanation of prices and the price level is based upon the demand for and the supply of gold (perhaps their fundamental theory) is not dealt with here for the sake of brevity. To attempt to combat fully their many misstate-ments, inaccuracies, and inconsistencies would lead too far afield for the purpose at hand. If their argument with respect to the requisite increase in monetary gold stocks is successfully met in the following critical discussion, the idea of the demand for and the supply of gold determining the level of prices is also disposed of, as will be shown shortly. For a thorough-going and able, albeit somewhat scathing, cri-tique of the Warren-Pearson fallacies in general, see Spahr, W. E., *The Monetary Theories of Warren and Pearson* (New York: Farrar & Rinehart, 1934); and see Hardy, C. O., *The Warren-Pearson Price Theory* (Washington: The Brookings In-stitution, 1935).

[2] Warren, George F., and Pearson, Frank A., *Prices* (New York: John Wiley and Sons, Inc., 1933), pp. 100, 82, and 90.

world gold production has not increased fast enough to maintain a stable price level with a normal increase in business and normal demand for gold.

The fallacy of which Professors Warren and Pearson accuse "some economists" (of starting calculations from an abnormally low point in gold production) can be passed over lightly in view of their own assertion that gold production has not increased sufficiently *since 1915* to maintain a stable price level, inasmuch as 1915 was the absolute peak year of gold production prior to 1932—a fact which they neglect to mention. This is a minor point, however, and its collapse by no means disposes of the argument that there has been a deficiency in the rate of output of monetary gold.

This view is further developed in an article by Professors Warren and Pearson appearing in the New York *Times* for July 23, 1933, the gist of which is as follows:

> From 1914 to 1928, the world's gold stocks increased 38 per cent, and the world's production of basic commodities increased by exactly the same percentage. Therefore the world gold supply was just about adequate to support pre-war prices, provided all the world returned to the gold basis. But prices in England in 1928 were 45 per cent above pre-war, and in the United States 41 per cent above pre-war. At that time the countries of the world were trying to return to gold. France returned on June 25, 1928, and the gold panic was soon on.

There are, however, certain hard facts of recent monetary history which this theory of a scarcity of gold does not seem adequately to explain. It is therefore pertinent at this point to inquire more fully into the matter of the gold supply. The table on page 42 indicates the increases in the monetary gold stocks of the CENTRAL BANKS and TREASURIES of 48 countries, comprising practically all of the commercial countries of the world, at the end of each year from 1913 to 1932. The table also gives figures for gold production, net gains to the western world from China and India, net changes in the supply of new gold, net changes in the aggregate of monetary gold reserves, and the annual percentage change in the aggregate of monetary gold stocks. The non-monetary demand represented by net imports into China and India is also shown.

TABLE V

GOLD: SUPPLY, DEMAND, AND STOCKS
(In Millions of Dollars, 23.22 gr. fine gold)

| | GOLD SUPPLIES | | | MONETARY GOLD STOCKS | | | DEMAND |
|---|---|---|---|---|---|---|---|
| Year | Mine Output | Released from India and China | Total Year's Addition | Total, 48 Countries | Change from Preceding Year | Per Cent Change | Non-Monetary Uses (India, China) |
| 1900 | 254 | — | 254 | 2,029 | 79 | — | 103 |
| 1913 | 460 | 4 | 464 | 4,857 | — | — | 220 |
| 1914 | 440 | 28 | 468 | 5,342 | 485 | 10.0 | 136 |
| 1915 | 470 | 12 | 482 | 6,236 | 896 | 16.8 | 89 |
| 1916 | 455 | — | 455 | 7,139 | 387 | 6.2 | 124 |
| 1917 | 421 | — | 421 | 7,139 | 514 | 7.8 | 185 |
| 1918 | 385 | 16 | 401 | 6,807 | −332 | −4.7 | 84 |
| 1919 | 366 | — | 366 | 6,794 | − 13 | − .2 | 304 |
| 1920 | 333 | 15 | 348 | 7,238 | 444 | 6.5 | 124 |
| 1921 | 330 | 11 | 341 | 8,029 | 791 | 10.9 | 76 |
| 1922 | 319 | — | 319 | 8,402 | 373 | 4.6 | 207 |
| 1923 | 368 | — | 368 | 8,635 | 233 | 2.7 | 239 |
| 1924 | 393 | — | 393 | 8,956 | 321 | 3.7 | 239 |
| 1925 | 393 | — | 393 | 8,973 | 17 | .2 | 322 |
| 1926 | 400 | 2 | 402 | 9,209 | 236 | 2.6 | 185 |
| 1927 | 402 | — | 402 | 9,567 | 358 | 3.9 | 157 |
| 1928 | 407 | — | 407 | 10,026 | 459 | 4.8 | 175 |
| 1929 | 403 | 2 | 405 | 10,305 | 279 | 2.8 | 134 |
| 1930 | 431 | 10 | 441 | 10,915 | 610 | 5.9 | 113 |
| 1931 | 459 | 155 | 614 | 11,258 | 343 | 3.1 | 40 |
| 1932 | 494 | 220 | 714 | 11,920 | 662 | 5.9 | 40 |

Source: National City Bank *Letter*, March, 1933, p. 43, and there credited to the *Federal Reserve Bulletin* and other sources.

It is to be noted that the above figures for the period beginning with 1913 are not for production of gold only, but include the net increases in *bank reserves*. They are thus not subject to deductions for non-monetary uses or absorption in hand-to-hand circulation and private hoards. Nor are they subject to the Warren-Pearson criticism of those calculations that neglect the total *monetary stocks* of gold—in fact, the table goes even farther than Professors Warren and Pearson seem willing to go, as will be shown shortly, in that it indicates the rate of increase in the *reserves of central banks*.

According to the table on page 42, the annual average increase in monetary gold stocks in central banks and governmental treasuries for the period 1900–1929 was 5.8 per cent; for the period 1913–1929, 4.8 per cent; and for 1929–1932, 5.0 per cent. For the decade of the 'twenties, the rate of increase was 4.27 per cent per annum, and for the period 1922–1929, it was 3.16 per cent per annum.

Inasmuch as the amount of the increase in monetary gold stocks as shown by the above table is about 88 per cent from 1914 to 1929, or more than double the 38 per cent indicated by Professors Warren and Pearson in the *Times* article quoted above, Mr. George E. Roberts of the National City Bank addressed an inquiry to Professor Pearson asking for an explanation of the discrepancy, to which Professor Pearson replied in part as follows: [1]

> * * * Gold stocks in central banks increased more rapidly than world stocks. In 1914, the central banks held two-thirds of this gold, and in 1931 practically all of it. The additions to central bank stocks represent 82 per cent of the total produced in the period. The data we used indicate that additions represent 54.5 per cent. The gold outside the central banks cannot be ignored. It was used to transact business and therefore should be added to central bank reserves to get the total gold. The location of the gold is relatively unimportant. Cotton and wheat sell for ounces of gold, and in the long run it makes little difference where it is located. This is not disputing the general belief that gold is used more efficiently when in the banks than when in private hoards.

Professor Pearson's contention that "cotton and wheat sell for ounces of gold" requires little comment. It clearly stamps him as one of the very few out-and-out present-day bullionists. But the notion that the location of the gold is relatively unimportant with respect to prices should not be allowed to pass unchallenged.

[1] See the National City Bank *Letter*, September, 1933, p. 135.

*Importance of Location of Gold Is Pivotal*

To arrive at their figure for total monetary gold for 1914 Professors Warren and Pearson add to the figure for the gold reserves of central banks and governments their own estimate of the amount of monetary gold outside of these banks and treasuries and outside of Asia. This estimated figure of $2,678 million added to the figure for the central banks and governmental treasuries gives them a total of $8,020 million for the world's total monetary stock of gold for 1914, and it is with the use of this initial figure that their percentage increase of 54.5 per cent from 1914 to 1928 is derived. What Professor Pearson evidently means by saying that "the gold outside the central banks cannot be ignored" is that it should be added to the central bank reserves as though it were capable of performing the same amount of money work as would an equal amount of gold in central bank reserves. It is to be noted, however, that he admits he is not disputing the general belief to the contrary.

Here is the crux of the whole matter, and here is the major fallacy of the Warren-Pearson argument. It makes a tremendous difference whether the monetary gold stock of the world is in the hands of the public circulating as gold coin or is being hoarded, in India for instance (in either case unavailable both to central banks and for purposes of international trade), or whether it is in the vaults of the central banks serving as a reserve base making possible the creation of multiple deposit currency. There is today little disagreement among economists that deposit currency constitutes the most important medium of exchange of modern commercial countries, that it performs 90 per cent or more of the money work of the United States, and that it is upon the gold reserve in the central banks that deposit currency is ultimately bottomed. Gold coin in hand-to-hand use performs substantially the same function as an equal sum in bank checks, whereas gold held in bank reserves supports a manifold volume of bank credit subject to circulation by means of checks.

It has already been mentioned in Chapter II that prior to the establishment of the Federal Reserve System one dollar in reserve supported approximately five dollars in bank credit, or deposit currency, and that after the Federal Reserve System was inaugurated the same (gold) reserve could support at the maximum expansion a credit structure about six times as great. The extent to which the introduction of the Federal Reserve System effected an economy of reserves in the United States has also been shown (see pages 24–28). The establishment of a central banking system in a country where one did not exist before, in other words, brings about immediately an economy of gold, virtually doubling or even tripling the expansive power of the banking system on the basis of a given amount of reserves—or, putting it another way, it enables the maintenance of the same credit structure with only one-half or one-third the amount of gold reserve previously necessary. The gold released from serving as a reserve base under the old system now serves as a basis for future credit expansion just as would that much new gold secured from the mines. And to the extent that the central banks attract gold to their vaults which formerly circulated as gold coin, or to the extent that the central banks absorb a larger proportion of the mine output of gold than formerly, further economies in the use of gold are effected.

Changes of these types have been taking place extensively since 1914.[1] The number of central banks in the world has increased markedly since that date. More and more, gold which formerly circulated as coin has become lodged in central bank vaults as reserves; and the central banks have been acquiring an ever-larger percentage of the mine output and of the world's total monetary stock of gold. As Profes-

[1] Cf. Dr. Melchior Palyi, "Some Problems of International Banking Policy," in The International Gold Problem (London: Humphrey Milford, 1932), p. 116: "It is undoubted that, from the point of view of the business community, a better use of the existing gold supply is being made today than before the War."

sor Pearson admits, the central banks held two-thirds of the monetary gold stocks in 1914, and in 1931 they held practically all of it (about 95 per cent). Newly produced gold went from the mines to the central banks in much larger proportions during the period following 1913 than before that date. In the twelve years ending with 1912 gold production amounted to $4,711 million and reporting bank reserves increased $2,222 million, or 47 per cent of the new production. In the twelve years ending with 1930 production of gold aggregated $4,531 million and the increase of bank reserves was $4,108 million, or 90 per cent of the new production. For the period from 1913 to 1932 production of gold amounted to $8,129 million and the net additions to central bank reserves were $7,063 million, or 86 per cent of the new production.[1] The extent to which economies in the use of gold as bank reserves have proceeded since 1914 utterly destroys any validity which might otherwise have attached to the 3-per-cent estimate before that date. What is now important is *the rate at which central banks acquire gold reserves*, for it is on the basis of reserves in central banks that credit is created.

As shown by Table V, the average rate of increase in central bank gold reserves for the period 1922–1929 was 3.16 per cent per annum, the smallest rate of increase for any comparable period since 1913, yet one which satisfies the requirement of Professors Warren and Pearson that monetary gold stocks should increase at the rate of 3.15 per cent per annum. It is to be stressed, however, that these figures are for central bank reserves, and not all monetary gold stocks, including those which circulate as coin. The distinction is important because a rate of increase today of 3 per cent per annum for central bank gold reserves, because of the increased number of central banks and the absorption by them of a greater portion of the mine output of gold, is doubtless equal in effect on prices to a 10 per cent per annum increase in monetary gold stocks prior to 1914.

[1] National City Bank *Letter*, March, 1933, p. 44.

The argument that monetary gold stocks should increase at approximately 3 per cent per annum is therefore entirely vitiated because of the superior credit expansion possibilities of gold in central banks as contrasted with gold in circulation as a medium of payment.

Since it is generally admitted that bank credit constitutes the most important medium of payment, the requirement of growth in the volume of media of payment consonant with the rate of increase of the physical volume of production and trade would be fully met if bank credit grew at the same rate as physical volume of trade. It follows, then, that if there is any validity in the 3-per-cent argument, a growth at that rate in the most important of the media of payment should suffice to accommodate a 3-per-cent rate of industrial expansion. It is therefore pertinent to note the rate of increase in bank credit since 1913.

The banking system of the United States was extended practically to its limit on the basis of its available reserves in that year. Following that date, in consequence of acquisitions of new gold reserves and the enhanced expansive powers of those reserves brought about by the establishment of the Federal Reserve System, the extension of credit proceeded at a dizzy pace. The deposits of all banks as of June 30, 1914, amounted to $18,566 million, and at December 31, 1929, they were $55,289 million, having increased by nearly 200 per cent. This represents a compound rate of increase for deposit credit of almost 7.5 per annum, from 1913 to 1929. Professors Warren and Pearson do not claim that there was any such increase in physical volume of production and trade, nor, therefore, that there was need for such an increase in the volume of the means of payment.

An analysis of the increase in deposits during this same period also throws interesting light upon credit expansion in member banks of the Federal Reserve System, contrasted with the same in non-member institutions. The deposits of non-member banks were $12,192 million on June 30, 1914, and by December 31, 1929, had increased to $21,420 million, a gain of 75 per cent. The deposits of the member banks were $6,374 million in 1914, and in 1929 they were $33,865 million, an increase of 430 per cent. It is thus apparent that greater credit expansibility was made available to member banks, as against non-members, by the creation of the Federal Reserve System. This comparison is subject to the strictures pointed out on pages 30–31, but a large part of the total increase in member bank deposits between 1914 and 1929 took place after 1921, and it was about this date that accessions to the Reserve System from the non-member ranks virtually ceased.

### Bearing of Gold Exchange Standard

Other measures effecting economies of gold, in addition to those attributable to the expansion of central banking and a greater absorption of monetary gold stocks by central banks, were brought into being by a number of countries when they returned to the gold standard following the War. Chief among these, perhaps, was the adoption of what is known as the "gold exchange standard," under which holdings of foreign exchange could serve as a currency base, side by side with gold.[1] Thus, for example, holdings of sterling or dollar credits might be counted as a reserve by the Bank of France, or other central banks abroad. While it is believed that the gold exchange standard was itself productive of undesirable disequilibria in the money and capital markets of the world prior to 1929, and of disastrous results after the depression set in, nevertheless the practice of counting foreign exchange holdings as part of a central bank's legal reserve constitutes a positive economy of gold. Such holdings, largely in the form of short-term claims on London and New York, are estimated to have been as high

---

[1] See *The Functioning of the Gold Standard*, by Professor Feliks Mlynarski, A Memorandum Submitted to the Gold Delegation of the Financial Committee of the League of Nations (Geneva: League of Nations, Document No. F. 979, 1931), p. 51: "Foreign exchange as a component of the fundamental reserve * * * is as good as gold. * * * By including foreign exchange in its fundamental reserve, the Bank raises its reserve ratio against its liabilities and can increase the amount of credit * * * ."

as two billion dollars prior to 1929, and to have had a practical significance nearly approximating that of an addition of two billion dollars in actual gold to central bank reserves during normal periods.[1]

### Significance of Gold Bullion Standard

It is further to be remarked that several countries, in returning to the gold standard after the War, adopted what is known as the "gold bullion standard," under which notes were not redeemable in gold coin as under the gold standard, but only in bars of gold bullion, and then only in large amounts. This also served to effect an economy of gold, in that it delimited the hand-to-hand circulation of gold. When in the normal course of trade gold coins found their way to the central banks, they were not reissued, but were melted into bars; as this procedure went on there was a constant contraction of gold coins in circulation. As these coins were melted into bullion, it was possible for the central banks to substitute for the gold in circulation deposit currency and notes to an amount many times that of the gold previously existing in the form of coins. This made possible an increase in the supply of the circulating media out of all proportion to the current production of gold, and accounts to a large extent for the increases in the gold reserves of the central banks, indicated in Table V, over and above the production of new gold from the mines. In other words, central banks not only took gold directly from the mines, but also added to their reserves most of the gold formerly circulating as coin.

### Increasing Use of Checks Effects Gold Economy

Lastly, the increasing popularity of the use of checks in certain countries which before the War were accustomed principally to paper currency and coin operated to effect

[1] "In the years 1924–1928 when the re-establishment of gold as an international standard was effected, a dozen countries or more increased their reserves of foreign exchange by some £120,000,000 in all. * * * This is exclusive of the Bank of France, which acquired no less than £250,000,000 of foreign exchange." Hawtrey, R. G., *The Art of Central Banking* (London: Longmans, Green & Co., 1932), p. 248.

a further economy of gold. As the use of "check-money" becomes more widespread, the need for gold coins as a circulating medium of payment is lessened.

### Cessation of Gold Production Would Have Resulted in No Shortage

All these measures—the extension of central banking, the adoption of the gold exchange and gold bullion standards, and the increasing popularity of checks—have resulted in such extensive economies of gold that the opinion may be hazarded that the world would not have suffered from a shortage of media of exchange had there been *no* gold produced from the mines after 1913, provided the monetary gold outside the central banks and treasuries in 1913 had all been transferred to the central bank vaults. Although at first blush this may appear as an exaggeration, a little reflection, it is believed, will prove its validity. Professor Pearson calculates the monetary gold outside the central banks in 1914 at $2,678 million. This amount of monetary gold performs no more money work than an equivalent amount of bank credit, or deposit currency (in fact, it is questionable whether it performs as much money work, because of its comparatively lower velocity of circulation). If this monetary gold were transferred to central bank vaults, a credit structure of approximately $75 billion might be erected upon the basis of this new gold reserve (if the central bank reserve ratio is 33 per cent and if the commercial banks' reserve ratio is 10 per cent), which should adequately satisfy the requirement of circulating media increasing at a rate corresponding to the rate of increase of the physical volume of production. Furthermore, the significance of the approximate $2 billion of foreign exchange also serving as a reserve base should not be overlooked. All in all, it would appear that the argument that additions to the monetary gold stock of the world must proceed at a rate of 3 per cent per annum was definitely inapplicable to the 1913–1929 period.

Indeed, what would appear to be conclusive of this whole question of an asserted shortage of gold, and at the same time indicative of the way in which central banking has economized gold reserves in recent years, is the fact that there was an actual surplus of gold reserves in 1928, as shown by the following calculation of the League of Nations: [1]

> The excess of gold reserves of 33% which, as explained above, is about the average cover * * * amounted at the end of 1928 to some $1,800 million. But fifteen countries hold over 90% of the gold reserves of the world [they are also the fifteen leading commercial nations of the world] and in these fifteen countries there was in 1928 a surplus of roughly $2,450 million. * * * The general conclusion to which these figures point is that * * * a theoretical surplus exists which about equals the amount of new gold likely to become available for monetary purposes during the next five years.

### THE QUESTION OF MALDISTRIBUTION OF GOLD

The idea that maldistribution of the world's gold supplies, with excessive concentration in the two countries, France and the United States, is the reason for the decline in prices, carries a greater degree of plausibility. This theory is advanced in the writings of Professor Cassel, as well as of a great many others. Thus, Cassel states: [2]

> Indeed, the sudden breakdown of commodity prices can only be explained by two events on the monetary side that have come into the foreground since the middle of 1929. * * * The second factor which since the middle of 1929 has tended to reduce the world's supply of means of payment is the very unequal distribution of gold caused by the tremendous gold imports into France and the United States.

### Maldistribution Merely Symptomatic

Professor Cassel, it should be noted, refers principally to the maldistribution *after* 1929 and *after* the fall of prices had already set in. Such maldistribution of gold is viewed

---

[1] *Interim Report* of the Gold Delegation of the Financial Committee of the League of Nations (Geneva: League of Nations, Publs. 1930; II, 26), p. 17.

[2] "Causes of the Fall of Prices," the London *Times*, "Annual Financial and Commercial Review," February 10, 1931, p. xxiv.

by the writers as symptom, not cause. It is the effect of a multitude of causes. Among these are war debts and reparations, national economic insecurity, and ill-considered political tinkering with the normal operation of international trade and the foreign exchange markets, to mention but a few such causes.[1] Also, a large measure of responsibility for the seeming failure of the gold standard and for the maldistribution of gold must be assessed against the workings of the gold exchange standard after confidence had become unsettled. With large amounts of short-term capital in the form of foreign credits loose upon the world money markets, it was only natural for those countries having the largest foreign exchange holdings to wish to repatriate that capital in the form of gold when confidence was tottering.[2] As France, for instance, sought to convert its holdings of foreign exchange into gold, the procedure effected a redistribution of gold and at the same time placed an unexpected strain upon the normal workings of the international gold standard proper. It must not be forgotten, however, that it was in 1931 and 1932 that most of this conversion of foreign credits into gold took place. The following comment of Dr. C. O. Hardy of the Brookings Institution goes to the heart of the question of maldistribution, it is believed:[3]

> With regard to the maldistribution of gold, it is almost sufficient to point to the fact that prior to the crisis of 1929 there was no appearance of a shortage of bank credit in any country but England. * * * Maldistribution is one way of saying the distribution of gold is different from what it was before the war. But the distribution of wealth, the production of commodities, is also different.

---

[1] "But it must not be forgotten that this 'maldistribution of gold' was in itself a result of existing barriers, economic nationalism, war debts and reparations, and the load of debt contracted since the War." *Monetary Policy and the Depression*, Publication of the Royal Institute of International Affairs (London: Humphrey Milford, 1933), p. 14.

[2] The amount of short-term capital in the form of foreign exchange holdings has been estimated at the staggering sum of 50 billion Swiss francs at the end of 1930. See the *Second Annual Report* of the Bank for International Settlements (Basle, 1932), p. 11.

[3] "Gold and Credit," *The Annals of the American Academy of Political and Social Science* (January, 1933), Vol. 165, p. 201.

It is quite true that the gold holdings of the Bank of France reached the enormous total of $3,218 millions in June, 1932. But this, it is to be emphasized, was long after the depression and the fall of prices had set in. The fact that the gold reserve of the Bank of France more than doubled from September, 1929, to June, 1932, might well be regarded as evidencing maldistribution as of the latter date, but it does not explain the start of the fall of prices in late 1929. The nationalistic hoarding of gold was a contributing factor in the precipitancy and persistency of that fall, once started, but it by no means follows, as Cassel and others contend, that the initiation of the price decline should be attributed largely to the pre-depression maldistribution of gold. For the fact remains that the most striking maldistribution of gold occurred after the decline in prices set in. And it appears more probable that the price situation itself brought about the alleged maldistribution, than does the converse argument.[1]

### CONDITIONS REQUISITE TO SATISFACTORY OPERATION OF GOLD STANDARD

Finally, it is frequently contended that the gold standard, as such, is the root cause of the present difficulties, and that as long as we insist upon having a standard of payments tied to gold, just so long will we continue to subject ourselves to the disastrous aberrations of the price level attributable to the failings of the gold standard. The problem of an ideal monetary standard is beyond the scope of this volume. It may be remarked in passing, however, that certainly the gold standard is not infallible; no conceivable system which is subject to human administration is infallible. But it must be remembered that the rules of the gold standard game have been flagrantly violated, not only since the

[1] "The movement of prices in different countries * * * helped to produce a maladjustment in the monetary systems of the world and in the distribution of gold. * * * In the last resort, international gold movements are due to the state of the balances of payments." *Course and Phases of the World Economic Depression* (Boston: World Peace Foundation, 1931; A League of Nations publication), p. 96.

start of the depression but ever since 1914. The gold standard admittedly requires experienced and skilled control in order to insure its relatively smooth working. Certain other conditions also are necessary, including a plasticity of and a reasonable agreement between costs and prices, readiness to accept payment of international debts in goods and services, and international goodwill as opposed to competitive nationalism, for it is only when these conditions are met that an international gold standard can function at all. The fact that ten billion dollars in short-term international indebtedness are circulating in the money and capital markets of the world is proof of the lack both of economic security and of international goodwill. The existence of this amount of "homeless" funds is damaging to internal economies so long as they fail to be converted into long-term investments through the normal operations of the capital market, and is an ever-present threat to the proper functioning of the gold standard. When, therefore, it is alleged that the gold standard has broken down, it is well to remember that scarcely any of the conditions necessary for its proper functioning have been realized, and that given the facts as they exist, no system could have survived the series of economic earthquakes which have shaken the world in the past twenty years.[1]

It is clear, then, that neither scarcity of gold on an absolute scale, nor deficiency in the rate of increase in the monetary gold stocks of the world, nor excessive demand for gold in relation to its supply, nor the inherent nature of the gold standard as such can be charged with primary responsibility

[1] See Hartley Withers, "Causes of the Crisis," the London *Times*, "Annual Financial and Commercial Review," February 9, 1932, p. xx: "Since the War the gold standard has never had a fair chance of serving the nations as the good and useful handmaid that she was before it—a fact to be remembered by the eager enthusiasts who have already decided that it must never be restored." See also the Inaugural Address of the late Brig.-Gen. Sir Arthur Maxwell as President of the Institute of Bankers, *Journal of the Institute of Bankers*, 1931, p. 506: "The real complaint which might be made against the gold standard is not that it has worked badly but that it has worked too well and too accurately and brought to light too clearly the disturbances in international financial relations." Further, see Professor Ralph A. Young, "The United States and Gold" *The Annals of the American Academy of Political and Social Science* (January, 1933), Vol. 165, p. 217.

for throwing the economic machine into reverse gear.[1] There is some measure of validity attaching to the view that the maldistribution of gold, after it was accomplished, was productive of evil results, but that suggests the need for analysis of those defects in the world's economic system which brought about the maldistribution, rather than concentration of attention upon the maldistribution itself as a causal factor explaining the start of the price decline.

## TOPPLING OF PRICES WAS LAST STAGE OF DECLINE FROM HEIGHTS OF WAR INFLATION

On the contrary, startling as it may appear to those who, without bothering to inquire into the facts, have found the necessary sacrificial offering in the gold situation, the view is held that one of the principal causes of the fall in prices has been an excess of gold [2]—excessive in view of the known economies in the use of gold as a basis for credit expansion—which permitted the erection of a superstructure of credit of such magnitude that when the rate of growth of that credit structure abated in 1928–1929, the fall in prices was the more precipitous. There is good evidence that the price decline starting in 1929 simply marks the culmination of a long period of inflation of bank credit based on gold beginning as early as 1897. Coupled with this is the fact that the Federal Reserve Board, by fostering credit inflation from 1922 to 1929 in an endeavor to sustain the price level, merely served to intensify the stresses and strains imposed upon the normal functionings of the gold standard by an inordinate bank credit inflation. When the Board reversed its "easy money" policy in 1929 and the bubble of inflation burst with the

---

[1] "The dislocation of the monetary and credit system that is nowadays going on everywhere is *not* due—the fact cannot be repeated too often—to any inadequacy of the gold standard. The thing for which the monetary system of our time is chiefly blamed, the fall in prices during the last five years, is not the fault of the gold standard, but the inevitable and ineluctable consequence of the expansion of credit, which was bound to lead eventually to a collapse." Ludwig von Mises, *The Theory of Money and Credit* (New York: Harcourt, Brace & Co., 1935), p. 20.

[2] "I may be exaggerating, but it seems to me that from a certain angle we can just as well speak about the over-abundance of gold as the scarcity of gold." Dr. Melchior Palyi, "Some Problems of International Banking Policy," *op. cit.*, p. 115.

stock market fiasco, ample impetus was provided for a headlong descent, making up in the short space of four years for the artificial tamperings with the normal economic forces at work to overcome the tumorous growth of War-time inflation. The writers strongly incline to the view that the 1929–1932 fall in prices was simply the last stage of a decline from the giddy heights of the War inflation of bank credit and prices. Had not the Federal Reserve Board interfered, a slow downward movement of prices (of the type normally following a major war financed by inflationistic measures) doubtless would and should have continued beyond 1922. The Federal Reserve Board could have provided an immeasurable service by directing its control activities to an endeavor to break the rate of fall and prevent the deflation from becoming precipitate, instead of the disservice it did perform by endeavoring to stabilize the price level from 1922 to 1929. Bluntly, our present difficulties are viewed largely as the inevitable aftermath of the world's greatest experiment with a "managed currency" *within* the gold standard, and, incidentally, should provide interesting material for consideration by those advocates of a managed currency which lacks the saving checks of a gold standard to bring to light excesses of zeal and errors of judgment.

## CHAPTER IV

# OVERPRODUCTION, UNDERCONSUMPTION, AND MALDISTRIBUTION OF INCOME AS CYCLICAL FORCES

No less plausible and even more widely accepted than the theories which are based upon the shortcomings of the gold standard are those which seek to find the solution of our recurring depressions in alleged overproduction of goods and services, or in underconsumption of the same, or in maldistribution of wealth and income. These are fundamentally similar notions, each being a variant of what is commonly known as the underconsumption theory of cycles.

## The Underconsumption Theory

The central thesis of the underconsumption theory concentrates attention upon the market for consumers' goods. If equilibrium is preserved in that market, it is argued, then the whole complex industrial machine continues in equilibrium, on the theory that the demand for equipment and machinery (capital goods) to make the consumers' goods is a derived demand from the consumers' goods market. Later phases of the discussion will show that, as the system actually works, the reverse of the above argument is substantially correct. It is not denied that *all* production is intended ultimately to promote the production of consumption goods; nevertheless, the output of capital goods is at times determined by considerations which are in some respects quite independent of the conditions prevailing in the consumers' goods market.

Common to all forms of the underconsumption theory is the argument that the industrial system as now organized fails to provide consumers with sufficient purchasing power to take the output of the industrial machine off the market. There is, it is alleged, a deficiency of consumers' income which brings on the fall of prices and depression. In order to preserve equilibrium between consumption and production in a capitalistic society with an ever-increasing output of consumption goods, so the theory runs, there must be an ever-larger consumers' income to buy those goods or else overproduction will occur.

The authors firmly believe that the unthinking acceptance of these theories has had a positive influence for evil, tending to prolong the depression by preventing the development of a proper understanding of its causes as a basis for combative action. Such theories unquestionably influenced the Hoover Administration, and the basic philosophy of the Roosevelt Administration's attempts at recovery are obviously predicated upon them.

### Variants of the Underconsumption Theory

As indicated above, there are three main variants of the underconsumption theory. The first, stressing the apparent surfeit of goods and attaching only secondary importance to income as such, is generally known as the overproduction theory. The second approaches the problem of depression principally from the standpoint of the alleged shortage of consumers' incomes, the underconsumption theory proper. The third emphasizes not so much the absolute deficiency in income as the disproportion between income consumed and income saved, finding the explanation of depression in the maladjustments in the distribution of incomes. All three theories have common roots, but enough *differentia* exist among them to justify according separate treatment to each. It will be the task of this chapter to attempt to refute the arguments of these theories as explanations of the cause of depression.[1]

---

[1] These theories, it may be remarked parenthetically, are mainly concerned with explaining the depression proper, or the collapse of a boom; they usually do not seek to explain the origin of the boom which precedes the depression. For this reason they are hardly entitled to be considered as theories of the business cycle; they are merely "depression" theories.

## OVERPRODUCTION CONTRASTED WITH ILL-ASSORTED PRODUCTION

John Stuart Mill's famous answer to the overproduction theory, first put forward in 1848 at a time when it was feared that labor-saving machinery involved loss of employment, is always deserving of repetition and is presented herewith *in extenso:* [1]

> The doctrine [of overproduction] appears to me to involve so much inconsistency in its very conception, that I feel considerable difficulty in giving any statement of it which shall be * * * clear * * * . First, let us suppose that the quantity of commodities produced is not greater than the community would be glad to consume: is it, in that case, possible that there should be a deficiency of demand for all commodities for want of the means of payment? Those who think so cannot have considered what it is which constitutes the means of payment for commodities. It is simply commodities. Each person's means of paying for the productions of other people consists of those which he himself possesses. All sellers are inevitably and *ex vi termini* buyers. Could we suddenly double the productive powers of the country, we should double the supply of commodities in every market; but we should, by the same stroke, double the purchasing power. Everybody would bring a double demand as well as supply: everybody would be able to buy twice as much, because every one would have twice as much to offer in exchange. * * * the remuneration of producers does not depend on how much money, but on how much of consumable articles, they obtain for their goods. * * * A general over-supply, or excess of all commodities above the demand * * * is thus shown to be an impossibility. * * * there is no over-production; production is not excessive, but merely ill assorted. * * * Thus, in whatever manner the question is looked at, * * * the theory of general overproduction implies an absurdity.

Nearly forty years later, in 1886, a British Royal Commission was appointed to inquire into the depression which had continued almost without a break for the previous ten

---

[1] *Principles of Political Economy* (London: Longmans, Green & Co., 1923), Ashley's edition, Book III, Chapter xiv, pp. 557–560.

years. A passage from the report of this Commission runs in part as follows: [1]

> * * * one of the commonest explanations of this depression or absence of profit is that known under the name of over-production; * * * general over-production is of course impossible.

At about the same time that British industry was experiencing the depression referred to, American industry was undergoing like difficulties, and the overproduction argument was also much in vogue in this country. Shortly after the report of the British Commission on Trade and Industry was made public, David A. Wells, a leading American economist of the time, offered an equally critical statement with reference to the overproduction theory, as follows: [2]

> No term has been used more loosely in the discussion of this subject of trade depression than that of 'over-production.' The idea that there can be such a thing as a general production of useful or desirable commodities in excess of what is wanted is an absurdity; but there may be * * * an amount of production in excess of demand at remunerative prices, or, what is substantially the same thing, an excess of capacity for production.

It is seen, then, that the idea of overproduction as an explanation of depression is an economic concept of long life,[3] and it is one which regularly provides the "popular" theory of the disastrous slumps in trade and industry. It was a frequent explanation of nineteenth century depressions, and "poverty in the midst of plenty" has become a commonplace of contemporary discussion. The world is represented as being drowned by the flood of its own output which it cannot consume; it is said to have brought on its

---

[1] *Final Report of the Royal Commission appointed to inquire into the Depression of Trade and Industry* (Cmd. 4893, 1887), p. xvii.

[2] *Recent Economic Changes* (New York: D. Appleton & Co., 1889), pp. 25–26.

[3] For a discussion of the development of the underconsumption theory from Lauderdale and Malthus, through Sismondi and Karl Marx, up to and including John A. Hobson and Messrs. Foster and Catchings, see A. H. Hansen's *Business Cycle Theory: Its Development and Present Status* (Boston: Ginn & Co., 1927), Chapters II and III.

present penury by the very diligence with which it has sought to devise aids to production.

It is necessary to be quite clear about what can validly be meant by "overproduction." It does not mean production of more than can be consumed, nor even of more than can be sold at *some* price. Any quantity of a thing that is actually desired can be sold, if the price be fixed low enough. There is no reason to believe that there is any industry (or any combination of industries) that can, even during prosperity, always sell what it could produce at whatever price it may choose, without any regard for the conditions of demand operative at that price. What economists mean when speaking of overproduction is that more has been produced than can be sold at a price sufficient to repay full cost of production, that is, to bring returns adequate to induce producers to continue producing at the same rate. Production may be in excess of demand at what the producers consider remunerative prices, as Wells points out; nevertheless, all that has been produced can be sold, but in some cases only at a loss.

## Price, the Key-Log

Price, then, is the key to the matter; and in any industrial jam, it is the key-log that has to be extricated before the economic system can again move smoothly forward. Production may be ill-assorted, as Mill puts it, or there may be partial overproduction. But there cannot be even partial overproduction—or at least not for any appreciable length of time, and not of sufficient dimensions to bring on a major industrial depression—if prices are "right." Much less, of course, can there be any such thing as "general overproduction." When partial overproduction makes its appearance, it is *prima facie* evidence that the price system is out of balance, that the pricing machinery is not performing its proper function of equating supply to demand. For right prices are prices that move goods, and there can be no jam of goods flowing into the market if prices are promptly adjusting themselves to the actual conditions of supply and demand. The smooth and proper functioning of the economic system is conditioned upon plasticity of prices. This does not require that price adjustments be instantaneous; neither does it contemplate, on the other hand, monopolistic and governmental efforts to withhold copper, cotton, wheat, or rubber from the market when prices are already too high to move all the supply off the market. Attempts to fix prices at a height which makes attractive the planting of rubber trees for future yield, the extension of wheat and cotton acreage, and the development of new mines, are not conducive to the avoidance of overproduction of those commodities at such artificially fixed prices.

*Enlarged Production Constitutes Enhanced Demand*

Here, then, are the fundamental points upon which all overproduction theories break down—that production gives rise to purchasing power, and that more of commodities that are desired cannot be produced than will be purchased if the prices of those commodities are right, or "market-clearing," prices. Classical economics may have become antiquated in the eyes of the new school of "experimental economists" who would revamp the economic system according to their idea of modernization, but no system of "new economics" can successfully eliminate as one of its components the keystone of the arch of Classical economics. Lack of appreciation of Say's *théorie des débouchés*, that production is the source of consumption, that enlarged production means enhanced demand, or, as in Marshall's statement, that "the National Dividend is at once the aggregate net product of and the sole source of payment for all the agents of production," is what causes the structure of the so-called new economics to collapse of its own weight.[1]

---

[1] Devotees of the new school of economics well may ponder the estimate of the late Allyn Young of one of their foremost leaders: "I do not see how one who looks backward through smoked glasses can look forward with open clear eyes." *Economic Problems, New and Old* (Boston: Houghton Mifflin Co., 1927), chapter on "The Trend of Economics," p. 247.

A sufficient reason for completely discarding the older economics is hardly found in the failure of the Classical School to integrate properly this cardinal principle of all economic theorizing with a fully developed explanation of the operation of the pricing system. Progress toward this goal was given impetus by the Austrian School and the School of Lausanne, and was further advanced by the eclecticism of Marshall and others of the neo-classicals before the turn of the last century; a unified exposition of the *modus operandi* of a competitive pricing system was finally realized by virtue of the work of the early twentieth century economists, Davenport, Taylor, Cassel, and Knight.

Failure to understand, or even to be acquainted with, the tenets basal to neo-classical economics is at the bottom of most of the bad economics which has had such a popular reception during the last few years, descending, as it has, upon a distraught and bewildered world ready to listen to and to believe in anything in the way of criticism of the existing economic order, without first bothering to inquire whether the assumptions of the older economics have been fulfilled. It explains why such an un-economic monstrosity as "Technocracy" could enjoy the vogue it did, and even become the subject of semi-serious disputation, as well as why the gross inconsistencies and contradictions of the original NRA were regarded so lightly by a people ready to grasp at any straw promising surcease from their troubles.

*Overproduction Apparent, Not Real*

If overproduction had been the cause of the depression, it would seem that the physical volume of production should have been increasing at an inordinate rate in the period before the crash; if there had been absolute overproduction on a large scale, an acceleration in the rate of increase of production should so indicate. The statement of Carl Snyder of the Federal Reserve Bank of New York, whose work in providing factual information regarding the physical volume of production is such as to make his testimony conclusive, is as follows: [1]

> Consider the last five or six years, to 1930. Therein the rate of industrial growth, so far as we may measure it, has been substantially identical with that of the pre-war average rate of growth * * * . The idea of an unusual rise in total production, preceding the crisis, was, so far as I can find, a fiction.

Moreover, if overproduction had existed prior to the crash, it should have been evidenced by a general increase of stocks of goods on hand, a general oversupply in the form of inventories which could not be marketed. Yet the fact that there was no increase of inventories during the late boom was iterated and reiterated by almost every writer up to the time of the crash.[2] *After* the crash, general overproduction *seemed* apparent—as is always the case—but it should be remarked that the existence of stocks of raw materials and semi-manufactured goods is generally overestimated at such times, for the reason that during a depression the stocks are entirely visible and greater attention is focused upon them. However, in the months following the crash, as Professor Åkermann has shown, the world's surplus stocks of basic commodities averaged much less than a normal year's supply.[3]

### Technological Unemployment

Inextricably connected with and an integral part of the overproduction theory of depressions is the notion that the cause of the overproduction is an over-rapid application of machinery to production. It is argued that inventions and technical progress have proceeded at so rapid a pace that goods are being produced in such excessive amounts that

[1] "Overproduction and Business Cycles," *Proceedings of the Academy of Political Science* (June, 1931), Vol. XIV, No. 3, p. 358.

[2] "It will be remembered that during this period economic analysts were continuously stressing the fact that no undue accumulation of unsold goods was in evidence." Moulton, H. G., *The Formation of Capital* (Washington: The Brookings Institution), p. 138. And see Snyder, *op. cit.*, p. 358: "We know, moreover, there was no great piling up of stocks or inventories in recent years, or in 1929."

[3] *Economic Forecast and Reality, 1928–1932* (Stockholm: Svenska Bokhandeln, 1933), p. 11. In the case of wheat Carl Snyder estimates an increase in the normal carry-over equivalent to about three weeks' normal consumption; *op. cit.*, p. 336.

they cannot be marketed. This is again a long-lived argument, which made its first appearance during the early days of the Industrial Revolution, and which experienced a pronounced recrudescence during the post-War years. Far-reaching technical improvements were introduced during the post-War period, so extensive and so impressive as to be widely heralded as the advent of a "Second Industrial Revolution," and, as unemployment existed concurrently with the extension of these technical improvements, it was perhaps inevitable that the one should be considered the cause of the other. As, despite boom conditions, there was still a lack of full employment of labor, it was natural that the pessimistic views of the effects of the introduction of machinery on labor which were widely held at the time of the First Industrial Revolution should be revived. A new phrase was coined to describe the phenomenon of unemployment during apparent boom conditions—"Technological Unemployment." [1] While inventions and the machine were not regarded as unmixed evils, the question nevertheless was raised whether there was not a *permanent* unemployment attendant upon the introduction of improvements —the usual sense in which the term "Technological Unemployment" is now used.

Technical improvements and inventions do save labor, it is true, and therefore tend to displace some labor in specific occupations; but "the effect of a technical improvement for the entrepreneur introducing it must always be a diminution in money (or displacement) costs per unit of output; if it does not there will be no incentive to adopt it; and if it does it will always lead to an increase in production." [2] Labor is displaced only if the demand for the commodity on which the laborer is engaged cannot be expanded by the

---

[1] In contrast with the First Industrial Revolution, however, there was a change of emphasis in the argument advanced against inventions and technical change. The earlier attacks were aimed directly at the machine as such as a displacer of labor, and sometimes eventuated in physical violence; during the recent period, the argument developed into more of a theoretical disputation regarding the socio-economic effects of technical progress.

[2] Nicholas Kaldor, "A Case against Technical Progress?" *Economica* (May, 1932), Vol. XII, No. 36, p. 186.

reduction in price which the improvement makes possible. It may happen, however, that the demand for the commodity is inelastic, in which case there must be a displacement of labor in the production of that particular commodity. A fact which is generally lost sight of, however, is that with the reduction in cost which the improvement makes possible, there will usually be a compensating increase in demand for some other commodity, *provided* the reduction in cost is passed on to the consumer in the form of a reduction in price of the finished article. The reduction in price consequent upon the cheapening of production will release a part of the income of the consumers for expenditure on other commodities, so that there will be an increased demand elsewhere in the market for goods on which the displaced labor can be employed. But for this absorption of displaced labor to take place readily, it is reiterated, prices must be plastic: attempts by entrepreneurs to realize immediately the full gain from the reduction in cost by capitalizing anticipated profits on the basis of artificially maintained prices, or refusals by laborers to accept (temporarily) lower wages in alternative occupations, eventually frustrate their own purpose.

The fact that technical progress may cause some economic dislocation is not disputed; an over-rapid increase of inventions may necessitate greater flexibility among costs and prices in order to preserve relative stability than would otherwise be required. There is a certain degree of validity in the concept of technological unemployment, and the more so if it be regarded—as it should be—as essentially a short-run phenomenon. It appears in some degree whenever our complex society experiences a period of industrial transition. Most major technological advances result in the displacement of some employees. Under "ideal" conditions these displaced laborers would quickly be reabsorbed elsewhere in the expanding industrial system, but actually neither men nor capital equipment are sufficiently mobile nor prices sufficiently flexible to prevent intervals of idleness, more or less prolonged. Some of the discharged laborers may be so advanced in years as to be debarred from entry into new fields of work in which wages are equal to those of their former occupations. In general, the more rapid the technical progress the larger will be the fraction of the labor group that at any given moment is suffering enforced idleness or is making painful occupational readjustments. But considered from the long-run viewpoint, it may safely be stated that technical progress never has reduced, nor is there any reason for thinking that it ever will *permanently* reduce, the percentage of the total population that industry is capable of employing in gainful activities. And, particularly important with regard to the point at hand, there is no clearly discernible relationship between such technological unemployment as did exist during the late 'twenties and the collapse of 1929. These two phenomena —technological improvements and unemployment—should not necessarily be considered as standing in the relation of cause and effect to each other; they may both be results of some other cause, or causes.

The long-run effect of inventions, technical improvement, and increased use of machinery, then, is to supplement rather than to displace labor, and to increase total production. When total production is increased, the share going to each factor of production is enlarged, and both total and per man real wages of labor increase, provided always that prices are decreased with improved productivity. Technical progress, therefore, cannot normally result in permanent unemployment, and even the displacement of labor as a temporary condition will not be of long duration if the adjustment of prices, including the price paid for labor itself, is sufficiently rapid.

### Excessive Credit Expansion Leads to Misapplication of Capital

The possibility of partial overproduction must be granted: production may be "ill-assorted," or there may be "an excess of capacity for production" at remunerative prices. Instances might be multiplied of overproduction in this sense in specific industries, both prior to 1929 and during the Depression, prominent among which are coffee, cotton, wheat, rubber, copper, and tin. The automobile industry was during and even before the Great Depression a notable example of an industry with capacity in excess of the apparent demand for its products. Excess capacity, however, is evidence of overinvestment, or of misapplication of capital. And therein lies the explanation of those cases of seeming overproduction. Overinvestment, which must be assigned the rôle of a positive disturbing factor, has its ultimate source in an excess of credit, however, and this returns the argument to the basic contention of the present study. One of the deeper causes of the recent depression was the overexpansion and overinvestment of capital in many lines of business at a *rate* so pronounced as to represent a positive misapplication of capital in view of the level of prices then prevailing, or which might have been expected to prevail in the future.

But the policy of overinvestment, with its attendant misapplication of capital, could never have been carried to the lengths that it was during the decade of the 'twenties if the banks and the Government had not supplied abundant credits at artificially cheap rates. This, together with the policies of hoarding, pooling, and valorization, also made possible by the inflation of bank credit, prevented the natural and gradual reduction of prices that might have been expected from improved productivity. Hence a disturbing factor in the situation was the overinvestment and misapplication of capital; the origin of the misapplication of capital, the reason for the misdirection of investment, was the excessive credit expansion brought about largely by the inflationistic bias of the Federal Reserve authorities, tinkering with the inherently inflationistic machinery of central banking in an ill-advised effort to maintain prices at an artificially stable level.

## The Underconsumption Contention

Closely analogous to the notion of overproduction as the cause of the depression is the other side of a Janus-faced argument, the "underconsumption" theory proper. The argument of the underconsumptionists does not stress the excess of goods, as such, as being the cause of the trouble, but rather directs emphasis to an absolute insufficiency of purchasing power in the form of money in the hands of *consumers* to take the entire output of the industrial process off the market. Consumption rather than production is the focal point of attack; demand is differentiated from supply, and lack of demand because of insufficient consumers' purchasing power is made the disrupting factor. It is asserted that the net money income of the final results of the productive process is not great enough to remove the gross product from the market.

### Underconsumption Idea May Have Partial Validity Temporarily

It is conceded that in one type of situation which sometimes exists the underconsumption idea may be granted partial validity. That is during and following a serious monetary and banking panic, when unreasoning fear is the dominant emotion, and the disposal of goods and property rights in favor of "hard" money is an almost universal immediate objective. Under such conditions, as Davenport puts it,[1]

The psychology of the time stresses not the goods to be exchanged through the intermediate commodity, but the commodity itself. The halfway house becomes a house of stopping. There sets in an abnormally developed emphasis upon money or credit as deferred purchasing power rather than as present purchasing power—on money for future purchases rather than as demand for present goods. The situation is one of withdrawal of a large part of the money supply at the existing level of prices.

[1] Davenport, H. J., *The Economics of Enterprise* (New York: The Macmillan Company, 1925), p. 320.

But such a situation cannot endure for long, and it obviously occurs in conjunction with a period of crisis, rather than preceding it. In other words, to attribute some reality to the underconsumption idea in the brief period during which such conditions prevail is merely to recognize facts for purposes of description, but in no sense to explain the causes of the total situation.

With respect to other than panic conditions, it is patent that the underconsumptionists are wholly unmindful of the significance of Say's Law (the briefest possible expression of which is that "the supply of goods constitutes the demand for goods"). But to offer this as a summary refutation of the underconsumption idea is hardly enough to lay bare the roots of the fallacy. These seem embedded in failure to distinguish properly between the gross product and the net income of society, and in lack of comprehension of the workings of the capitalistic, many-stage, process of production, in which gross income necessarily must exceed net income.

### Refutation of Underconsumption Theory

Even if the system is in a condition of stationary equilibrium—that is, no net saving is being made—the gross product of economic activity will be considerably greater than the net income. The amount by which the first exceeds the second represents the repair and replacement of existing equipment—costs that must be covered if the system is to avoid retrogression. Indeed, it is not even necessary that the current money income of consumers should be equal to the net product produced, because of corporate and other business savings used to maintain and replace the existing stock of capital goods. Therefore, the net income in the form of money payments to *consumers* neither ordinarily will nor should be great enough to enable them to command the entire gross product of industry.

Furthermore, as our economic system is organized at present (the roundabout, many-stage, "capitalistic" process of production) the gross income—the total volume of money payments—necessarily exceeds the net money income or the net output of consumers' goods. There are many stages of payments which go to make up the gross income but which are not involved in the computation of net income. The larger number of payments is not from consumers to producers, but is made between producers and producers, and tends to cancel out in any computation of net income or of net product value. "In fact, income produced or net product is roughly only about one-third of gross income." [1] What is cost for one producer is in part income for some other producer, but part of that income the latter has to pay out in costs to other producers in another stage of the productive process (for intermediate products, raw materials, supplies, etc.), and so on. All that is necessary in order that equilibrium be maintained is that consumers' incomes equal the cost of producing *consumers' goods;* the total of producers' payments necessarily exceeds that of consumers' incomes.

But ours is a "progressive" economy, and not one in stationary equilibrium. It is one in which real saving is continually being made and being converted into real physical capital, and it is the net saving of the system which makes its progress possible. In such a situation the refutation of the underconsumption argument becomes even more convincing. If real saving is to take place—if the capital equipment of the society is to increase—then the gross product of the society very evidently must exceed the amount spent on consumption goods: the gross product must include that amount which makes possible the increase in capital equipment. A portion of the gross income must be put to the task of creating additional capital equipment in order to increase net income in the future. Not only must some of the total income be diverted from current consumption uses in order to maintain the stock of real capital, but some part of it must be used in ways which will result in an annual

---

[1] Slichter, Sumner, *Towards Stability* (New York: Henry Holt & Co., 1934), p. 7 (*note* to p. 6).

addition to that stock if the society is to progress. If all gross income were converted into net income it would mean not only that no progress would be possible, but also that the existing stock of capital goods would not be maintained, and the system would become retrogressive.[1]

This whole question, it is believed, is successfully disposed of by Dean A. B. Adams when he says:[2]

> If the physical volume of the current output of consumers' goods should equal the physical volume of all goods produced currently, there could be no accumulation of permanent capital— there could be no real savings. If real savings are to be made, the total volume of production must exceed the physical volume of consumers' goods flowing to the market. Real investment is an ultimate demand for goods just as the purchase of consumers' goods is an ultimate demand. When consumers and real savers purchase a physical quantity of goods equal to the physical quantity of production for that period, there can be no over-supply of goods or shortage of money income. Real savings and investment do not cause a shortage of consumers' money income, but they make industrial progress possible.

If this analysis is correct, there is no reason to believe that industrial depression is brought about by an absolute deficiency of consumption. Rather, the writers incline to the position of Professor Robbins:[3] "It may prove to be no accident that the depression in which most measures have been taken to 'maintain consumers' purchasing power' is also the depression of the widest extent and most alarming proportions." The same thought is expressed by Professor Åkermann:[4] "The theories of price-level stabilization and consumption credit were unable to predict the crisis—

---

[1] In fact, it is just this situation which has come to pass during the present depression—and it is precisely because of this fact that the present depression has persisted! *Cf.* Slichter, *op. cit.*, p. 6, *note:* "The estimates of the Bureau of Foreign and Domestic Commerce * * * indicate that during the present depression the income paid out as salaries, wages, interest, dividends, net rents and royalties, and withdrawals of owners has exceeded the net income produced." See also Chapter VII, this volume.

[2] *Profits, Progress and Prosperity* (New York: McGraw-Hill Book Co., Inc., 1927), p. 18.

[3] "Consumption and the Trade Cycle," *Economica* (November, 1932), Vol. XII, No. 38, p. 430.    [4] *Op. cit.*, pp. 45–46.

their adoption was indeed a cause of the crisis; the same theories moreover seem unable to remedy the depression: indeed they have only contributed to make things worse."

## Maldistribution of Income as a Possible Cyclical Force

Another variant of the underconsumption theory is that which maintains that depressions are brought about by the unequal distribution of income. The emphasis is placed upon a *relative* deficiency in consumers' incomes, or else upon a *relative* oversupply of savings in the hands of the capitalist class. The argument commonly runs thus: the incomes of property owners, entrepreneurs, and *rentiers* in general are so great a proportion of the total national income that they are unable to spend all their incomes on consumption goods, and therefore they must save and invest heavily in new capital developments. These savings of the capitalist class are so great that, when turned into new capital goods which soon beget more consumers' goods, the end-result is overproduction, because the consumers (laborers) do not command a sufficient percentage of the national income to enable them to take the additional supply of goods off the market.

This theory is based on the assumptions that the quantity of savings made and invested currently when the industrial system is operating at reasonably full capacity is large enough to produce a boom, and that investment of savings in new capital goods causes the physical supply of consumers' goods on the market to increase more rapidly than the increase in consumers' income. Because the percentage of national income going to capital is so great, it is argued, the capitalists are able to meet their living expenses with the lesser portion of their incomes, and the remaining larger portion cannot readily be expended otherwise than for new investments. This inordinate amount of saved income going to the creation of new capital equipment not only brings on and magnifies the boom, but also provides self-correction, for when the stream of new consumers' goods flowing from these new capital goods reaches the market, prices fall abruptly and industrial activity slows down, and the share going to capital is reduced during the depression.

The over-saving, or maldistribution of wealth theory, like the overproduction and underconsumption ideas, again indicates lack of understanding of the dual relations of production and consumption. Proponents of any of these doctrines would do well to ponder the dictum of Alfred Marshall:[1] "Economics from beginning to end is a study of the mutual adjustments of consumption and production: when the one is under discussion, the other is never out of mind." Savings, it is true, do reduce the amount of money income which is available for the purchase of consumers' goods, but savings do not reduce the amount of purchasing power which is available for the purchase of *total* goods and services. In any time period, the income which is saved and invested (in creating capital goods) plus the income used to purchase consumers' goods equals the value of total production during that period; the demand for goods equals the value of total current production; the demand for goods is equal to the supply of goods. Where (as is normally true) savings from the current national income are invested in "goods used for the production of goods," the total income of the economy is *spent for goods* (and services)—part for the stream of consumers' goods flowing into market, and part for the current stream of capital goods. There can be no oversupply of consumers' goods so long as the output of goods in general is being adjusted as between the production of consumers' goods and capital goods in the same proportions as is the total national income between spending and investing; or, stated more concretely, if 85 per cent of the total annual production is in the form of consumption goods and services, and if 85 per cent of the annual monetary income of the nation is "spent" (not invested), there is bound to be

---

[1] *Principles of Economics* (London: Macmillan & Co., Eighth Edition, 1930), p. 712, *note*.

sufficient purchasing power available to clear the markets of that output of consumers' goods.

It is therefore illogical to assume that either the absolute amount of savings or the size of the distributive share going to capital can initiate a boom. So long as the percentages remain relatively constant as between the share going to capital and the share going to labor (consumers), there is nothing inherent in any particular method of distributing the national dividend which will cause disequilibrium in the productive process, even though the total volume of production is increasing. Progressive expansion of the national income normally accompanies capital accumulation; indeed, as already shown, the aggregate net income cannot grow unless there be saving (disregarding technical progress and population growth). Nor need the basis of apportionment between saving and spending be considered as a disequilibrating factor, so long as the proportion remains the same: as Bickerdike and others have shown, a uniform rate of accumulation of capital is not inconsistent with economic stability.[1] What would result from a diversion of 50 per cent of the national dividend to savings, instead of the usual estimates of 10 to 20 per cent, would be that the rate of progress would be greater, prices and the rate of interest would fall, machinery would do more of the work of the productive process, the aggregate national real income would be greatly increased, and labor would have more leisure to enjoy the fruits of that enlarged income.

The views of the authors are largely compatible with Professor Hansen's contention that disturbances to the even flow of our industrial life are attributable in the main to *fluctuations* in the *rate* of capital accumulation.[2] In fact, it is just these fluctuations in the rate of capital accumulation which create instability, and which constitute the business cycle. But there is little reason to believe that alterations in the rate of voluntary saving can be of such magnitude or

[1] Hansen, A. H., and Tout, H., "Annual Survey of Business Cycle Theory: Investment and Saving in Business Cycle Theory," *Econometrica* (April, 1933), Vol. I, No. 2, p. 139.        [2] *Ibid.*, p. 119.

swiftness as to bring about the change in the rate of invest-ment which is the central feature of the present exchange-economy business cycle. Furthermore, the available statis-tics on the distribution of the national income do not show any such alteration in the proportion of the share going to capital as is assumed by the maldistribution-of-income theory—indeed, the reverse is true, as is observable in the following table:

TABLE VI

DISTRIBUTION OF NATIONAL INCOME IN THE UNITED STATES BY FUNCTIONAL SOURCES

| YEAR OR YEARS | WAGES AND SALARIES | ENTREPRENEURIAL INCOME (Includes Rent) | INTEREST AND DIVIDENDS |
|---|---|---|---|
| 1910 | 48.9 | 36.5 | 14.7 |
| 1913–1917 | 57.5 | 32.4 | 10.5 |
| 1918–1922 | 62.9 | 29.4 | 7.7 |
| 1924–1927 | 65.5 | 26.3 | 8.2 |
| 1928 | 65.1 | 24.7 | 10.2 |

Source: *Encyclopedia of the Social Sciences*, article on "National Income," Vol. XI, p. 218.

## Banking Policy a Disturbing Factor

It is indisputable that the rate of investment, change in which is the dominant characteristic of the business cycle, does fluctuate over wide limits. Wherein, then, is the chief source of variation in the rate of investment? The thesis of this volume is that it is to be found in the elasticity of the banking system, and subsequent chapters will be devoted to an elaboration of this contention. The banking system is able to provide the funds which permit investment in capital goods at a rate in advance of the increase of voluntary sav-ings by the society in question. It is this availability of loanable funds which makes possible the misdirection of real capital that results in partial overproduction. It is the means of payment forthcoming from the banking system that makes possible the financing of excessive capital-creation activities, and it is the cessation or slackening of this increase of media of payment that operates to reverse the period of expansion.

There is even reason to believe, however, that depression need not necessarily ensue from an expansion in the rate of accumulation of capital goods *per se*, provided prices decline *pari passu* with the increased productivity brought about by this increase in investment. The fall in prices would in itself serve to constitute an effective check upon *inordinate* capital development because it would bring about a decline in the rate of return going to capital; as the rate of return to capital declined consequently upon the fall in prices the rate of accumulation of capital goods would tend to diminish. Under such conditions the system is automatically self-corrective. It is just this self-corrective process which is essential to the smooth functioning of the economic machinery. And it is in this way that the system would work were it not for the disturbing factor of credit. The injections of new credit not only permit an increase in the rate of capital accumulation, but also tend to disrupt progressively the normal equilibrium relationships between costs and prices over many sectors of the pricing front. The fundamental disequilibria are not discernible until the new credits are withdrawn or cease to increase, when it then becomes apparent that the anticipated earnings of capital based on the prevailing (artificially pegged) price level will not be realized, and the creation of capital goods ceases abruptly. The cessation of the production of new capital produces depression, and is at the same time the dominant characteristic of depression.

In order to guard against misinterpretation, it may be well to state explicitly that it is a particular type of banking policy, and not banking as such, at which the criticism of the above paragraphs is aimed. Banking is not necessarily and inherently malevolent in its effects; on the contrary, as will be shown in later chapters, it is an institution that may readily be utilized in pursuance of beneficent ends.

## CHAPTER V

# POST-WAR DEVELOPMENTS IN AMERICAN BANKING

The banking crisis of March, 1933, marked the end of an epoch in American banking—a strange epoch, more puzzling in all of its ramifications than any previous period in American banking history. The beginning of this epoch dates from the passing of the Federal Reserve Act in 1913, its foundations were laid during the period of War inflation, but its most astonishing chapters were written during the approximate decade 1922–1932.

The present chapter does not attempt to deal with the details of the panic of 1933, which was merely the grand finale to this highly dramatic period; the crisis proper has been adequately treated by others in separate individual studies. It is important, however, to direct attention to some of the more significant changes in American banking which were developing principally from 1922 onward, setting the stage for the collapse of 1929, the great wave of bank failures from that date on through 1932, and the final crash in 1933. And for an understanding of the more immediate causes of the depression it is essential that the developments taking place in the American banking system be clearly in mind, as the changes occurring in the banking system were intimately connected with the structural changes in the economic system which led up to the depression. The central thesis here set forth is what may be termed a bank credit theory of the depression; the explanation of the depression is bottomed squarely on the inflation of bank credit which occurred between 1922 and 1929. The present chapter, therefore, depicts certain aspects of the banking and credit background of the recent structural changes in the economic system; the structural changes themselves produced by the operations of the banking system will be dealt with in the following chapter.

## Unprecedented Expansion and Contraction of Capital Credit

The period under review was characterized principally by the greatest expansion and contraction of investment credit, *i.e.*, capital credit, on record.[1] The years 1922 to 1929 (inclusive) witnessed an expansion of credit in the form of loans and investments by the commercial banks of this country of almost 14 billion dollars, taking the form exclusively of an expansion of investment credit—principally investments in securities, increased loans on securities, and increased loans on real estate. From the end of 1929 to the end of 1932 there was witnessed a deflation of bank credit for the commercial banks of almost exactly the same amount (the extent of the deflation to the end of 1933 being even greater).[2] Although the earlier years were not marked by an appreciable expansion of credit by the banks for commercial purposes, unfortunately those following 1929 were marked by a deflation of such credit relatively greater than the deflation of investment credit, with a resultant hampering of business activity because of the restrictions on commercial credit available to the business community.

## Factors Underlying Credit Expansion

This investment-credit expansion was attributable in large part to the growth of banking reserves beginning in 1922, aided by the influx of gold from abroad, but induced principally by the credit expansion activities of the Federal

[1] "Investment inflation" and "investment credit" are used here in the sense employed by Professor F. A. Bradford in an article, "Social Aspects of Commercial Banking Theory," *American Economic Review* (June, 1933), Vol. XXIII, No. 2, p. 217 ff., and by Professor E. C. Harwood in his book, *Cause and Control of the Business Cycle* (Boston: Financial Publishing Company, 1932).

[2] The foregoing figures, as well as those presented in following pages, unless specifically cited, are taken from the *Federal Reserve Bulletin* and the *Annual Reports* of the Federal Reserve Board. To reduce the annotation, specific citations are dispensed with as much as possible.

Reserve Banks. The increases in the gold stock were more in the nature of a permissive factor in the expansion of credit for the banking system, as the gold went principally to swell the reserves of the Federal Reserve Banks; it was the utilization of their surplus reserves by the Federal Reserve Banks to increase the reserves of the member banks which represented the initiating source of the expansion of credit. A second source of the inflation of bank credit was resident in the nature of central banking as such: the member banks were enabled to replenish, or to add to, their reserve balances by rediscounting with (borrowing from) the Federal Reserve Banks—an operation common to central banking, but impossible on a large scale under the old National Banking System. A third, and in certain respects an even more important, factor in the expansion of credit was the more effective use to which the reserves of the member banks were put, made possible by the progressive reduction of average reserve requirements as a result of the shift of demand deposits to the time deposits category; as "average" reserve requirements declined it was possible for the banks to continue expanding credit even without positive additions to their reserve balances. A final factor assisting in the expansion was the reduction in reserve requirements made by the Federal Reserve Act as originally passed and as later amended; it is obvious that a banking system with a reserve-deposit ratio in the neighborhood of 10 per cent can expand credit more rapidly and more extensively than one with a ratio of 20 per cent or more. It should be pointed out that the last three factors are important more as explanations of why the inflation was so prolonged and extensive, rather than primarily as originating factors; the primary initiating source of the expansion was the action of the Federal Reserve Banks in increasing the reserves of the member banks. In brief, then, the direct sources of the inflation are all traceable to provisions of the Federal Reserve Act, and more specifically, they are directly connected with the development and operation of the system of central banking created by that

Act. None of the factors named above was in effect before 1913; and the inflation of 1922–1929, as we have known it, would not have been possible without the facilitating offices of the Federal Reserve System.

### EFFECTS OF INVESTMENT CREDIT INFLATION

The immediate effects of this investment credit inflation were marked by important and interrelated changes in the character of bank loans and investment assets.    There developed an indirectness in the processes of bank credit financing, bank credit entering into the channels of production and trade through operations in the securities and capital markets rather than in direct loans to business men to finance short-term transactions.    The liquidity of banks declined in general to such an extent that they were ill-prepared to cope with the situation which arose when the stock market crash placed an unduly severe pressure on the banking structure. As a result of the plethora of bank credit funds and the utilization by banks of their excess reserves to swell their investment accounts, the long-term interest rate declined and it became increasingly profitable and popular to float new stock and bond issues. This favorable situation in the capital funds market was translated into a constructional boom of previously unheard-of dimensions; a real estate boom developed, first in Florida, but soon was transferred to the urban real estate market on a nation-wide scale; and, finally, the stock market became the recipient of the excessive credit expansion. These three booms—the constructional boom proper, the real estate booms, and the stock market hysteria—combined to produce structural changes in the economic system which were directly involved with the immediate origins of the depression. This trinity of booms contributed to sustain a seeming prosperity, the tragic speciousness of which was not widely apparent until after the bubble had burst. Hence the remote effect of the investment credit inflation was the depression, to be followed by the unprecedented bank failures terminating in the Banking Panic of 1933.[1]

## THE EXTENT OF INFLATION

The growth of deposits for all the banks in the country from June, 1921, to December, 1929, was over 19 billion dollars. This is to be compared with 18.6 billion dollars in total deposits for all banks, in June, 1914. Thus the growth of bank credit during this brief period exceeded the growth of bank credit throughout the history of banking in this country up to 1914. This expansion, it is to be noted, occurred during a period of relative stability of prices, as measured by the wholesale commodity price indexes, and is therefore not strictly comparable to the War-time period of inflation and rising prices, when an increase of deposits of practically the same amount took place. During the War, inflationary developments followed a regular and more conventional spiral pattern; price increases were preceded and occasioned by additional issues of credit, and as prices rose it became necessary for business men to call into use ever-larger amounts of bank credit to carry their inventories

[1] The best treatments of the changing developments in American banking during this period are the study prepared for the National Industrial Conference Board by Professor Ralph A. Young of the University of Pennsylvania, entitled *The Banking Situation in the United States* (New York: National Industrial Conference Board, 1932), and *The Banking Situation*, by Professors Willis and Chapman (New York: Columbia University Press, 1935). In certain respects even more valuable, because in the nature of "spot" analyses, are the writings of Dr. B. M. Anderson, Jr., economist of the Chase National Bank. Much the same may be said of the work of Professor H. Parker Willis of Columbia University. In a whole series of articles beginning as early as 1923 Anderson repeatedly pointed out the evils attendant upon Federal Reserve credit expansion for the banking system as a whole, the most important of these being "Cheap Money, Gold, and Federal Reserve Bank Policy" (*Chase Economic Bulletin*, Vol. IV, No. 3), "Bank Money and the Capital Supply" (*Ibid.*, Vol. VI, No. 3), and "Bank Expansion Versus Savings" (*Ibid.*, Vol. VIII, No. 2); for others dealing with this same question, consult the bibliography at the end of this volume. Professor Willis, in his regular articles contributed to *The Banker* (London) and in two articles in *The North American Review* ("The Failure of the Federal Reserve System," Vol. 227, No. 5, and "Who Caused the Panic of 1929?" Vol. 229, No. 2), displays his keen understanding of what was taking place. Those who complain that economists were not conversant with the nature of the developments of this period need only glance back at what was then being written by these two men. Their writings, and the study of Professor Young, have been drawn upon in the preparation of this chapter. For a foreign viewpoint, see R. W. Goldschmidt, *The Changing Structure of American Banking* (London: Routledge, 1934).

at the inflated price level. In contrast, the peace-time inflation of the 'twenties involved an anomalous and more startling expansion of bank credit than occurred during the War.

The net demand deposits plus time deposits of the Reporting Member Banks rose from $13,256 million in De-
cember, 1921, to $21,131 million in October, 1929, an increase
of about $8 billion, or approximately 60 per cent in eight
years. The net demand and time deposits of all the member
banks increased during the same period from $20,900 mil-
lion to $32,269 million, or approximately 55 per cent. The
net demand and time deposits of all the commercial banks
of the country (excluding mutual and other savings banks,
and private banks) expanded from $29,307 million to $42,580
million, an increase of 45 per cent. All of the banks of the
country, as mentioned above, increased their deposits by
over $19 billion, from $35,742 million June 30, 1921 (figures
for all banks being unavailable December 31, 1921), to
$55,289 million December 31, 1929, an increase of 55 per
cent in this instance also. The (geometric) rate of increase
per annum for the commercial banks was almost 5 per cent,
for the member banks and for all banks almost 6 per cent,
and for the Reporting Member Banks over 6 per cent.

Yet during the same period no such startling increase
was occurring in the gold reserves of the Federal Reserve
Banks. Although it is true that they did increase rather
rapidly during the early years of this period, in October,
1929, the gold reserves were but $85 million greater than in
December, 1921. Strictly speaking, it is the reserve balances
of the member banks lodged with the Reserve Banks which
represent the true basis of member bank credit expansion;
nevertheless it is the gold reserves of the Federal Reserve
Banks which constitute the *ultimate* reserve of the member
banks. The extent of the inflation of bank credit in the
System may therefore be measured by comparing the total
net demand deposits plus the time deposits of the member
banks with the gold reserves of the Reserve Banks, as is
done in Table VII.

TABLE VII

GOLD AND DEPOSITS, ALL MEMBER BANKS, 1921-1929

(In Millions of Dollars)

| | DECEMBER, 1921 | OCTOBER, 1929 | PER CENT CHANGE |
|---|---|---|---|
| Federal Reserve Banks' Gold Reserves | 2,875 | 2,960 | 3 |
| Member Bank Net Demand plus Time Deposits | 20,900 | 32,269 | 54 |
| Ratio Deposits to Gold Reserves | 7 to 1 | 11 to 1 | |

While the gold reserves of the Federal Reserve Banks increased 3 per cent from the end of 1921 to October, 1929, deposits increased 54 per cent. The credit structure in the member banks, which in 1922 was 7 times the gold reserves, had by 1929 been reared to 11 times the gold reserves; one dollar of gold in the Reserve Banks supported $7 of member bank deposits in 1921, but by 1929 there was $11 in deposits for each dollar in gold reserve.

Further, taking the reserve balances of the member banks with the Federal Reserve Banks as a more conclusive measure of the expansive possibilities of the member banks, it is found that the increase in total member bank credit from 1922 to 1929 was 16 times the increase in member bank reserves during this period. In other words, for each dollar added to member bank reserve balances, member bank credit increased 16 dollars.

The banking years from 1922 to 1929, then, were characterized by a great credit inflation—an absolute quantitative inflation viewed from any angle, and a relative inflation viewed with respect to the needs of trade and in consideration of the price level. The distinguishing characteristic of this bank credit inflation was that it represented an inflation of investment credit, as only a small part of the expansion was in the form of increased commercial credit.

THE INITIATING SOURCE OF THE INFLATION

The primary sources of this investment-credit expansion were first, the growth of banking reserves beginning in 1922, and secondly, the more effective or more "economical" uses to which those reserves were put. One reason for the increase in banking reserves was the influx of gold from abroad, and the passage of that gold through the high-tension transformer of the bankers' banking system of this country into a very much more "efficient" reserve base than a similar amount of gold would have constituted before 1914. Another highly important reason for the growth of reserves was the action of the Federal Reserve Banks in increasing the reserve balances of the member banks through the medium of open-market purchases. A further factor aiding in the increase of banking reserves was the action of the member banks in borrowing from the Reserve Banks. The member banks were enabled to make a more effective use of these increased reserves by virtue of a declining average reserve-deposit ratio, brought about by the relatively more rapid growth of time deposits compared to demand deposits, and were able to continue expanding credit even after reserve balances ceased to increase. And the reductions in legal reserve requirements wrought by the Federal Reserve Act and its amendment in 1917 made possible a greater expansion of credit on the basis of a given increase of reserves than would have been possible prior to 1914.

Operating in conjunction with all of these factors was a process through the medium of which the expansion of credit was facilitated—the purchases of investments on the part of the banks. The banks used their new reserves made available by Federal Reserve open-market action to purchase investments, thereby creating new deposits in the banking system. These new deposits took the form largely of time deposits, and hence reduced the average reserve-deposit ratio of the banking system, freeing reserves which in turn could be utilized in the purchase of more investments or to create new deposits by means of direct loan extensions.

All of these factors were acting and reacting upon each other in such a degree of interdependence and circularity of cause-and-effect relationships as to make it well nigh impossible to unravel all of their various ramifications while they were in progress. During one phase of the period the activity of one factor may have represented the dominant force working for the upward expansion of credit, and at another point in time a second factor may have occupied that rôle, but usually one was not making its effect fully felt without the assistance of others, and frequently all were working more or less in unison. There is but little difficulty, however, from an analysis of the statistical evidence and from their own public utterances,[1] in assessing primary responsibility for the expansion of credit upon the members of the Federal Reserve Board and upon the central banking system through which the Board's experimentation found expression. Federal Reserve action was the underlying motivating force operating during this period, and tended to accentuate the action of the other forces at work. While

---

[1] In support of this contention, the testimony of Dr. A. C. Miller of the Federal Reserve Board is of special interest: "In the year 1927, if the Committee will look at the curve [relating to Federal Reserve holdings of Government securities], you will note the pronounced increases in these holdings in the second half of the year. Coupled with heavy purchases of acceptances it was the greatest and boldest operation ever undertaken by the Federal Reserve System, and, in my judgment, resulted in one of the most costly errors committed by it or any other banking system in the last 75 years. I am inclined to think that a different policy would have left us with a different condition at this time. You notice that as the volume of these securities voluntarily purchased by the Federal Reserve increases; in other words, as the Federal Reserve puts money into the market, not because member banks asked for it by offering paper for rediscount, but in pursuance of an affirmative policy of our own which in effect said,

'We shall not wait to be asked to provide increased money through rediscounts; we will operate upon our own responsibility and through our own instrumentality, to wit, the purchase of U. S. Government obligations—'

there followed an increase in the reserve balances of the member banks * * * . That [1927] was a time of business recession. Business could not use and was not asking for increased money at that time. But the banks do not want to and in fact do not carry uninvested moneys or idle reserves. Here, then, in 1927, came an accession to their reserves for which they had to find a use." *Hearings on the Operation of the National and Federal Reserve Banking Systems*, pursuant to Senate Resolution 71, Part 1, p. 71. [Hereinafter referred to as *Hearings on the Operation of the Banking Systems*.] (Washington: Government Printing Office, 1931.)

all the factors mentioned are important as explaining the extent and duration of the credit expansion, nevertheless it should be borne in mind that the primary initiating source of the inflation was the open-market policy of the Federal Reserve Board, leading to an expansion of member bank reserve balances.

An increase in the gold reserves of the Reserve Banks would not have set in motion the chain of events working for inflation had not the Federal Reserve Board and the Federal Reserve Banks made use of the influx of gold to finance Reserve credit expansion. Gold in the vaults of the member banks does not count as legal reserve as defined by the Federal Reserve Act, and the greater portion of the gold received from abroad by the member banks in the early years of this period was paid into the Federal Reserve Banks by the member banks, not to increase member bank reserve balances with the Reserve Banks, but for the purpose of liquidating existing member bank indebtedness. Increases in the gold stocks of the Reserve Banks are only a permissive and facilitating factor in credit expansion for the member banks; unless the gold is used to increase member bank reserve balances in some way, there is no increased basis for member bank credit expansion. It is significant that the Federal Reserve Banks were possessed of ample surplus reserves to finance a considerable expansion of credit even before the new influx of gold began in the post-War period. Furthermore, gold continued to come in during the year 1923, yet member bank reserves and member bank credit did not increase appreciably in that year because it was a year of Federal Reserve credit contraction; also in 1927 gold flowed out in large quantities at a time when member bank reserves and member bank credit were expanding rapidly. It is conceded that to the extent that gold received from abroad was lodged in non-member bank vaults it did increase the ability of those banks to expand credit; however, by far the larger part of the total commercial bank credit expansion during this period was in the member banks, and it is with this expansion that we are principally concerned.

Nor would the central banking system, as an inanimate credit mechanism, by and of itself have produced the credit expansion had not the directing force of the Board impinged upon it. Nevertheless the machinery of the central banking system—the hyper-elasticity inherent in any central banking system—underlay the process of credit expansion. We could have had some sort of controlling body akin to the Federal Reserve Board under the National Banking System, but no errors of such a controlling body could conceivably have brought about so great an expansion as the recent one, witnessed under a system of central banking working in conjunction with the existing commercial banking system. It was the action of the Federal Reserve Banks in making available to the member banks an enlarged basis for credit expansion by increasing the reserves of the latter which must be regarded as the initiating force in the expansion of total bank credit; the open-market and rediscount rate [1] policies of the Federal Reserve Board were the dominant factors in stimulating the expansion of credit.

## OPEN-MARKET PURCHASES SIGNIFICANT

The fundamental index of credit-expansion ability for the banks in this country is the relationship between their reserves and their deposit liabilities.[2] If the reserves of the member banks increase, these banks are in a position to increase their outstanding credit. Member bank reserves did increase during this period as a consequence of action taken by the Reserve authorities. During three different years—1922, 1924, and 1927—the Federal Reserve Banks

---

[1] See p. 89 and pp. 92 ff.

[2] "In the Federal Reserve System, a buffer is created between the credit superstructure and the gold base, a buffer which is found in member bank reserve balances. These balances are the effective reserve base of the credit structure, and excessive fluctuations can and do take place in their volume, quite unlike the movements of the gold reserves of the country." Edie, L. D., "The Future of the Gold Standard," in *Gold and Monetary Stabilization*, p. 119.

embarked upon a policy of Reserve credit expansion.[1]  As Reserve Bank credit expanded through the medium of open-market purchases (chiefly Government bonds), member bank reserves were increased, and on the basis of the excess reserves thus created the member banks were enabled to expand their own credit.  In addition to this means of inducing increases in member bank reserves, the Federal Reserve Banks extended the invitation to the member banks to assist in the expansion of Reserve credit by reducing rediscount rates to a point where it became profitable for the member banks to borrow from the Reserve Banks, and thereby replenish their reserves.

The table on page 90 shows the relations of Federal Reserve open-market purchases, increased reserves for the member banks, increased investment purchases, and increased deposits.

It is observable that 90 per cent of the increase in member bank reserves occurred in the three periods of Federal Reserve expansion, that all of the increases in investments and in net demand deposits were concentrated in those years, and that 80 per cent of the increase in total deposits coincided with Reserve credit expansion.  Net demand deposits plus time deposits increased more in *both* 1922 and 1924, and in 1927 the increase was but slightly less, than the *combined* increase for *all* of the other five years of this period.  The sequence of events leading to inflation clearly seems to have consisted of increased Federal Reserve open-market purchases, which resulted in increased member bank reserves; the new reserves were used by the member banks to add to their investment holdings, thus creating new deposits in the banking system.

What Dr. Miller describes as the condition in 1927, and the effect of the Reserve System's activities in that year,

[1] "But in that period [1922–1929] there were three periods when the Federal reserve credit did increase, and that was when we were buying Government securities.  From February to June, 1922 * * * from April to December, 1924, * * * and in 1927, the last quarter. * * * " Testimony of C. S. Hamlin of the Federal Reserve Board before the Senate Banking and Currency Committee, *Hearings on the Operation of the Banking Systems*, Part I, p. 165.

TABLE VIII

OPEN-MARKET PURCHASES AND MEMBER BANK RESERVES,
INVESTMENTS, AND DEPOSITS

(In Millions of Dollars)

| | INCREASE 1922 | INCREASE 1924 | INCREASE 1927 | TOTAL INCREASE 3 YEARS (1922, 1924, 1927) | TOTAL INCREASE 8 YEARS (DECEMBER, 1921, TO OCTOBER, 1929) |
|---|---|---|---|---|---|
| Open-Market Purchases | 464 * | 636 † | 468 ‡ | § | § |
| Member Bank Reserves (December daily avgs.) | 167 | 300 | 181 | 648 | 713 |
| Member Bank Investments (December call) | 1,527 | 1,159 | 1,371 | 4,057 | 3,688 |
| Net Demand Deposits (December call) | 1,754 | 2,092 | 1,083 | 4,929 | 4,503 |
| Net Demand plus Time Deposits (December call) | 2,948 | 3,246 | 2,508 | 9,344 | 11,359 |

* October 19, 1921, to June 17, 1922.
† September 29, 1923, to December 13, 1924.
‡ June 25, 1927, to December 17, 1927.
§ Not cumulated, because no progressive increase.

is merely a repetition of the history of the expansions of 1922 and 1924. Business neither demanded nor needed additional credit for commercial purposes in those years. But as Miller says, banks are not in the habit of carrying uninvested idle reserves (or were not in those days, at least), and being faced with a condition of lack of demand for commercial loans on the part of the business community, the banks were virtually compelled to find an earning outlet for these accessions to their reserves by purchasing investments. But increased investment purchases, as pointed out in Chapter II, just as much as direct loan extensions, create increased deposits in the banking system. It was principally through the medium of increased purchases of investments that the original impetus to the upward expansion of credit came from the banks, rather than from requests of business men for increased commercial credit facilities.

Following shortly upon the expansion of investment holdings in each of these three years, loans on securities, largely connected with stock market speculation, began to increase.[1] Part of the increased deposits in 1922 came from increased loans on securities; this was even more true of those engendered during the 1924 expansion; and the greater portion of the increased deposits following upon the 1927 expansion came from this source.

The Board did not long persist in its policy of increasing Reserve credit during any single expansion period. Instead it actually reversed its policy in this respect, in each instance, and sought to reduce Federal Reserve credit by selling securities. It would be natural to expect that the contraction of Reserve credit would bring about a reduction of the reserve balances of the member banks (for the sale of securities by the Federal Reserve Banks operates to "mop up" member bank reserves, just as their purchase increases them) and thus force a contraction of total member bank credit. This is probably what would have happened had it not been for a set of developments [2] taking place concurrently, that tended to nullify the attempts to effect a contraction of member bank reserve balances.

### FACILITATING FACTORS IN THE INFLATION

Having considered the forces that initiated and generated the inflation, it will be in place to comment upon its long duration and the unprecedented height to which it attained.

There was no upward secular trend of Reserve credit outstanding during the period from 1922 to 1929; total Reserve Bank credit stood at $1,450 million in October,

---

[1] "Investments * * * began to increase in the late fall of 1921 and increased steadily after that time. * * * Loans secured by Government obligations and 'all other loans', which comprise the bulk of commercial loans, followed [declined] upon the same course both relatively and absolutely as total loans. But loans secured by stocks and bonds, which represent in part stock-exchange loans, * * * increased. * * * " Ninth *Annual Report* of the Federal Reserve Board (1922), p. 7.

[2] See pp. 92–101, below.

1929, as against $1,548 million in December, 1921, and was, in fact, much larger in 1920 than in 1929 (a high of $3,522 million in October, 1920, and of $1,643 million in December, 1929, respectively). There was, however, an upward trend in member bank reserve balances, with total member bank reserves $713 million larger in October, 1929, than in December, 1921. Even this expansion of reserve balances does not serve fully to explain the 55 per cent increase in total credit, because member banks' net demand deposits and time deposits increased 16 times as fast as did their reserves. This was perhaps the most unusual aspect of this most unusual period; the explanation of it contains the clue to the magnitude of the increase in bank credit.

One of the explanations for the rapid expansion of credit during the period under review was the reduction of legal reserve requirements for the member banks effected by the Federal Reserve Act. A banking system with an average reserve ratio of 10 per cent can maintain a total credit structure approximately double that when the reserve ratio is 20 per cent, and expansion on the basis of a given increase in reserves can proceed to twice the extent in the former case as in the latter. This in part explains why expansion was more extensive on the basis of an absolute increase in the volume of reserves than would have been possible under the National Bank Act; had the reserve requirements of the National Bank Act been retained in the Federal Reserve Act, the expansion of the 'twenties could not have been so pronounced. This does not, however, account fully for the magnitude of the inflation, nor does it in any sense explain the continued expansion of member bank reserves.

A more important reason for the prolongation of the expansion of member bank credit was the action of these banks in borrowing from the Federal Reserve Banks in order to replenish reserves. Federal Reserve policy was integrally connected with the process of member bank rediscounting. Each time that the Federal Reserve Banks embarked upon a policy of open-market purchases they also

eased rediscount rates. Member bank borrowing did not
follow promptly upon the reductions in the discount rate;
indeed, the accessions to member bank balances were used
in part, to pay off existing indebtedness to the Reserve
Banks. It was not until the Reserve Banks reversed their
open-market policy and began to sell securities that rediscounting on the part of the member banks began to increase.
A chart showing Reserve Bank open-market purchases and
member bank borrowing would indicate an almost perfect
inverse correlation between the two.

The sale of securities by the Reserve Banks normally
has an effect opposite to that accompanying their purchase—
it tends to contract member bank balances with the Federal
Reserve Banks, and hence to reduce their reserves. Reversals in rate policy, however, did not coincide with the
reversals in open-market policy; rediscount rate increases,
forcing a diminution of rediscounting, came later in time
than the sales of securities on the part of the Reserve Banks.
Chart I on the following page depicts graphically the relations between Federal Reserve discount rate policy and
member bank rediscounting activities.

Open-market purchases of securities ceased in June, 1922,
but the rediscount rate was not raised until March, 1923.
When the Reserve Banks began to sell securities following
June, 1922, the member banks offset the contraction in
reserve balances, which would otherwise have followed, by
rediscounting with the Reserve Banks, and thus were able to
maintain their total reserves virtually intact. Rediscounts
increased from $396 million in August, 1922, to $873 million
in October, 1923; reserve balances for the member banks
stood at $1,820 million June 30, 1922, and were $1,839 million
September 30, 1923. In December, 1924, the Reserve Banks
again reversed their open-market policy of expansion, and
again sold securities; as rediscount rates were low at that
date, member bank rediscounting rose from $228 million in
November, 1924, to $688 million in December, 1925, before
the increased rediscount rate became an effective check

upon member bank borrowing. Member bank reserves increased from $2,182 million in December, 1924, to $2,219 million in December, 1925. And when the open-market policy of 1927 was reversed by the Reserve Banks in December of that year, rediscounting again increased, and continued into

CHART I

REDISCOUNT RATE AND VOLUME OF
REDISCOUNTING, 1922-31

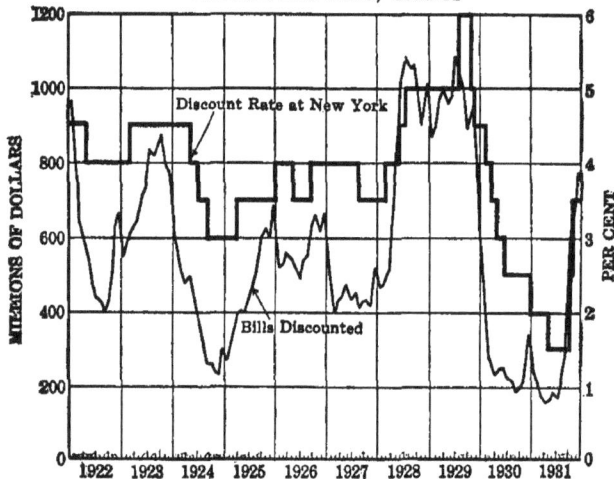

Source: Hardy, C. O., *Credit Policies of the Federal Reserve System* (Washington: The Brookings Institution, 1932), p. 229. Reproduced by permission.

August of 1928 before successive rate increases checked it. It is true that rate increases in this last instance followed rather promptly on the reversal of open-market policy; but, as inflation and the stock market boom had by this time manifested unmistakable "runaway" tendencies, it was found that more drastic rate increases were necessary to discourage further member bank borrowing.

Thus, each time that the Reserve Banks sought to reverse their open-market policy of expansion by selling securities, that action was rendered ineffectual by rediscounting on the part of the member banks; the reserve balances which had been built up at the instance of Reserve Bank open-market purchases were maintained at approximately the same level by the member banks on their own initiative through the simple process of borrowing from the Federal Reserve Banks. But it should not be concluded that Federal Reserve policy aiming at credit contraction would have been ineffective in any event; had the Board and the Reserve Banks seen fit to act more vigorously and more resolutely—that is to say, had rate increases been more positive, and had they occurred simultaneously with the sales of securities—it is improbable that the situation would have gotten so far out of hand.

Rediscounting by the member banks served to replenish their reserves and operated to prolong and heighten the inflation. Each period of Federal Reserve open-market operations tended to lift member bank reserves to a new plateau, and the member banks in replenishing their reserves by borrowing were able to maintain their reserves at approximately that same level until the next period of open-market purchases came along. The successive periods of open-market purchases began in each instance from a higher plateau of absolute reserves, so that reserves were progressively pushed upward and there was therefore no necessity for member banks to make positive reductions in total bank credit outstanding.

DISPROPORTIONATE GROWTH OF TIME DEPOSITS RESULTED IN PROGRESSIVE DECLINE IN AVERAGE RESERVE-DEPOSIT RATIO

A factor of even greater importance than the two foregoing in explaining the continuation and the magnitude of the inflation was the conversion of demand deposits into time deposits, which brought about a progressive decline in the average reserve-deposit ratio for the banking system. It was the most deceptive of the factors at work, and went almost wholly unobserved at the time.[1] It serves to explain why member bank credit continued to expand during periods when Federal Reserve action was seeking to effect

[1] Anderson and Willis, as mentioned, being conspicuous exceptions.

credit contraction, and why total credit was expanding even when member bank reserves were not increasing. It is also the clue to the explanation of why total member bank credit could expand 16 times the increase in member bank reserves, and hence why credit expansion was so rapid and so pronounced during the periods of open-market purchases of securities.

The disproportionate growth of time deposits in the banking system beginning with 1922 was one of the most striking aspects of this whole period of credit growth.[1]  As time deposits comprised an ever-increasing proportion of total deposits, the *average* reserve ratio required against deposits declined.    This is attributable to the fact that the legal reserve required to be maintained against time deposits in National Banks (and other member banks) was (at that time) only 3 per cent, whereas against demand deposits it ranged from 7 to 13 per cent according to the classification of the banks. A shift in the proportion between demand deposits and time deposits in favor of the latter reduces the average required reserve-deposit ratio, and hence frees reserves which may be used as the basis for further credit expansion. A declining average reserve ratio operates to increase the excess reserves in the banking system just as much as positive increases in reserves induced by Federal Reserve open-market purchases or member bank borrowings.  As a result of the reduced reserve ratio, the banks were not only able to maintain the existing credit structure on the basis of a given absolute volume of reserves, but actually to increase total credit outstanding without any positive additions to that same volume of reserves.

[1] "The change noted in the composition of loans and investments of member banks has been accompanied by a corresponding change in the character of their deposits.  Since 1922 net demand deposits of reporting member banks have increased 27 per cent, while their time deposits have increased 93 per cent, and the proportion of time deposits to the total of time and net demand deposits has increased from 23 to 31 per cent. * * * Looking at the developments in the condition of member banks as a whole in recent years, the outstanding changes have thus been in the direction of a larger proportion of long-term investments and of loans on securities and of a corresponding increase in the proportion of time deposits, as compared with deposits payable on demand."  Thirteenth *Annual Report* of the Federal Reserve Board (1926), p. 8.

The following table shows the comparative growth of net demand deposits and time deposits for the Reporting Member Banks from 1921 to 1929.

TABLE IX

REPORTING MEMBER BANKS, NET DEMAND AND TIME DEPOSITS

(In Millions of Dollars)

Monthly averages of weekly figures

| DECEMBER | NET DEMAND DEPOSITS | TIME DEPOSITS |
|---|---|---|
| 1921 | 10,247 | 3,009 |
| 1922 | 11,146 | 3,720 |
| 1923 | 11,127 | 4,083 |
| 1924 | 13,184 | 4,855 |
| 1925 | 13,173 | 5,357 |
| 1926 | 13,032 | 5,768 |
| 1927 | 13,872 | 6,419 |
| 1928 | 13,399 | 6,842 |
| 1929 (October) | 3,633 | 6,839 |
| Per Cent Increase | 33% | 127% |

From December, 1921, to October, 1929, the increase in net demand deposits in the Reporting Member Banks was roughly 33 per cent while the increase in their time deposits was 127 per cent, or an average annual percentage increase of time deposits four times that of demand deposits. The comparative growth of time deposits in the Reporting Mem-

TABLE X

REPORTING MEMBER BANKS IN NEW YORK CITY, NET DEMAND AND TIME DEPOSITS

(In Millions of Dollars)

Monthly averages of weekly figures

| DECEMBER | NET DEMAND DEPOSITS | TIME DEPOSITS |
|---|---|---|
| 1921 | 4,219 | 290 |
| 1922 | 4,325 | 539 |
| 1923 | 4,234 | 609 |
| 1924 | 5,372 | 814 |
| 1925 | 5,204 | 792 |
| 1926 | 5,094 | 902 |
| 1927 | 5,570 | 1,034 |
| 1928 | 5,305 | 1,198 |
| 1929 (October) | 5,561 | 1,258 |
| Per Cent Increase | 32% | 333% |

ber Banks of New York City was even more rapid, as shown
in Table X.

### BANK CREDIT EXPANSION VERSUS DIRECT SAVING AS AFFECTING GROWTH OF TIME DEPOSITS

It seems highly probable that most of the growth of time
deposits was a product of bank credit expansion, rather than
of direct saving, as some observers have contended.[1] Open-
market operations are usually carried out in the larger
cities. If there had been a general growth of saving throughout the country, it is to be supposed that the growth in time
deposits in the smaller cities would have kept pace, at least
to a considerable degree, with that in larger cities. The
evidence of Table XI, however, is that the increase in time
deposits was especially pronounced in those centers most
affected by open-market operations of the Reserve Banks;
the percentage increase for the banks in Central Reserve
Cities (New York and Chicago) was thrice the increase for
those outside Reserve Cities, and in absolute amount the
growth of time deposits in Reserve Cities alone (63 in number in 1929) exceeded that for the country banks.

TABLE XI

NET DEMAND AND TIME DEPOSITS, ALL MEMBER BANKS

(In Millions of Dollars)

| December | BANKS IN CENTRAL RESERVE CITIES | | BANKS IN OTHER RESERVE CITIES | | BANKS OUTSIDE RESERVE CITIES | |
|---|---|---|---|---|---|---|
| | Demand Deposits | Time Deposits | Demand Deposits | Time Deposits | Demand Deposits | Time Deposits |
| 1921 | 4,343 | 528 | 4,150 | 2,109 | 4,685 | 3,814 |
| . . . . | . . . . | . . . . | . . . . | . . . . | . . . . | . . . . |
| 1929 | 7,058 | 1,755 | 5,970 | 4,888 | 5,833 | 6,590 |
| Per Cent Increase | 63% | 232% | 44% | 132% | 24% | 72% |

[1] The contrary view is advanced by W. Randolph Burgess, *The Reserve Banks
and the Money Market* (New York: Harper & Brothers, 1927), pp. 37–38: "The
writer's tentative conclusion from these figures and other evidence is that time
deposits in commercial banks are to a considerable extent genuine savings deposits * * * ." And see the article by Elmer Hartzell, "Time Deposits," in the
*Harvard Business Review* (October, 1934), Vol. XIII, No. 1.

The most pronounced growth in time deposits, further-more, coincided with the periods of rapid Reserve credit expansion. It may be observed from Table IX, above, that 55 per cent of the increase in time deposits for the Reporting Member Banks was concentrated in the three years 1922, 1924, and 1927. For the Reporting Member Banks in New York City, 64 per cent of the total increase in time deposits occurred in these three years. During the year 1922, time deposits in the Reporting Member Banks in New York City rose by 86 per cent, and in the following year only 13 per cent; in 1924, time deposits increased 34 per cent, and during 1925 there was an actual decrease of 3 per cent; time deposits increased rapidly again in 1927, with Reserve credit expansion, and slowed down in 1928 when that expansion ceased. What is true of New York holds also for Chicago, these being the two cities where the major portion of open-market operations are usually conducted.

Thus it is seen that the greatest growth of time deposits coincided in points of time with the Federal Reserve open-market purchases of securities, and that this growth of time deposits was in each instance relatively greater than the growth of demand deposits. Chronologically and causally, the order of developments was as follows: Federal Reserve open-market purchases resulted in expansion of member bank reserve balances; this served to instigate increased purchases of investments by the member banks; and the credit generated thereby took the form largely of time deposits. The Reserve Banks pumped credit into the money market, inducing increased reserves in the banking system; the banks used the new reserves to purchase investments (later, to make loans on securities) which created more deposits in the banking system, and the increased deposits, being unneeded by business men and corporations as demand deposits for current transactions, were shifted to time deposits which would draw interest. This greater relative growth of time deposits operated to reduce the average reserve-deposit ratio, hence freeing reserves which in turn could be used by the banks further to increase their investments and their loans on securities without any absolute increase in reserves.

## PAYMENT OF INTEREST ON TIME DEPOSITS A FACTOR IN THEIR EXPANSION

It should be remarked at this point that another of the changes introduced by the Federal Reserve Act assisted in the greater relative growth of time deposits. The preference displayed by corporations and business men with idle bank balances on hand for having those balances in the form of time deposits was largely influenced by the interest to be earned on time deposits. It was mentioned in Chapter II that the Federal Reserve Act sanctioned the payment of interest on time deposits by member banks, making this privilege fully and legally available for the first time to the National Banks. Without this inducement to carry idle funds in the form of time deposits it is unlikely that such deposits would have increased so rapidly; and had they not done so, the reduction in the average reserve ratio which assisted so materially in the expansion of credit probably would not have been so extensive.

## FEDERAL RESERVE BOARD COGNIZANT OF TIME DEPOSIT DEVELOPMENTS

That the Federal Reserve Board was fully aware of the existence and nature of these developments is evidenced by its *Annual Report* for 1927:

> The continuous growth of time deposits in recent years at a rate more rapid than the growth in demand deposits has resulted in an increase in the proportion of the banks' deposit liabilities that is represented by time deposits. This more rapid growth of time deposits, which require only 3 per cent reserve, has been an important factor in the past six years in enabling member banks to increase their loans and investments by $11,000,000,000 on the basis of $756,000,000 added to their reserve balances. This

expansion during the past six years at the rate of $15 of credit to $1 of reserve has reduced the average required reserves * * * .

In its *Annual Report* for 1926 the Board had also called attention to this growth in time deposits, and the significance of that development for the reserve situation:

> Another phase * * * in the operations of member banks arises from the fact, already mentioned, that time deposits have been increasing much more rapidly than demand deposits. Since legal reserve requirements against time deposits are 3 per cent, while against net demand deposits they range from 7 to 13, the increase in the proportion of time deposits has had the effect of decreasing the average amount of reserves * * * . This decline in ratio means that member banks were able to comply with legal reserve requirements with a considerably smaller amount of reserves than would have been necessary had the proportion of time to demand deposits remained unchanged or, to put it another way, to add a large amount to their loans and investments without a corresponding increase in their reserves. As a matter of fact, reserve balances of member banks have not increased since the end of 1924, while there has been since that time a growth of about $2,900,000,000 in the total amount of credit extended by these banks.

The core of the explanation, then, of why credit could expand at a rate faster than the expansion of reserve balances and why total outstanding credit reached such an altitude is found in the declining average reserve ratio of member banks. Considering the Reporting Member Banks alone, the reserve balances at the end of 1924 stood at $1,690 million and in June, 1929, they were $1,672 million—an actual decrease of $18 million—yet the loans and investments of the Reporting Member Banks expanded by the amazing total of $3,729 million between these dates!

## THE PARADOX OF INCREASING MEMBER BANK CREDIT COMBINED WITH RISING RESERVE RATIO OF FEDERAL RESERVE BANKS

This factor also serves to explain the seemingly anomalous situation of *increasing member bank credit* at times when *the reserve ratio of the Federal Reserve Banks* was also increasing; a rising reserve ratio for the Reserve Banks would ordinarily indicate that Reserve Bank reserves were *not* being used to finance credit expansion. It was this condition of a rising reserve ratio for the Reserve Banks which confused European observers of the American gold and credit situation, and caused some of them to believe that the United States was "sterilizing" gold. Even such a careful student of banking and credit conditions as Cassel was led to the misstatement that [1] "* * * in * * * the United States there was an aversion from using the fresh gold acquired for any such purpose [credit expansion], and to a large extent the gold was simply buried in the vaults of the Central Banks." Far from lying buried and unused in the vaults of the Federal Reserve Banks, the gold was being used more effectively to finance a period of inflation than during any like peace-time period in history.[2]   A high, and at times rising, reserve ratio for the Federal Reserve Banks might suggest that the gold was lying idle in the vaults of the Reserve Banks; but the habit of European economists of looking at the central bank reserve ratio overlooks the essential importance in this country of the magnitude of the excess reserves of the member banks.   Member bank credit increasing at a rate 16 times faster than the increase in members' reserves, and gold reserves in 1929 less than 7 per cent of the total credit outstanding for all banks in the country, are facts incompatible with the idea of sterilization of gold.

It should now be apparent that the expansion of the 'twenties was almost exclusively an outgrowth of changes in our banking system introduced by the Federal Reserve Act. It is partly for this reason that the inflation is denominated a central banking phenomenon. But even the introduction of a central banking system would not have permitted so rapid and so extensive an expansion of credit without the

---

[1] *The Crisis in the World's Monetary System* (Oxford: Oxford University Press, 1932), p. 71.
[2] "We have made a more intensive utilization of gold than any other country except England." John H. Williams, in *Gold and Monetary Stabilization*, p. 149.

concurrent changes in reserve requirements and those respecting time deposits. And at the same time it is improbable that the expansion would have gotten under way had it not been for the action of the central banking authorities in initiating the inflation.

### THE NATURE OF THE INFLATION

The inflation of 1922–1929, the extent of which is set forth in the first section of this chapter, has been characterized as an "investment inflation," or capital inflation. Banks during this period were tying up an increasing share of their resources in assets not readily liquidated; they were extending to business men and to industry, or through their banking operations they were enabling business men and industry to acquire, long-term or capital credit, with fixed assets of one character or another pledged as security. Further, the banks were becoming intimately entangled with the capital market by engaging in extensive security-market financing. The proportion of their assets which represented commercial credit in the strict sense progressively constituted a decreasing proportion of their total resources, while the proportion which went into investment

TABLE XII

LOANS AND INVESTMENTS, ALL MEMBER BANKS, 1921, 1928, AND 1929

| ITEM | PERCENTAGE DISTRIBUTION | | | INDEX NUMBERS JUNE, 1921, BASE | |
|---|---|---|---|---|---|
| | 1921 | 1928 | 1929 | 1928 | 1929 |
| Loans and Investments | 100 | 100 | 100 | 145 | 148 |
| Loans | 75 | 69 | 72 | 133 | 142 |
| Commercial Loans | 53 | 36 | 36 | 98 | 100 |
| Loans on Securities | 19 | 26 | 28 | 206 | 229 |
| Loans on Real Estate | 3 | 7 | 8 | 300 | 314 |
| Investments | 25 | 31 | 28 | 179 | 167 |
| In Government Securities | 11 | 12 | 12 | 165 | 162 |
| In Other Securities | 14 | 19 | 16 | 189 | 171 |
| Total of "Capital" Loans and Investments | 47 | 64 | 64 | 200 | 214 |
| Commercial Loans | 53 | 36 | 36 | 98 | 100 |

or capital assets consistently increased, taking the form of
loans on real estate, loans on securities (largely stock exchange lending), and outright purchases of investments.
These facts are brought out in Table XII, which shows the
percentage distribution of loans and investments for all member banks, and index numbers of these items computed on
the basis of the figures for 1921 as 100.

According to Table XII Loans declined from 75 per cent of
Total Loans and Investments in 1921 to 69 per cent of the
total in 1928; Commercial Loans declined from 53 per cent
to 36 per cent, while Loans on Securities and Loans on Real
Estate increased from 19 per cent to 26 per cent and from
3 to 7 per cent, respectively. Investments rose between the
same dates from 25 per cent of Total Loans and Investments
to 31 per cent, almost all of the increase being represented
by Investments in corporate and other securities. Furthermore, although Loans on Securities and Loans on Real
Estate are technically classified as *loans*, the actual character of many such assets was such as to cause them to
stand in much the same relation to the process of inflation
as did *investments* proper; the proceeds of a considerable
portion of these loans, in other words, were used for purely
"investment" purposes, rather than to expedite commercial
and industrial activities. Investments increased 79 per cent
between 1921 and 1928, while all Loans were increasing
but 33 per cent and Commercial Loans were actually declining; there was a slight decrease in Investments from 1928
to 1929, apparently because banks sold their investment
assets in order to increase their Loans on Securities and on
Real Estate. It is also significant that the sale of these
securities during 1928 and 1929 depressed the bond market
in those years and caused a rise in the rate of interest on
corporate securities.

A more complete presentation of the nature of the 1921–
1929 inflation is found in Table XIII, submitted by Dr. Miller of the Reserve Board in his testimony before the Committee on the *Hearings on the Operation of the Banking Systems*

(Part I, p. 138), and presumably accessible only to Reserve System officials prior to that time.

(Part I, p. 138)

TABLE XIII

LOANS AND INVESTMENTS OF ALL MEMBER BANKS
(In Millions of Dollars)

| JUNE | INVESTMENTS | LOANS ON SECURITIES | LOANS ON URBAN REAL ESTATE | ALL OTHER LOANS | TOTAL LOANS AND INVESTMENTS |
|---|---|---|---|---|---|
| 1921 | 6,002 | 4,400 | 875 | 12,844 | 24,121 |
| 1922 | 7,017 | 4,500 | 1,100 | 11,565 | 24,182 |
| 1923 | 7,757 | 4,950 | 1,350 | 12,450 | 26,507 |
| 1924 | 7,963 | 5,350 | 1,575 | 12,279 | 27,167 |
| 1925 | 8,863 | 6,718 | 1,875 | 12,062 | 29,518 |
| 1926 | 9,123 | 7,321 | 2,161 | 12,579 | 31,184 |
| 1927 | 9,818 | 8,156 | 2,449 | 12,533 | 32,756 |
| 1928 | 10,758 | 9,068 | 2,624 | 12,611 | 35,061 |
| 1929 | 10,052 | 10,095 | 2,750 | 12,814 | 35,711 |
| Increase | 4,050 | 5,695 | 1,875 | −30 | 11,590 |
| Per Cent Increase | 67% | 129% | 214% | .... | 48% |

*Commercial Loans Strikingly Stable*

This table is deserving of careful examination. It is to be observed that total loans and investments for all member banks show an increase of $11,600 million during the eight-year period, all of which took the form of increases in investments, increases in loans on urban real estate, or increases in loans on securities. The commercial loans ("all other loans") were actually less at the end of the period than at the beginning, and their stability throughout the period is worthy of notice. After the one rather sizable increase from 1922 to 1923, representing largely a recovery from the extremely drastic deflation of commercial credit during the 1920–1921 depression, commercial loans varied less than $400 million for the remainder of the period.

While the commercial loans were displaying this pronounced stability, the investments of the member banks were increasing by 67 per cent, their loans on securities were expanding by 129 per cent, and their loans on urban real estate were advancing by 214 per cent. The effects of this upward thrust of bank credit were first revealed through the medium of increased investments, but shortly afterward they became apparent in connection with the "loans on securities" category.  It is not difficult to trace the real beginnings of the stock market boom to the expansion in loans on securities engendered by the Federal Reserve credit expansion of 1924, with such loans increasing 26 per cent between June, 1924, and June, 1925.  Loans on securities were approximately two-thirds of the investments total at the beginning of the period, yet they exceeded the investments at the end of it.  In 1921, loans on real estate were 3 per cent of total loans and investments, but in 1929 were 8 per cent, contributing almost one-sixth of the absolute increase in total loans and investments.

It is apparent that the indictment of the American banking system by the late Paul M. Warburg made before the National Monetary Commission and prior to the establishment of the Federal Reserve System, unfortunately still held good in 1929: [1] "The European financial system is constructed upon discounts as its foundation; the American system is constructed upon bonds and stocks as its foundation."  Indeed, the above figures seem to indicate that the foundation had simply been considerably enlarged—and commensurately weakened—by the operations of the Federal Reserve System itself.

### EFFECTS OF THE INFLATION

It is observable that the inflation of bank credit from 1922 to 1929 had three highly significant effects upon the banking and financial system and upon business.  First, the liquidity of all banks declined, rendering the banking system particularly susceptible to the vagaries of an unstable stock market.  Secondly, an abnormal "roundaboutness" developed in the way in which bank credit was extended to the business community by the banks.  And thirdly, there was engendered

[1] Quoted by Phillips, C. A., *Readings in Money and Banking* (New York: The Macmillan Company, 1921), p. 707.

a marked investment or capital boom, which sustained business activity at an artificial level and whose inherent instability was not easily recognizable.

### Liquidity of Banks Impaired

The most striking aspect of the declining liquidity of the banking system had to do with the reduction in the proportion of commercial loans in bank portfolios. The discount foundation, slender enough at the outset, was further weakened during the course of this investment credit inflation. Commercial banks, in other words, were largely forsaking commercial banking operations in favor of dealings in credit extensions of a long-term or capital nature.

These departures from the tested tenets of sound banking were recognized as early as 1926 by the Federal Reserve Board in its *Annual Report* for that year (p. 10):

> The changing character of the business of member banks in recent years has thus been characterized by an increased use of their resources in long-time investments and in loans not arising out of the current requirements of trade and industry * * * . This is a development which, though it may in some cases result in strengthening the position of individual member banks, represents a departure from the original conception of the Federal reserve banking system as of a cooperative undertaking among commercial banks engaged primarily in the financing of the current operations of productive industry and trade. As long-time trends these changes in the character of the business of the member banks are significant both because they tend to decrease the proportion of short-term, self-liquidating paper in the assets of member banks and because they result in relatively smaller reserve holdings against the deposits of these banks.

This decrease in the proportion of short-term, self-liquidating assets served to lessen the liquidity of the banks and to reduce their ability, both relatively and absolutely, to meet their deposit liabilities upon demand or short notice; at the same time the growth of assets of a long-term character made it increasingly difficult for the banks as a whole to realize upon those assets by conversion into cash if necessity for such action arose.

There is a vast difference between liquidity and "shift-ability." Liquidity denotes ability to realize direct amortization of the loan, the making of which gave rise initially to the asset in the bank's portfolio; shiftability implies ability to obtain cash by transference of that asset to some other bank or person ready and able to take it over. But if all banks engage in a program of building up their investment assets at the expense of their self-liquidating assets, shiftability is found to be impaired, if at all attainable, should all banks later attempt to improve their cash positions by transferring their investment assets elsewhere. Outside of the banking system itself, there is usually an insufficiency of liquid resources in any nation to absorb a wholesale liquidation of investment assets, and when all banks are mutually embarrassed with a surplusage of investment assets, no place to shift such assets can be found. This was the situation that developed in the closing months of 1931 when the wave of bank failures made it imperative that banks improve their cash positions; their wholesale efforts to convert investment holdings into cash resulted in one of the most precipitate drops in bond prices on record.

## Two Aspects of Liquidity

It is conceded that an argument of considerable plausibility can be offered in support of the thesis that there is no such thing as "liquidity" for the banking *system* in time of difficulty—even in the case of short-term, self-liquidating paper.[1] The authors incline to the position, however, that the traditional principles of basing banking operations on short-term transactions in self-liquidating commercial paper are still largely valid and fundamentally sound. The views on banking liquidity of the late Professor J. Lawrence Laughlin, of the University of Chicago, may well be recalled: [2]

[1] See especially the article by Professor Fritz Machlup, formerly of the University of Vienna, "The Liquidity of Short-term Capital," *Economica* (August, 1932), Vol. XII, No. 37, pp. 271 ff.

[2] *Money, Credit and Prices* (Chicago: The University of Chicago Press, 1931), Vol. II, p. 724.

Here is the crux of the whole matter. * * * Short-term loans on salable goods on the way from the producer to the consumer are the most liquid loans a bank can make; for when sold the goods bring in the cash with which to meet the debt. * * * Therefore, the solvency of a bank is always tested by the character of the assets in its loan items; if of a high class and short-time they can be rediscounted for cash.

Two aspects of liquidity are brought out in this excerpt from Professor Laughlin: the one, that short-term or commercial loans are self-liquidating in character; the other, that they are rediscountable for cash. To provide adequate rediscount facilities was one of the principal objectives sought in the establishment of the Federal Reserve System, and rediscounting is one of the primary functions of all central banking systems. But apart from the rediscounting feature attaching to short-term loans, a commercial bank should be able readily to improve its reserve position by simply refusing to make new loans and calling for the repayment of outstanding loans as they mature.

The theory of the "self-liquidating" loan is that the transaction which presumably was facilitated by the original making of the loan should itself provide the funds with which to discharge the loan. In this way, a bank can speedily reduce its loans, and, as reduction of loans and reduction of deposits go hand in hand, it can improve its reserve-deposit ratio and hence its liquidity in a comparatively short space of time, even without resort to rediscounting, provided that a substantial portion of its loans are actually "self-liquidating" in character. And the rediscounting privilege is still available, in the event that it appears desirable to enhance the liquidity of the bank even more hastily.

It should be clearly understood that the above analysis relates principally to a well-managed commercial bank, and that its applicability to the commercial banking *system* is in some degree limited. Liquidity of the individual bank can bring liquidity to the system only in a restricted sense. It is apparent that simultaneous attempts to liquidate by all banks could hardly fail to bring economic activity to a virtual standstill; the effects of attempts to liquidate the entire banking system, if it could be done, would be even more disastrous than those which result from illiquidity of the units of that system. There is, nevertheless, a solid residuum of truth in the older doctrine that the banking system is less vulnerable and more stable if the individual banks are in a genuinely liquid condition. If the individual components of the banking system are liquid, there is much greater likelihood that an incipient banking crisis can be kept under control and prevented from spreading into a disastrous financial conflagration.

### Decline in Ratio of Gold to Deposits Suggests Declining Liquidity

Aside from this decline in the liquidity of the banking system with regard to the character of the assets involved, the liquidity of the system declined in another respect during this period, that is, in the proportion of its ultimate reserves to deposit liabilities. The following table compares the deposits of all commercial banks with the gold reserves of the Federal Reserve Banks. While it is true that the gold reserves of the Federal Reserve Banks do not properly indicate the total reserves of all commercial banks, the overlapping and pyramiding of reserves which was one of the weaknesses of the National Banking System, in appreciable measure still obtains. The non-member commercial banks carry the greater part of their reserves as deposits with the member banks, just as the member banks carry *all* their (legal) reserves in the form of deposit balances with the Federal Reserve Banks, so that in effect the reserves of the Federal Reserve Banks constitute the ultimate reserves for the entire banking system.

Thus liquidity declined for the banking system by one-third, viewed from the standpoint of one interested in the proportion of ultimate reserves held against deposit liabilities. If a 10-per-cent reserve ratio is considered a satisfac-

TABLE XIV

INDIVIDUAL DEPOSITS, ALL COMMERCIAL BANKS, AND GOLD
RESERVES OF THE FEDERAL RESERVE BANKS

(In Millions of Dollars)

| JUNE | DEPOSITS | TOTAL GOLD RESERVES, FEDERAL RESERVE BANKS | RATIO OF GOLD TO DEPOSITS |
|------|----------|-------------------------------------------|---------------------------|
| 1922 | 29,867 | 3,022 | 10.1 |
| 1929 | 42,580 | 2,858 | 6.7 |

tory one for the safe conduct of banking operations and for
proper liquidity, certainly a 7-per-cent ratio indicates an
illiquid condition, since the ability of the banks to meet
demands for cash is greatly impaired.

### Credit Extension by Indirection

Intimately related to the declining liquidity of the banking system and to the decline in importance of commercial
loans, there developed an increasing indirectness of the
relationship between the banking process and the financing
of production and trade.   By using their growing reserves
to purchase investments and to make loans on securities
and on real estate, the banks were increasing the deposits of
the system and hence were furnishing increasing amounts
of credit to the business community; but in this way bank
credit reached the processes of production and trade through
the capital and securities markets, rather than through direct
loans to business men to finance short-term commercial
transactions.   The decline in commercial loans cannot be
charged entirely to the unwisdom of the bankers; part of
this decline was due to decreased demands for credit on the
part of business men actuated by a desire to get out of debt
to the banks after their unpleasant experiences in the stringency of 1920–1921.   Nevertheless, the indirect extensions of
credit initiated by the action of the banks assisted in facilitating this debt-reduction policy.

The utilization of increased reserves to purchase investments forced down the long-term rate of interest so that
corporations found it profitable to float bonds and stocks,

using the proceeds to retire their bank loans.[1]  In absorbing
these new issues the commercial banks were indirectly supplying additional bank credit funds to industry, but at the
same time this very process operated to reduce their direct
loans to business men and corporations.  In the course of
time, in fact, this increased flotation of corporate securities
in an especially favorable capital market virtually surfeited
some of the issuing corporations with liquid funds for which
they found a profitable use in the stock exchange call-loan
market, adding new fuel to the already raging flames of
stock market speculation.  These call loans in the stock
market made by corporations constituted a large part of
the "loans by others" item appearing in the monthly statements of brokers' loans.

### An Inherently Instable Boom

The most important effect of the abnormally low interest
rates and the inflation, as these were related to subsequent
cyclical developments, was the stimulation of a marked
boom in the construction of capital goods.  By injecting new
credits into the business situation *via* the securities and
capital markets the banks financed a constructional boom
of immense proportions, as well as a real estate boom.[2]
The early flotations of securities, as just mentioned, enabled corporations to retire much of their previously in-
curred indebtedness to banks.  Additional issues of new
securities were also absorbed by the banks, seemingly quite
willingly and without misgivings; the continuation of this
process served to depress further the long-term rate of interest and at the same time to generate new deposits.  The

[1] "The decrease in commercial loans was due, in addition to the smaller volume
of business activity, also to the fact that corporations floated securities at the prevailing low rates and used the proceeds to reduce their bank loans."  Fourteenth
*Annual Report* of the Federal Reserve Board (1927), p. 5.

[2] "The growth in member bank credit * * * therefore * * * was not entirely
in response to current requirements of trade and industry, but included an element
of growth of credit for longer term purposes, and particularly for the financing of
building operations and real-estate transactions."  Thirteenth *Annual Report* of
the Federal Reserve Board (1926), p. 6.

proceeds of the later issues were used in a variety of ways. Industrial plant extensions, public utility construction, and increased and improved mechanization of industry were all financed thereby. Real estate bond issues were brought out on a scale unmatched in previous history. States and municipalities sold bonds to the banks and used the new credit to further street and highway construction, school building programs, water works, and other construction of a capital nature. Our export trade was stimulated by extensive over-seas lending, again assisted by the banks. Finally, the stock market received a new impetus from the abundant credit made available to it by the banks, beginning principally during the Reserve credit expansion of 1924 but with its most important developments proceeding from the 1927 expansion. All of these factors, plus the new use to which the superabundant credit was put in connection with the highly important matter of installment financing, helped to carry business activity on the false bottom of credit inflation long enough for the term "New Era" to become a byword; they all contributed to the prosperity of 1928 and 1929, the intrinsic weaknesses and spurious character of which were not widely recognized until the decline began in the autumn of 1929.

It was through these various booms of a capital nature that the "cheap credit" policy of this period found its chief outlets. The net effect of these influences was to produce an alteration in the structure of production; that is to say, there was a more than proportionate increase in the production of capital goods as compared with consumption goods. Investment (in the sense of the creation of real capital equipment) financed by bank credit was proceeding at a rate in advance of the accumulation of real savings. The disproportionate increase in investment activity and the stock market boom would not have developed had it not been for the aiding influences of the banking system; without the effects of this disequilibrium between investment and saving the declining liquidity of the banking system by itself probably would not have brought on utter collapse.

The relation of this disequilibrium between saving and investment to the depression is treated at length in the next chapter; the part played by the stock market collapse in contributing to the length of the depression is dealt with in Chapter VII.

## CHAPTER VI

# THE FUNDAMENTAL CAUSES OF THE GREAT DEPRESSION

It has been asserted (Chapter IV) that fluctuations in the rate of creation of fixed capital are the dominant feature of the business cycle. It was also stated that the source of fluctuations in the rate of investment was the elasticity of the banking system, what Hawtrey labels "the inherent instability of credit." A highly important result of an exceptional increase of investment is the misdirection of capital which characterizes a boom period, the setting of the stage for future depression. The present chapter, which is directed toward the task of developing a generalized theory of business cycles, as well as to an explanation of the causes of the Great Depression, centers the cycle in a disequilibrium between investment and saving, and sets forth the cause of that disequilibrium as residing in the capacity of the banking system to generate lending power at a rate in excess of the growth of voluntary saving.

DEVELOPMENTS IN BUSINESS CYCLE AND MONETARY THEORY

If the explanation of the causes of the depression and the theory of business cycles here set forth seem to follow closely those theories of the "Trade Cycle" advanced by Hayek and Keynes it is simply because the writers agree with Professors Hansen and Tout that the contributions of these men represent "the most signal recent developments of business cycle and monetary theory." [1] Developed on the Continent by members of the New School of Vienna, principally Mises, Hayek, and Haberler, on the foundations pointed out by the Swede, Knut Wicksell, this theory was also being for-

[1] "Investment and Saving in Business Cycle Theory," *Econometrica* (April, 1933), Vol. I, No. 2, p. 119.

mulated in the writings of D. H. Robertson and J. M. Keynes in England, largely independently of knowledge of the work of the Austrian writers. It is found most fully developed in Keynes' *Treatise on Money* and in Hayek's *Monetary Theory and the Trade Cycle* and his *Prices and Production* (which, as Hayek properly states, are to be considered as complementary expressions of his theory). Mention must also be made of Robertson's concise, but difficult, *Banking Policy and the Price Level* (Keynes awards full credit to Robertson for influencing his own thinking along these lines), and of Mises' *Theory of Money and Credit*.[1]

Although the attempt to resolve the problem of the business cycle in the divergences of investment and saving that are largely traceable to the operation of the banking system explains certain features of the last cycle for which the exclusively monetary forms of explanation are not adequate, not all of the refinements of Keynes' and Hayek's analyses are acceptable. And bearing in mind that the principal aim of the present work is an explanation of the depression, there are certain dissidences between the theory developed here and those of both of these men. The similarities will be apparent to readers at all conversant with their views, however, and the indebtedness of the authors will be obvious.

### AN INTEGRATED EXPLANATION

Any attempted explanation of the recent depression in the United States should not only be concerned with its

---

[1] Keynes has a succinct statement of his theory in his chapter, "An Economic Analysis of Unemployment," in *Unemployment as a World Problem*. Other brief expositions of virtually the same theory as that advanced here are to be found in Lionel Robbins' *The Great Depression*, Chapter III, and his article "Consumption and the Trade Cycle," *op. cit.*; in Professor H. F. Fraser's *Great Britain and the Gold Standard*, Chapter V; Professor Haberler's chapter, "Money and the Business Cycle," in *Gold and Monetary Stabilization;* and E. F. M. Durbin's chapter in *What Everybody Wants to Know About Money*, edited by G. D. H. Cole. E. C. Harwood's *Cause and Control of the Business Cycle* makes use of the same idea as applied to the American post-War banking situation. H. G. Moulton's "Commercial Banking and Capital Formation" in the *Journal of Political Economy*, Vol. XXVI, Nos. 5, 6, 7, and 9, is probably the first attempt by an American economist to formulate a similar theory—even though Moulton has apparently departed somewhat from his former position in his recent book, *The Formation of Capital*. An excellent critique of the theories of Keynes and Hayek is that of Professors Hansen and Tout in *Econometrica, op. cit.*

causes but should also seek to explain why it has been of such unprecedented amplitude. The theory here advanced departs from those of the above-mentioned writers principally in the greater emphasis it places upon the introduction and subsequent functioning of a system of central banking in the United States, and upon the banking and credit policies of the Federal Reserve Board as they found expression in the operation of that system. For the rôle played by the Federal Reserve System is at the heart of the explanation of the boom, as well as of the duration of the ensuing slump, and the policies of the Board as expressed in the System's operation are intimately connected with that explanation.

From this standpoint, the theory here developed may be called a "central banking" explanation of the depression. The depth and duration of the depression are held to be the ineluctable consequences of the preceding boom. That boom could never have lasted as long as it did, nor could it have assumed the proportions it attained, under the old National Banking System. The boom and depression were therefore proximately caused by central bank credit expansion.

In its more general aspects, however, the explanation here given might perhaps best be described as an eclectic theory of the business cycle. For an attempt is made to relate the various "real" or structural aspects to those monetary phenomena which together form the cycle (money here being used in the wide sense to include bank credit, or what Robertson and Keynes call Bank Money). Further, a *rapprochement* of these two (the "structural" and the monetary) explanations with that known as the equilibrium view of business cycles is sought. The integration does not extend to the inclusion of those eleven factors which Professor Clark calls "strategic" ones, nor yet so far as Sir Josiah Stamp's "eighteen valid, but not always universal, causes," nor are many of Irving Fisher's "nine main causes" incorporated. Rather, the concern here is with those consistently fundamental or basically causal factors, the monetary and the non-monetary phenomena. The non-monetary factors

take their form principally in an expansion of the creation
of real capital, or investment activity, and result in a loss of
equilibrium, while the monetary factors serve to explain
how the increase of investment which brings about the loss
of equilibrium has its start.  Indeed, the object is not so
much to explain the influence of isolated factors as it is to
integrate three separate or particularistic theories into one
consistent explanation of the entire cycle of boom and
depression.

### DOMINATING EXPLANATORY CONSIDERATIONS

Briefly stated, the dominating argument of the present
chapter is devoted to a consideration of the importance of
investment[1] in the modern exchange economy and its
relation to the recent boom and depression; to the disequilibrium between the rate of capital creation (investment) and the rate of accumulation (voluntary saving); to
the rôle of the rate of interest, as expressed both in the
"natural" rate of interest and the "market" rate of interest,
in contributing to the disequilibrium between investment and
saving; to the part played by profits; to the general lack of
equilibrium throughout the whole economic system precipi-
tated by the disequilibrium between saving and investment,
and the importance of this general loss of equilibrium in
prolonging the depression; and to the rôle of the banking
system in producing the fluctuations of the market rate of interest about the natural rate, making possible the creation of
real capital in advance of the rate of voluntary saving, and
thereby originating the disequilibrium in the first instance.
Finally, the importance of the stock market crash of 1929
(both in its aspects as the immediately precipitating cause

[1] The term "Investment" is used herein to mean the positive act of converting
loanable funds that come onto the capital market, arising in the first instance either
as "true" savings out of money incomes or as "created" bank credit, into tangible
capital equipment or real physical capital. Savings are usually used by investors to
buy bonds (or stocks), and the proceeds of these bond sales are used to finance the
construction of new building, the purchase of new machinery, etc.  The term investment is used throughout to mean the latter process, rather than that of the savers
when they "invest" their saved money income by purchasing bond and stock
issues.

of the ensuing depression and in its effects as a factor contributing to the continuing stagnation), the significance of rigidities in the price-cost-wage structure, and the relation of the banking system's difficulties after 1929 to the continuance of depression, are subjected to scrutiny and analysis.

### COMPLEXITY OF PRESENT-DAY COMPETITIVE ECONOMIC ORDER

Many writers have emphasized the connections between the increasing severity of business cycles and the evolution of our modern competitive, free-enterprise, price-profit-exchange economic order. With the growth of indirect exchange the pricing system has become more complicated, and division of labor has become more extensive. And concurrently with the increased division of labor, the Industrial Revolution introduced the roundabout, capitalistic, time-consuming process of production, which hit full stride in the last quarter of the nineteenth century. Division of labor necessarily implies a considerable time-interval between the first stages of production and the final emergence of consumable goods. And the growth of transportation facilities, by greatly broadening market areas, itself contributed to more intensive specialization and wider geographical division of labor.

### INHERENT DISEQUILIBRATING FORCES

But this very complex organization of the modern competitive-exchange order contains certain inherent disequilibrating factors. Production being for the market, which is typically an impersonal and distant one—distant not only spatially but also in point of time—the entrepreneurs in a competitive-exchange economy cannot possibly have complete foreknowledge of the demand conditions for their products. Production, therefore, cannot possibly be adjusted perfectly to the demands of consumers; not only must each producer guess as best he can *what* and *how much* consumers desire, but he must also endeavor to adjust his plans to the actions of his competitors. Uncertainty is a necessary concomitant of the roundabout, time-consuming, capitalistic process of production. If production could always be exactly proportioned to consumption there would be but scant opportunity for dislocations to arise.

It is an empirically verifiable fact, however, that production does not run such an even course as consumption. And it is this very fact, coupled with the inherent "roundaboutness" of capitalistic production, tending to develop time lags between cause and effect, which is one of the contributing factors in the oscillatory swings of business which we have come to call the cycle. The time lags in themselves go a long way towards explaining this tendency to oscillation, or wave-like movements of the volume of production. The economic situation might be likened to that of a steam heating plant thermostatically controlled: this seems a more realistically comparable analogy in the realm of the physical than the frequently utilized illustration of the pendulum. Time lags do not play an important part in the behavior of a pendulum; although its swings are oscillatory, the arc is fixed, and the reversals are calculable and almost instantaneous. Not so in the case of the thermostat: as the temperature falls, and more fuel is added, the initial effect is simply to drive the temperature even lower by temporarily stifling the free-burning fire.  As the new fuel eventually takes effect in the form of increased heat, however, a tendency to force the temperature upward to a greater degree than was intended becomes apparent, and the thermometer moves above the desired point of equilibrium.[1]

### Oscillation Greatest in Capital Goods Industries

Now the chief industries in which the time lags are most apparent and those in which the tendency to oscillation is greatest are those which make the capitalistic process of

[1] The authors are indebted to Professor F. H. Knight for the suggestion of this analogy.

production what it is—those which are engaged in adding to the stock of capital goods, to the creation of fresh "tools" of production, generally known as the instrumental or constructional industries, or producers' goods industries. These are also the industries, it should be emphasized, which produce the lack of balance for the productive system during boom and depression. Indeed, it is scarcely too much to say that the fluctuations in the production of capital goods *are* the business cycle—they are at least the counterweight, the balance wheel, determinative of the fluctuations in the general volume of production.[1]

As early as 1872, Jevons pointed out that: "It [the cause of commercial fluctuations] seems to be in the *varying proportion which the capital devoted to permanent and remote investment bears to that which is but temporarily invested soon to reproduce itself.*"[2] And an American business man and engineer long connected with the iron and steel and construction industries, George H. Hull, wrote in 1911,[3] "The difference between periods of prosperity and periods of depression is chiefly * * * a decrease in the rate of production of permanent wealth, such as buildings, railways, ships, goods, materials, etc." Similar statements could be multiplied at length,[4] for it is now generally recognized by those

[1] "The tendency to intensified fluctuations of derived demand, including the demand for * * * durable consumers' goods, as well as producers' goods, is of basic importance * * * . If it could be controlled in all its manifestations, the primary result would be a great stabilization of the average rate of productive activity by cutting off those fluctuations of production which exceed the fluctuations of consumers' current expenditures. As a secondary result, consumers' expenditures would themselves be made far more stable than they now are. Thus the effects of stabilization would be cumulative, and the back of the business cycle would be broken." Clark, J. M., *Strategic Factors in Business Cycles*, p. 191.

[2] Jevons, W. Stanley, *Investigations in Currency and Finance* (London: Macmillan & Company, 1872), 1884 edition, pp. 27, 28.

[3] *Industrial Depressions* (New York: Frederick A. Stokes & Co., 1911), p. 27.

[4] *Cf.*, for example, the following random selections: "We may now define, with precision, * * * *a period of boom is one of special increase in the production of fixed capital; a period of decline or a depression is one in which this production falls below the point it had previously reached*" (Cassel, *The Theory of Social Economy*, p. 550); "The most characteristic feature of a modern industrial boom is the utilization of an abnormally large proportion both of the past accumulations of consumable goods and of the current production of consumers' goods to elicit the production, not of other consumable goods, but of construction goods" (Robertson, D. H., *A Study of Industrial Fluctuations*, London: P. S. King & Son, 1915, p. 157); "For, while a diagram showing the output of the instrumental industries would be a curve

properly conversant with the problem of business cycles that it is these fluctuations in the production of capital goods which constitute the chief characteristic of the modern business cycle. But to describe the most typical feature of the cycle does not in itself serve to explain the cause of the fluctuations. The aim here is to explain the interdependence of these various structural, or "real," phenomena connected with the fluctuations in capital goods production with those monetary causative factors which are usually neglected by those writers who concentrate their attention upon the fluctuations in the production of producers' goods, without endeavoring to analyze the causes of the fluctuations.

The technical fact, then, that the time lags just discussed are most pronounced in the producers' goods industries helps explain the fundamental rhythmic character of the progress of the productive process. There is an obvious reason why this is so. The construction of plants and equipment for the purpose of manufacturing consumption goods is several steps farther away from the consumers' demands than the processes of making those consumers' goods, and is therefore more subject to miscalculations. Unfortunately, as Keynes points out,[1] the statistics on the production of new capital goods are incomplete. There are certain categories of producers' goods that are sufficiently representative, however, for which the relevant statistics of production are comprehensive enough to be considered as indicative of major tendencies.

PRODUCTION OF IRON AND STEEL AS "TRADE" BAROMETERS

The production of pig iron, for instance, is a partial indicator of the production of fixed real capital, and pig iron production has been called "the barometer of trade" on

with large rises and large falls, one showing the output of consumers' industries would consist of rises interspersed with horizontal movements, like the outline of a flight of stairs" (Pigou, A. C., *Industrial Fluctuations*, London: Macmillan & Co., 1929, 2nd ed., p. 18).

[1] "There is no single set of figures which measures accurately what should be capable of quite precise measurement—namely, the rate at which the community is adding to its investment in Fixed Capital." *A Treatise on Money*, Vol. II, p. 97.

account of its use in all types of construction activity and in the production of machinery.  Cassel states of it that,[1] "When we consider all the uses of iron, we see clearly that it is not only unequivocally the most important material of fixed capital, but is so generally used as such that * * * the annual production of iron may therefore be taken as a measure of the annual production of fixed capital."  The following table gives the figures for the physical volume of pig iron production around the significant turning-points in the last three major depressions prior to the Great Depression.

TABLE XV

PRODUCTION OF PIG IRON AT VARIOUS DATES

(In Thousands of Long Tons)

| | | |
|---|---|---|
| 1871—1,665 | 1891—8,280 | 1904—16,497 |
| 1872—2,549 | 1892—9,157 | 1905—22,992 |
| 1873—2,561 | 1893—7,125 | 1906—25,307 |
| 1874—2,401 | 1894—6,657 | 1907—25,781 |
| 1875—1,869 | 1895—5,329 | 1908—15,936 |

Source: Burns, A. R., *Production Trends in the United States* (New York: National Bureau of Economic Research, 1934), Table 44, p. 294.

TABLE XVI

PRODUCTION OF PIG IRON AND OF STEEL, 1919–1932

(In Thousands of Long Tons)

| YEAR | PIG IRON | STEEL |
|---|---|---|
| 1919 | 31,015 | 34,671 |
| 1920 | 36,926 | 42,133 |
| 1921 | 16,688 | 19,784 |
| 1922 | 27,220 | 35,671 |
| 1923 | 40,361 | 44,944 |
| 1924 | 31,406 | 37,932 |
| 1925 | 36,701 | 45,394 |
| 1926 | 39,373 | 48,296 |
| 1927 | 36,566 | 44,935 |
| 1928 | 38,156 | 51,544 |
| 1929 | 42,614 | 56,433 |
| 1930 | 31,752 | 40,699 |
| 1931 | 18,426 | 25,945 |
| 1932 | 8,781 | 13,681 |

Source: Burns, *op. cit.*, p. 296.

[1] *The Theory of Social Economy*, p. 548.

The production of pig iron and of steel during more recent years, covering the period from 1919 and including two major depressions as well as two minor cyclical dips (1924 and 1927), is shown in Table XVI. The figures for the production of steel have been added because it has come to assume an even greater importance than pig iron in the production of capital goods. It will be readily apparent from an inspection of these tables that the output of pig iron and of steel reaches a peak just before the downturn of the cycle, and then declines drastically during the ensuing depression.

The distinguishing objective characteristic of boom periods, then, is an accelerated rate of growth of investment in fixed real capital. The boom of the 'twenties was marked by even greater investment activity than previous ones.[1] The growth of steel production in the United States from 1921 to 1929 shows an annual average (arithmetic) increase of 35 per cent, which is considerably greater than Åkermann's comparable figure for the rate of growth of world steel production.

CONSTRUCTIONAL ACTIVITY IN UNITED STATES DURING
PRE-DEPRESSION PERIOD PRODIGIOUS

Of the absolute volume of fixed real capital produced during this period as represented by construction, Keynes has the following to say: [2]

[1] Cf. Åkermann, *Economic Forecast and Reality, 1928-1932*, p. 3: "It should be stressed that the recent boom period probably more than any previous one was marked by an intensive and accelerated production of fresh capital goods, and that the creation of means of production and other fixed real capital had never before shown such rapid expansion. To substantiate this assertion we shall confine ourselves to referring the reader to the following table showing the average growth of the world's production of pig-iron up to the turn of the century—and steel—after the turn of the century—during the different boom periods. The increase is calculated from the year when the depression was most pronounced to the year when the boom was at its height.

AVERAGE ANNUAL PERCENTAGE GROWTH

| | | |
|---|---|---|
| 1858/1864..........6.9 | 1885/1890 ........ 8.1 | 1908/1913........16.8 |
| 1865/1873..........7.5 | 1893/1900 ........ 9.1 | 1914/1917........13.6 |
| 1876/1883..........8.1 | 1900/1907 ........12.3 | 1921/1929........21.0" |

[2] "An Economic Analysis of Unemployment," in *Unemployment as a World Problem*, pp. 5-6.

Let us consider the United States first, because the United States has held throughout the key position. The investment activity in this country was something prodigious and incredible. In the four years 1925–1928 the total value of new construction in the United States amounted to some $38,000,000,000. This was—if you can credit it—at the average rate of $800,000,000 a month for forty-eight months consecutively.

This figure is virtually twice the supposed present value of all of the American railroads, and represents an amount in dollars almost half the market value of all the stocks listed on the New York Stock Exchange in 1929.

CHART II

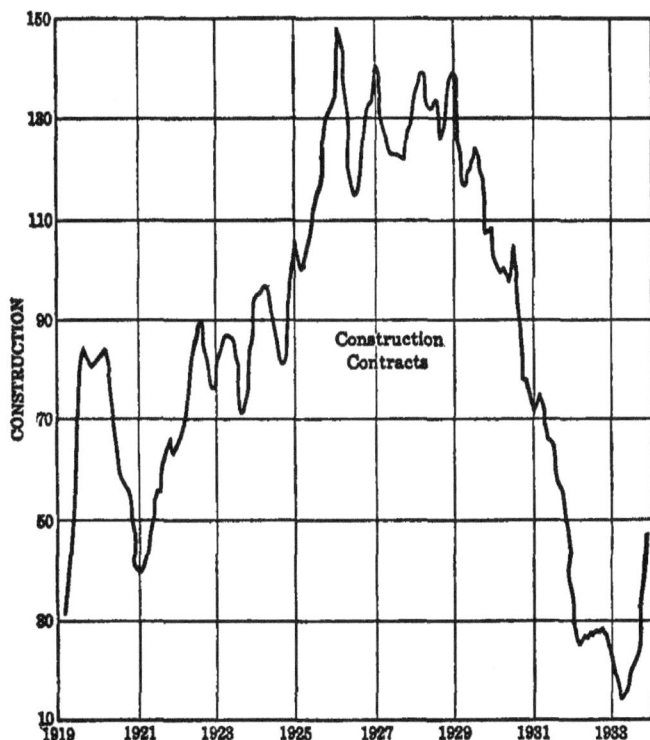

Source: *The Annalist* (January 19, 1934), Vol. 43, No. 1096, p. 103.
Reproduced by permission.

The behavior or course of construction activity (as represented by construction contracts awarded) during the recent boom and depression is shown in Chart II, using index numbers based upon monthly averages for 1923–1925 as 100. It may be observed that the index rose by more than 100 points from 1921 to 1926, and declined 120 points from 1929 to 1933.

The production of machine tools is another valuable indicator of the fluctuations in the production of capital goods. Machine tools represent what may almost be called capital in pure form, the real "produced means of production." J. M. Clark in his *Strategic Factors in Business Cycles* says that the correlation of machine tool production with the business cycle is "virtually perfect" (p. 230); the League of Nations publication *World Production and Prices, 1925–1932* [1] states (p. 66): "The mechanical engineering industry of the United States has suffered more than that of any other country; and, further, it has suffered more than any other American industry." The index of machine tool orders published in the *Survey of Current Business* [2] (1922–1924 monthly average as a base of 100) declined from a high of 336 in February, 1929, to a low of 13 in February, 1933—a decline of 96 per cent.

### Production of Consumption Goods Relatively Stable

It is to be observed, furthermore, that the production of consumption goods is not subject to the violent fluctuations characterizing the production of capital goods. Consumption tends to be maintained relatively well even in severe depressions, at least as compared with the alterations in the production of capital goods. The conditions during the eight-year period, 1925–1932, with respect to the production of consumption goods and of goods constituting fixed real capital, or producers' goods, are indicated in the following table.

[1] Geneva: League of Nations, 1933.
[2] June, 1929, No. 94, p. 26, and Vol. 13, No. 4, p. 48.

TABLE XVII

COMPARATIVE PRODUCTION OF PRODUCERS' AND CONSUMERS' GOODS
IN UNITED STATES

(1925–1929 average = 100)

| | 1925 | 1926 | 1927 | 1928 | 1929 | 1930 | 1931 | 1932 |
|---|---|---|---|---|---|---|---|---|
| Producers' Goods | 93 | 99 | 92 | 104 | 113 | 83 | 54 | 29 |
| Consumers' Goods | 97 | 97 | 102 | 100 | 104 | 88 | 89 | 82 |

Source: *World Production and Prices, 1925–1932*, p. 56.

The comparative behavior of production goods and consumption goods is shown graphically in Chart III, which also serves to portray what Pigou calls the "stair-step" movement of consumption goods. The output of producers' goods was lower in 1932 than at any time during the present century, while the output of consumers' goods declined in that year to a point only slightly below that prevailing in the 1920–1921 depression and but very slightly lower than the 1901–1930 average. Fluctuations in consumers' goods production are obviously induced by fluctuations in producers' goods production.

CHART III

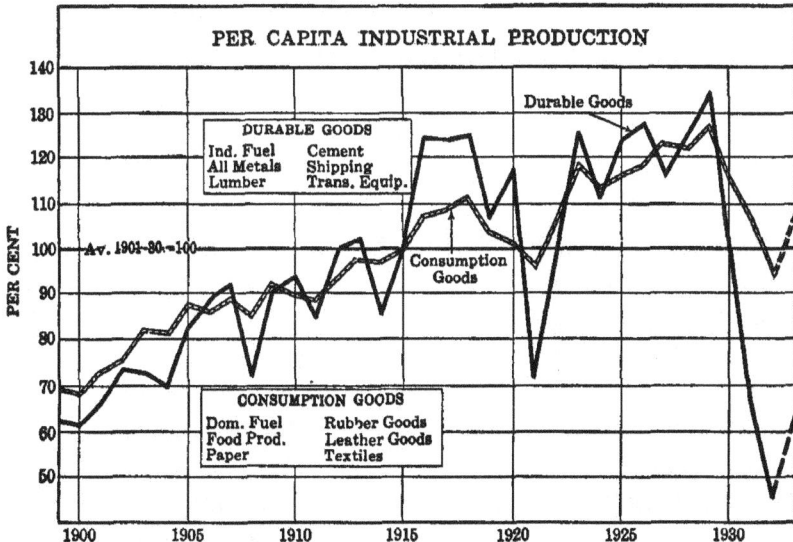

PER CAPITA INDUSTRIAL PRODUCTION

Source: The Cleveland Trust Company *Bulletin* (August 15, 1933), Vol. 14, No. 8.
Reproduced by permission.

DISPARITY BETWEEN INVESTMENT AND SAVING CAUSES
CYCLICAL SWINGS IN BUSINESS ACTIVITY

Now, it can hardly be said with any great degree of conviction that the rate of increase of public saving is subject to such vacillations as are exhibited by the fluctuations of investment indicated by the above historical data on the rate of capital development, imperfect as the evidence may be. The habits of persons with respect to voluntary saving are relatively fixed and unchanging, except possibly over such long periods of time that they may be disregarded for the purposes of a discussion restricted to such a relatively short-run phenomenon as the business cycle. In an economy marked by a relatively uniform rate of progress, it may be assumed that the rate of public saving approximates fairly closely to that rate of progress: as Cassel states,[1] "in the uniformly progressive exchange economy, *the total income as well as both its parts—consumption and capital accumulation—increases in the same percentage as the capital.*"

If, then, there occur oscillations in the rate of capital accumulation which are not in consonance with the rate of saving (it is *public* or "real" saving that is now under consideration) it follows logically that it is the disequilibrium between investment and saving which causes the cyclical oscillations in business activity. If the rate of capital development always coincided with the rate of saving, it is hardly conceivable that business cycles of the character and severity to which we are accustomed would occur. A constant rate of capital formation and a constant rate of saving are mutually determinative of equilibrium—not only *must* there be, in a condition of equilibrium, a coincidence of the rate of capital accumulation and the rate of saving, but, when those conditions are present, equilibrium *will* result.

This, however, in no wise explains why and how disequilibrium between the rate of capital accumulation and

[1] *The Theory of Social Economy*, p. 62.

the rate of saving may arise. It is therefore necessary to inquire into the genesis of such maladjustment.

## GENESIS OF SAVING AND INVESTMENT DISPARITIES

An opening attack on the problem may be made by pointing out that, in a money economy or one predicated upon indirect exchange, the demand for and the supply of capital goods do not meet in their natural forms, but in the form of (demand for and supply of) money: the supply of loanable funds coming into the capital market and being converted into fixed capital equipment has its price expressed as a (money) rate of interest. The "money market," very significantly elastic, is in many respects allied with the "capital market." Hence disequilibrium between investment and saving is a characteristic of the money exchange economy.

## OSCILLATION OF MARKET RATE OF INTEREST ABOUT NATURAL RATE SUPPLIES CONDITION FOR DIVERGENCE BETWEEN RATE OF INVESTMENT AND RATE OF SAVING

Underlying the disequilibrium between investment and saving is the disequilibrium between what has come to be called the "natural" rate of interest and the market rate— between the realizable rate of return on invested capital and the price paid for loanable funds as expressed in the market rate of interest.[1] It should be stressed that the

---

[1] The conception of the "natural" rate of interest has been the subject of much controversy, ridiculed by Gregory as a "stalking ghost," and as Hardy points out, "impervious to inductive proof or disproof" ("Savings, Investment, and the Control of the Business Cycle," *Journal of Political Economy* [June, 1931], Vol. 39, No. 3, p. 390). But whether subject to precise measurement or not, the idea of a "natural" rate of interest (or some equivalent term) nevertheless has a useful significance. The "natural" rate of interest might be defined as the marginal "yield" rate of interest—the currently realizable yield on capital at new investment margins, for, as Marshall says, "the rate of interest applies strictly to new investments only" (*Principles*, p. 592). Marshall seems to have had something in mind akin to a "natural" rate of interest when he speaks of "the general rate of interest"—"the phrase 'the general rate of interest' applies in strictness only to the anticipated net earnings from new investments of free capital" (*ibid.*, p. 553). Alternatively, the "natural" rate might be designated the "real" marginal productivity of capital— even though not subject to statistical proof it can hardly be denied that there is a productivity rate which measures the currently realizable return to capital. Professor Knight's definition that interest is "the ratio between perpetual annual in-

market rate of interest here under consideration is the *long-term* rate of interest, the rate for long-term capital (bonds), and not the short-term rate for commercial loans.[1]  The long-term *market* rate of interest is subject to inductive examination, and it is a well-known fact that it fluctuates rather rapidly, and within wide limits.  It tends to oscillate, in other words, about the natural rate.  This relationship between the two rates of interest, the natural rate and the market rate, may be stated in another way by saying that the two rates move in a reciprocal relationship to each other, the market rate standing above the natural rate at one phase of the business cycle and below the natural rate at another phase of the cycle.

Granting, then, the possibility of this divergence between the natural and the market rates of interest—deferring, temporarily, inquiry into the reason for, or the causation of, this possibility—it supplies the necessary and sufficient con-

come and the cost of income-yielding goods at the margin of growth" (*Encyc. Social Sciences*, Vol. VIII, p. 135), is similar to the use of the term here. Keynes' definition that "the natural rate of interest is the rate at which saving and investment are exactly balanced" (*Treatise on Money*, Vol. I, p. 155) is also similar, but involves somewhat different placement of emphasis; the authors hold that saving and investment *are* balanced when the "natural" rate and the market rate are in equilibrium (as does Keynes himself elsewhere in his *Treatise*). If only those sums coming on to the capital market as supply of loanable funds represented the real savings of the public, the market rate and the "natural" rate would not long diverge from one another; for "the margin of growth" is conditioned by the rate of accumulation of free capital seeking investment.  Furthermore, inability to measure the "natural" rate ought not to occasion either regret nor anxiety; indeed, the very idea of inductive measurement is foreign to the concept of such a rate.  For the "natural" rate of interest is simply an abstraction, a concept that is indispensable if certain types of equilibrium adjustment within the economic system are to be defined with any degree of precision.  Thus regarded, it is apparent that the "natural" rate is closely akin to the "equilibrium price" that is so familiar as an analytical tool in present-day neo-classical economics.

[1] It is on this point, it seems, that Keynes makes a fundamental error in placing what measure of emphasis he does on the influence of the short-term market rate of interest in the business cycle, by not recognizing that the growth of working capital is a function of what he himself considers the basic factor, the growth in investment capital.  Increased working capital, represented by short-term commercial loans, is itself an outgrowth of the enhanced activity engendered by the increased investment activity, and the short-term rate of interest is a function of the long-term rate, not the reverse.  In his evidence before the Royal Commission on Gold and Silver Inquiry (which Keynes himself edited in publishing Marshall's *Official Papers*, and therefore should have been familiar with), Marshall had stated that "the average rate of discount is determined by the average level of interest in my opinion," and "my position is that the mean rate of discount is governed by the mean rate of interest for long loans" (*Official Papers*, p. 51).

dition for the divergence between the rate of investment and the rate of saving. It contains the essence of the next link in the chain of causation, the possibility of the emergence of profit, and "profits are the mainspring of change in the existing economic order. Strictly, * * * we should say that it is the *anticipated* profit or loss on new business, rather than the actual profit or loss on business just concluded which is the mainspring of change." [1] If the market rate of interest is below the natural rate, if business men can make use of loanable funds at a cost which is less than the marginal rate of return to capital, there is a possibility of profit by using those loanable funds to make new investments. In such conditions business men will, and do, succumb to the lure of the anticipated profit and proceed to make new investments in the endeavor to make those prospective profits a realized certainty.[2] That is to say, entrepreneurs will sell new bond issues on the capital market to secure the funds with which to finance the construction of new capital equipment when the market rate of interest falls below the natural rate.

But if these new bond issues met only the savings of the public coming onto the capital market in the form of real saved money income, such discrepancy between the market rate and the natural rate could hardly endure for long. The ability of the entrepreneurs to embark upon new investment activity would be strictly limited to the funds made available by savers. And the supply of savings seeking investment in the bond market being relatively fixed, the greater demand for these funds on the part of the entrepreneurs would rapidly cause the disparity between the market rate of interest and the natural rate to disappear—the market rate would be forced up equal to (or above) the natural rate so that the prospect of profit would cease.

[1] Keynes, J. M., *A Treatise on Money*, Vol. I, pp. 140 and 159.
[2] " * * * the attractiveness of investment depends on the prospective income which the entrepreneur anticipates from current investment relatively to the rate of interest which he has to pay in order to be able to finance its production * * * ." *Ibid.*, Vol. I, p. 154.

Under the conditions contemplated by static equilibrium theory, no doubt this is what would obtain. In the static analysis, it is essential for the maintenance of equilibrium that investment equal saving, and so long as the supply of loanable funds coming on the capital market is limited to those sums saved by the public from current income this equilibrium would prevail (at least within relatively narrow limits). In our modern credit economy, however, banks have the ability to create purchasing power, *i.e.*, loanable funds or "liquid capital," that enables borrowing entrepreneurs to get command over labor and materials for the purpose of producing new capital equipment. Such funds (but for rising-price tendencies) serve no less effectively in this connection than an equal amount of "real" savings.

## MANUFACTURE OF "BANK MONEY" CREATES DISPARITY BETWEEN MARKET AND NATURAL RATES OF INTEREST AND ALTERS STRUCTURE OF PRODUCTION

It is the process of creating credit on the part of the banks, then, that makes possible the violent fluctuations in the rate of investment. Not only does the action of the banks bring about the disparity between the market and natural rates of interest which introduces the initial prospects of profit, but by supplying entrepreneurs with funds in amount greater than the saved income of the public the banks help to produce an alteration of the structure of production [1] and make possible, for a time, actual realized profits for certain classes of entrepreneurs.

---

[1] The term "structure of production" is by no means used here as synonymous with the Hayekian sense of that term, to mean an *elongation* of the vertical structure of production. It is in his use of that notion that Hayek's theory is untenable, in the writers' opinion, or at least the use of the concept "elongation of the structure of production" is unnecessary to the main parts of Hayek's thesis. The term "structure of production" *does* have a useful significance, however, when confined to mean the *proportion* between producers' goods production and consumers' goods production—between consumption and investment. An alteration of that proportion in favor of the increased production of producers' goods brings about a disproportionality of the whole productive process, which is itself the seat of the trouble. Hereafter, therefore, the use of the term "structure of production" will be considered as referring to this proportion between the production of capital goods and consumption goods.

When banks create credit and place it at the disposal of entrepreneurs who wish to use it for new capital development, the supply of loanable funds which is directed to the capital-producing industries is augmented. It was shown in Chapter II that by purchasing investments banks could create credit in much the same way as they do by granting direct loans or by discounting. This is the avenue by which newly created bank money enters the economic system upon the voluntary action of the banking system.[1] That is to say, when the banks are confronted with a situation of mounting reserves and relatively slight demand for credit on the part of the business community, they actively create new credit in the system by adding to their investment portfolios.

The effect of these new purchases of investments, however, is not only to create new deposits in the system, but also to force up the price of bonds, or conversely, to lower the long-term market rate of interest.[2] The purchase of investments by the banks represents new demand for bonds

[1] Malthus, T. R. (in the *Edinburgh Review* [February, 1811], Vol. XVII, No. XXXIV, pp. 363–365) said that none of the writers he was acquainted with " * * * has ever seemed sufficiently aware of the influence which a different distribution of the circulating medium of the country must have on those accumulations which are destined to facilitate future production," and further, "the question of how far, and in what manner, an increase of currency tends to increase capital appears to us so very important, as fully to warrant our attempt to explain it * * * . It is not the *quantity* of the circulating medium which produces the effects here described, but the *different distribution* of it * * * on every fresh issue of notes * * * a larger proportion falls into the hands of those who consume and produce, and a smaller proportion into the hands of those who only consume. * * * an increased issue of notes tends to increase the national capital, and by an almost, though not strictly necessary consequence, to lower the rate of interest."

[2] *Cf.* Keynes, *A Treatise on Money*, Vol. II, p. 358: " * * * the purchase and sale of securities by the banks for their own account have been the dominating factor in determining the turning-points in the price level of bonds." And *cf.* Riefler, W. W., *Money Rates and Money Markets in the United States* (New York: Harper & Brothers, 1930), p. 119: "Through their own purchases and sales of investments, therefore, commercial banks have exercised a marked pressure on the market for bonds and contributed to a considerable extent to the agreement in relative movements between bond yields and short-term money rates." And see Steiner, W. H., *Money and Banking* (New York: Henry Holt & Co., 1933), p. 859: "Long-term investment credit impinges upon short-term commercial credit at several points. In time of depression, banks tend to use surplus reserves to purchase bonds. This tends to raise bond prices and make long-term financing more attractive. It also creates deposit currency which tends in part to offset the decline in the velocity of circulation that occurs at such times and in part to enable borrowers to retire their debts to the banks."

(new supply of capital funds) and operates as a marginal determining influence on bond prices, and hence upon the market rate of interest.[1] This forcing down of the market rate of interest creates the disequilibrium between the existing natural rate of interest and the new market rate, and with the market rate below the natural rate, activity in the capital market is stimulated. Entrepreneurs and corporations become interested in taking advantage of the profit possibilities created by the disparity between the two rates of interest, and seek to embark upon new investment undertakings by floating bond issues at the attractive market rate. For even small divergences of the market rate of interest are alluring to entrepreneurs interested in new capital development, and serve to direct activity to hitherto unexploited fields of investment.[2]

If the banks exhibit willingness to absorb these new bond issues, they do so by placing in the hands of those entrepreneurs and corporations floating the bonds the additional fresh purchasing power with which to finance further capital developments. This may not be *"real"* savings in any sense, yet the funds placed at the disposal of the entrepreneurs represent as effective purchasing power as does an equal amount of funds diverted from the purchase of consumers' goods to the purchase of bonds by real savers.[3]

---

[1] "For the value of a security is determined, not by the terms on which one could expect to purchase the whole block of the outstanding interest but by the small fringe which is the subject of actual dealing;—just as current new investment is only a small fringe on the edge of the totality of existing investment." Keynes, *A Treatise on Money*, Vol. II, p. 361.

[2] "On this point, Wicksell was very explicit, pointing out that the rate of investment is capable of being affected by small changes in the rate of interest, *e.g.*, ¼ per cent, which could not be supposed to affect the mind of the speculator." *Ibid.*, Vol. I, pp. 198–199.

[3] "The elasticity of credit undoubtedly facilitates and speeds the process of capital accumulation by enabling business men to secure and spend at any time larger amounts of capital funds than have been furnished for the purpose by prior savings. * * * They [the banks] do have power to create additional purchasing power in the form of bank deposits placed at the disposal of borrowers. This purchasing power does not come out of anyone's *prior* abstinence; but it initiates * * * an increase in production, with the result that increases of capital goods do not require equivalent prior sacrifices in consumption." Clark, J. M., *Strategic Factors in Business Cycles*, p. 192 and *note*, pp. 192–193.

## PIVOTAL IMPORTANCE OF DEGREE OF STABILITY IN RATE OF INCREASE OF INVESTMENT

It is this creation of new purchasing power by the banking system in excess of the voluntary savings of the public which produces the disequilibrium between investment and saving and alters the whole structure of production. Investment in the sense of capital creation runs ahead of saving, which is to say that there results an increase in the rate of production of producers' goods disproportionate to the rate of production of consumption goods. It is this disproportionality of the process of production, this alteration in the structure of production in the sense of a more rapidly increasing output of producers' goods than of consumers' goods, which characterizes the upswing of the cycle. For as Professors Hansen and Tout point out,[1] it is not the absolute amount of saving or of investment at one time or another which is of importance for business cycle theory, but rather the stability or lack of stability in the *rate* of investment. It is when the fluctuations in capital-creation activities become too great during a short-run period for the economic system to adjust itself to them with sufficient promptness, through its normal workings, that trouble results.

## BANK CREDIT EXPANSION ACCELERATES RATE OF INVESTMENT INCREASE

Pronounced frictions are set up in the operation of the economic machinery when the rapidity of shift in the center of gravity of productive activity is excessive. Moreover, friction as a factor in economic dynamics occupies a much more disruptive rôle when violent shifts in production from consumers' goods to producers' goods and back again are concentrated within a short period of time than when such shifts in production are spread over a long period. Even though the shifts in the distribution of resources between the production of the different classes of goods (producers' and

[1] "Investment and Saving in Business Cycle Theory," *op. cit.*, p. 119.

consumers') may in the longer period be of greater magnitude than during the shorter period, it is the violent changes during the short period that generate disequilibrium for the entire economic system. If an alteration of the structure of production in favor of a proportionally larger output of producers' goods is extended over a considerable period of time (as a result of a slow but steady increase in the proportion of the national income that is saved) the economic system is able to adjust itself with a minimum of disturbance to such continuing incremental changes. It is signally important for business cycle analysis, in other words, that the *rate of increase of investment* during the upswing of the cycle is more rapid than would be possible without the intermediation of the banking system in the process. It is because the creation of new credits by the banking machinery speeds up this rate of investment increase during the short-run period, therefore, that we have cyclical upheavals in magnified measure.

CHART IV

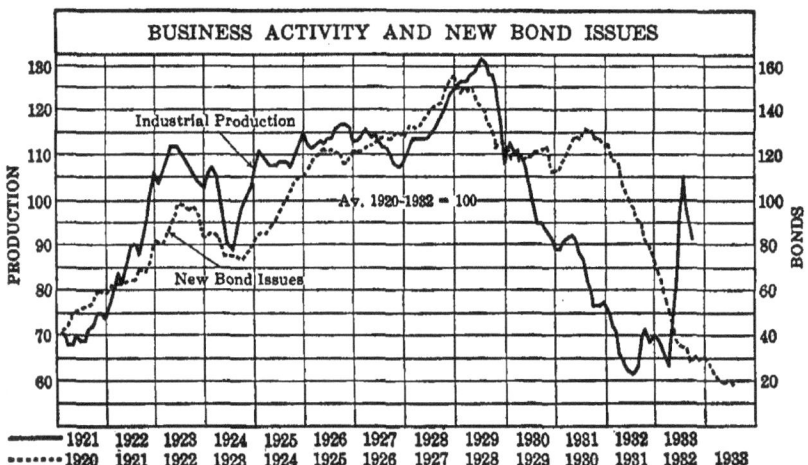

BUSINESS ACTIVITY AND NEW BOND ISSUES

Source: The Cleveland Trust Company *Bulletin* (October 15, 1932), Vol. 14, No. 10.
Reproduced by permission.

The connection between new capital flotations and productive activity is shown on the preceding chart. The index of new bond issues is moved up one year, so that the peak of new bond issues at the beginning of 1928 appears on the chart in the year 1929 for industrial production. The peak for new bond issues therefore came about 20 months before the break in industrial production. This is but natural, since considerable time elapses between the issuance of securities and the translation of their proceeds into productive activity. And if an inverted index of bond yields were superimposed on this chart, its highest point would coincide almost exactly (January, 1928) with the peak for new issues—new bond issues began to decline, in other words, when interest rates began to rise.

### "Created" Purchasing Power Enhances Profits in Circular Fashion

The disequilibrium between investment and saving set up by the banks in taking over new bond issues with created purchasing power has still other important influences. The process brings about an increase in the money income of the economic system, and for a time it increases the absolute amount of profits of the entrepreneurs.

The use of the newly created bank credit by bond-issuing corporations to finance new investment activity will increase the profits of those concerns to which the new money is turned over in exchange for materials, machinery, and other supplies and equipment. It will do so in one of two ways, or possibly both. The new monetary demand appearing in the market may force a rise in prices for materials, machinery, and equipment, thus enabling the selling corporations to reap profits because their costs do not rise as fast as the prices of their salable products; or, additional profits may arise, even with no increase in prices, simply because of the larger volume of orders that makes possible the renewed utilization of existing plants and equipment without a proportionate increase in costs.

Moreover, the increases in the rate of investment and in the rate of profits, originally set in motion by the banking system, are cumulative by virtue of this (absolute) increase of profits. For when business profits are increasing the total volume of saving tends to increase also, as it is customary for corporations to employ a large part of their profits in further plant extensions and purchases (or creation) of capital goods. Indeed, it is generally true that the bulk of savings comes from corporate saving. A circular process thus results: a widening circle of profits begets additional new investment activity, the latter in turn gives rise to yet larger profits and so on.

The stimulation of new investment activity by the action of the banking system, as well as the profits engendered thereby, have also the effect of increasing the incomes of the public, and this in turn tends to give an upward fillip to activity in the consumers' goods industries. Some part of the new profits will be paid out in increased dividend disbursements, thus increasing the purchasing power of the stock-holding classes. The money incomes of the laborers will also be increased; this again may occur in one of two ways, or both. Either wage rates may be bid up, on the one hand, or men previously unemployed or limited to part-time employment may now find full-time employment, on the other hand. In both cases money incomes, and hence monetary purchasing power, will be greater than before.[1] As the greater part of laborers' incomes is spent on consumption goods there will therefore ensue a stimulation of the consumers' goods industries. It is thus seen that the disequilibrium between investment and saving originally set in motion by the banking system has an inflationary influence on all phases of productive activity.

The origin of the excess reserves in the banks of the system

---

[1] "As the system actually operates, spending more on one thing is quite likely to mean spending more on other things also, and *vice versa*. This is by reason of the combined action of two basic causes. One is an elastic credit system, which makes it possible to spend more for one thing without at the same time spending less for something else. The other is the fact that setting more people at work making any one thing gives them more spending power to use in buying other things so that the result is not less demand for other things, nor even the same amount as before, but actually more. If more is spent for capital equipment, more will also be spent for consumers' goods, not in spite of increased capital expenditures but because of them." Clark, J. M., *Strategic Factors in Business Cycles*, p. 139.

(the member banks of the Federal Reserve System, primarily) which made possible the increased purchases of investments leading to the disequilibrium between the market and the natural rates of interest should be commented on at this point. It has already been shown (Chapters II and V) that the credit-creating activities of the Federal Reserve Banks led to an increase in the reserves of the member banks: by open-market purchases the Federal Reserve Banks induced new excess reserves in the commercial banking system. It has also been shown how the banks utilized these new reserves to expand credit on their own account by purchasing investments. By referring to Chart IV it may be seen that new bond issues increased most rapidly during those three years when the Federal Reserve Banks were actively engaging in open-market purchases. Hence the originating influence in the whole chain of causation leading to inflation was the policy of the Federal Reserve Banks in embarking upon Reserve-credit expansion. The creation of a central banking system introduced a markedly greater expansibility in the banking structure of the country, and the operation of this central banking system during the post-War period constitutes a sufficient explanation of the origin of the new credits.

## EXAGGERATED CHARACTER OF RECENT CYCLE ATTRIBUTABLE TO CENTRAL BANKING OPERATION

Here, then, is the fundamental explanation of the recent credit cycle, and in large measure, of the alternations of boom and depression—the credit-creating capacity and activities of the central banking system, Mises' "inflationistic ideology" of the central banks.[1] Federal Reserve credit expansion serves to explain the origin of the excess reserves

[1] Hayek criticizes Mises' explanation of the origin of the new credits as emanating from this "inflationistic ideology" of the central banking system—see his *Monetary Theory and the Trade Cycle*, especially pp. 145 and 150. But Hayek's claims for his "perfectly endogenous" theory are unconvincing to the writers for the very simple reason that his explanation of how the banking system creates credit (perfectly valid except for this one point) when a "certain amount of cash is newly deposited" never satisfactorily explains where the newly deposited cash comes from!

for the member banks of the system; the utilization of these excess reserves by the commercial banks to buy securities brings about a divergence of the market and natural rates of interest, thus creating the possibility of profit for entrepreneurs who undertake new capital development; stimulated by this prospect of profit, entrepreneurs bring out new bond issues to finance the new capital developments; and when these bonds are purchased by the banks new purchasing power is created which has the effect, not only of creating a disequilibrium between investment and saving, but also of causing the prospective profits to become realizable and at the same time of increasing the income of the public; and the actual realized profits in turn accelerate the rate of increase of investment.

It follows, then, that the height of the recent boom and the depth of the depression are fundamentally the outcome of Federal Reserve credit expansion. The recent cycle may therefore properly be designated a central banking phenomenon. The exaggerated character of the last boom and slump is understandable only in the light of the superimposition of a central banking system upon our former system. And an understanding of what was taking place in our banking system, largely as a consequence of the enactment of the Federal Reserve Act, is essential to an explanation of the causes of the depression. If the recent cycle has proved so puzzling to so many students of its devious course and manifold phases, it is because the full effects of the creation and operation of this central banking system upon the commercial banks have not been widely nor adequately understood; nor, furthermore, have the influences of the changing structure of the American banking system upon the structure of production been fully realized.

### Foregoing Analysis Compatible with Explanation of Earlier Cycles

At this stage of the argument it may occur to the reader that since no central bank existed in this country prior to

1913, the above analysis is therefore inapplicable to former depressions. Before examining this possible objection, however, it may be well to repeat once again that we have never had a boom and a depression quite so extensive as the recent ones, and that the rôle played by the operation of our central banking system must be an integral part of any theory attempting to explain *that* boom and depression. The extent of a boom generated by commercial bank expansion (without the intermediation of the central banks in initiating the conditions for the boom) was certain to be limited by the reserves of the banks, reserves which under the old system were scarcely subject to replenishment; and had the last boom been less extensive it is hardly possible to conceive of the depression being so severe and so protracted.

Moreover, it is believed that the framework of the foregoing analysis is largely applicable to the depressions which occurred prior to the Federal Reserve System; only in matters of detail is it inadequate or out of focus when brought to bear upon earlier cycles. The banks in New York City occupied the rôle of central banks for the commercial banking system prior to 1913. During depression, excess reserves of the banks outside New York City were transferred to the banks in New York City where they would command an interest return; the New York banks, faced with mounting reserves which they naturally desired to put to earning use, in the absence of demand for commercial credit used the new reserves to purchase investments, forcing down the long-term market rate of interest, and thus a cycle was generated.[1] The major variations between the patterns of the earlier cycles and that of the last cycle arise out of the fact that the New York banks were limited to the excess reserves deposited with them by the outside banks (subject to the qualification of accessions to their reserves from new gold inflows from abroad)—they could not "manufacture"

[1] See Allyn A. Young's *An Analysis of Banking Statistics for the United States* (Cambridge: Harvard University Press, 1928).

reserves in quite the same way as could the Federal Reserve Banks, and hence former booms were not so pronounced.

### THE IMMEDIATE, INCITING CAUSE OF DECLINE

In order to conclude this portion of the analysis, it remains but to inquire into what force or factor, operating as an immediate and inciting cause, stops the expansion, brings the boom period to an end, and initiates the decline. It is the cessation (or reduction) of the new "excess" flow of credit, brought about either by positive credit contraction or by a deceleration of its rate of growth. The slackening of the rate of credit growth (or the complete stoppage of the creation of new credits) is an effect of the stringency of bank reserves. And here again Federal Reserve policy played a dominating rôle in the latest cycle, for when the Federal Reserve Banks reversed their "easy money" policy in 1928 and 1929 the reserves of the member banks ceased to increase rapidly. As the banks no longer had expanding reserves to use for the purchase of investments, the withdrawal of this marginal determining influence on the price of bonds caused the long-term market rate of interest to rise. The effect was to bring about a convergence of the market and the natural rates of interest toward an equilibrium point, or, possibly, an actual rise of the market rate slightly above the natural rate, destroying the prospect of further profit from that quarter.[1] A comparison of the rate of credit growth with the course of bond prices shows that bond prices began to decline (the market rate of interest began to rise)

---

[1] Cf. Henry Thornton in his *An Enquiry into the Nature and Effects of the Paper Credit of Great Britain* (London: Knight and Compton, 1802), pp. 261–262: "As soon, however, as the circulating medium ceases to encrease, the extra profit is at an end * * * ." And see Hayek, *Monetary Theory and the Trade Cycle*, p. 176: " * * * in order to bring it [the crisis] about * * * *it is quite enough that the banks should cease to expand the volume of credit;* and sooner or later this must happen. Only so long as the volume of circulating media is increasing can the money rate of interest be kept below the equilibrium rate; once it has ceased to increase, the money rate must, despite the increased total volume in circulation, rise again to its natural level and thus render unprofitable (temporarily, at least) those investments which were created with the aid of additional credit."

early in 1928, at the same time that the growth of credit began to slacken.[1]

## Both Market Rate and Natural or Productivity Rate of Interest Vary toward Convergence

The convergence of the two rates of interest and the dissipation of the possibility of profit from new investment activity does not come solely from a rise of the market rate, however. The realizable rate of return to capital at many investment margins tends to fall in the later stages of a boom at the same time (though perhaps not in the same degree) that the market rate is tending to rise. This is the effect of two causes that have been gathering momentum cumulatively, but independently of each other. The first cause is the increase in the costs involved in the production of capital goods: as the costs of labor and materials advance, it follows that more dollars (liquid loanable funds) are required in order to produce a given item of physical capital than were necessary at an earlier stage of the cycle. In other words, a larger investment of liquid capital must be made in order to create (or buy) capital equipment of given technical capacity, and, if prices of finished products fail to advance equally with costs, the ratio of return to investment is progressively reduced.

The second cause is simply the operation of the principle of diminishing returns at numerous investment margins. Carried along on a wave of unquestioning optimism, many entrepreneurs blithely enter into further new investment commitments without adequate regard for the effects either of their own activities or of like actions on the part of other concerns in the same industry. So long as the market rate of interest is even slightly less than the rate of return (per dollar of cost) realized currently on new capital equipment, the situation constitutes an invitation to still further creation of capital goods, for men are ever prone to regard existing

[1] As a matter of fact, banks early in 1928 not only ceased to make new investment purchases but also sold bonds in order to finance speculation in stocks.

conditions as permanent.  There appear to be opportunities
for continued profits in the future in the further creation of
new capital equipment, and these seeming opportunities
could actually be realized if existing price relationships
were to continue; yet the very entrepreneurial actions that
are inspired by such a situation operate to destroy these
price relationships.  Thus, opportunities for profits (not
*profits*, it should be emphasized, but *opportunities for profits*)
are vitiated and rendered spurious, but so quietly and so
imperceptibly that many entrepreneurs and investors are
wholly unaware of what is taking place until the critical
point is definitely passed.  This results in "over-investment"
at many investment margins—that is, in many industries
the total stock of capital equipment is augmented so greatly
that the realizable productivity or rate of return per unit
of physical capital is appreciably reduced.

The movements of the two interest rates in opposite
directions, then—the discontinuance of the growth of credit
raising the market rate on the one hand, and the reduction
of the natural or productivity rate on the other hand—
operate to bring the rates back together or to destroy the
divergence between them that formerly was favorable to
new capital development.  Practically, however, the market
rate of interest is subject to wider fluctuations, and more
rapid ones, than is the natural rate.  And it follows, therefore, that the slackening of the rate of credit growth is the
more drastic influence in ending the boom.

### That Natural Rate of Interest Varies Is Peculiarly Important

Yet what is sought to be emphasized is the fact that *both*
rates tend to fluctuate.  This is of importance in understanding why depression, once under way, persists, for if
the natural rate were always a fixity the cycle would become
the purely monetary phenomenon that Mr. Hawtrey insists
it is and might easily be cured by purely monetary means.
All that would be necessary to restore the profitableness of

new investment would be to lower the market rate by appropriate bank action, and revival would proceed apace. It is not so simple as this, however, for as D. H. Robertson points out,[1]

> While there is always *some* rate of money interest which will check an eager borrower, there may be *no* rate of money interest in excess of zero which will stimulate an unwilling one. Secondly, * * * the assumption * * * that the total magnitude of the money supply lies entirely within the discretion of the banking-system and not at all within that of the public, seems to have only limited validity for such periods.

The convergence of the two rates of interest destroys the profit prospects which obtained when the market rate was below the natural rate. This leads to a slackening of new investment activity. And when investment ceases to increase at the old rate or actually begins to decline, the disequilibrium between investment and saving which characterized the boom period comes to an end. Investment declines to an equilibrium with saving or, as is usually the case, falls below it.

The decline in investment activity means that the period of positive realized profits is at an end. An alteration in the structure of production the reverse of that which obtains during a boom sets in: the production of producers' goods declines more rapidly than does the production of consumers' goods. The unemployment that prevails in the durable goods industries makes its influence felt throughout the whole process of production and over the whole system of interdependent prices. In short, depression is in full progress.[2]

This is not to imply that all that would be necessary for continued prosperity would be an avoidance of the cessation of the increase of credit—conscious efforts aimed at prolonging the increase in credit might indeed prolong the

---

[1] *Banking Policy and the Price Level*, p. 81.

[2] "The whole matter may be summed up by saying that a boom is generated when investment exceeds saving and a slump is generated when saving exceeds investment." Keynes, J. M., "An Economic Analysis of Unemployment," *op. cit.*, p. 21.

boom, but by so doing would almost certainly induce increasing maladjustments in production which would prolong the eventual depression, whether initiated by monetary or non-monetary influences.

The point to be emphasized is that it is usually the cessation of the excess flow of credit which brings about the disequilibrium between saving and investment that leads to depression. It is not intended to indicate, however, that there need be an *immediate* relation between the slowing down of credit increase, the decline in investment activity, and the onset of depression; other influences may be at work, as will be pointed out in Chapter VII, to prolong the boom, for a time, beyond the beginning of the decline in investment activity. Nevertheless, it is this pattern which almost invariably prevails. How long the boom may proceed after the onset of a positive decline in the durable goods industries is simply a question of the comparative strength of these other influences.

### Sound Theory Essential to Accurate Forecasting

The foregoing analysis of the course of the business cycle, largely theoretical in nature as it is, not only fits the course of events in this country from 1922 to 1929, and after, but embodies, it is believed, the explanation of the fundamental causes of the depression. No attempt will be made to review further the innumerable historical details from which might be gathered much factual evidence in support of the theory. The purpose here is not so much to provide an historical picture of the development of the boom and the subsequent depression as to seek the deeper, underlying, and fundamental causes of the depression itself. The historical factual material was being carefully observed by students of cyclical patterns, but to little benefit, since most American observers were thoroughly misled by what actually occurred. It was the use of the theory on which the foregoing explanation is based, or one markedly similar, on the other hand, that enabled Hayek to predict in April of 1929 the approach of the crisis in this country, and Åkermann, with better timing even than Hayek, to write on the first day of October, 1929,[1]

> * * * American economic life is now about to enter upon the final phase of a boom period that began already in the middle of 1921. * * * American monetary policy * * * can hardly be said during these years to have favored the tranquil course of industrial expansion. Under direct or indirect American monetary influences savings capital has been attracted to speculative investments, which are now beginning to prove unprofitable.

Sound theory of the cycle is prerequisite to accurate forecasting alike in the realm of business and the domain of economics.

### RECENT CYCLE THEORIES DIVERSELY DEFICIENT

Most American observers who were concerned with the structural view of business cycles were unable fully to appreciate the monetary aspects of the situation; those who were advocates of the purely monetary theory were so obsessed with the stable-price-level complex that they were unable properly to assess the importance of the underlying structural phenomena which were developing. The price stabilization complex common to most of the older monetary explanations of the business cycle is itself sufficient to warrant their rejection as something less than comprehensive theories of the cycle. The movement of wholesale prices occupies a central rôle in the usual monetary theory, and this concentration of attention upon the superficial phenomena of changes in the value of money has militated against an understanding of the channels through which newly created credit entered the economic system and of the effect of this new credit upon the structure of production. Further, there are certain aspects of the recent situation which render the usual monetary theory practically useless as an explanation of the late boom and depression; commodity prices as measured by the wholesale price index in this country were remarkably stable from 1922 to 1929, as is well known, so

[1] *Economic Forecast and Reality, 1928-1932*, p. 28.

that one point definitely established by the monetary experimentation involved is that stability of the price level is a doubtful safeguard against depression.  Nevertheless, the fact that those descriptive studies of the cycle which emphasize the inordinate increase of fixed capital during a boom fail to take account of the originating influence of credit expansion detracts from the importance of the non-monetary explanation as a generalized theory of business cycles.  An attempt has been made in the above explanation to bridge the gap between the monetary and the non-monetary theories: to describe the structural changes which characterize the cycle, and to explain their origin.

The equilibrium theory has not as yet been set forth; the integration of the third view of the cycle with the two foregoing into a single whole has not yet been accomplished. The following chapter, which may be considered a continuation of the present one, will essay that task; it is also concerned with the explanation of the duration of the depression, and with the relation thereto of the stock market crash of 1929.

## CHAPTER VII

# THE FUNDAMENTAL CAUSES OF THE GREAT DEPRESSION (*Continued*)

The greater part of the discussion centering upon an analysis of the causes of the depression and the development of a theory of business cycles has up to the present been concerned principally with an analysis of the causes of the boom. Little attention has been devoted as yet to the course and nature of the depression proper, or even to the immediate cause of the onset of depression. The foregoing chapter dealt with two phases of the theory of business cycles here being advanced, but no attempt was there made to present the third and last phase. Endeavor will be made in the present chapter to complete the task—to accomplish a synthesis of the third widely held theory of the cycle, the equilibrium view, with the preceding two, the monetary and the structural theories. This requires some consideration of certain salient features of the depression itself; in particular it necessitates an inquiry into the causes of its unforeseen prolongation, inasmuch as the disequilibria to which attention is directed in the exposition of the equilibrium theory are intimately connected with the duration of the depression.

## FORECASTERS LED INTO ERROR BY PREVIOUS CYCLE PATTERNS

No attempt will be made, however, to inquire minutely into either the history or all of the aspects of the depression. Analysis, as has been stated before, rather than description, is here the major aim. Nevertheless, some familiarity with conspicuous events of recent economic history is essential for an understanding of the severity and duration of

the depression, as well as for the completion of an explanation of its causes. Almost all of the accepted signs that had
marked the end of depression in the past were in evidence
by the summer of 1931, misleading careful students of cycle
theory and of older depression patterns to predict recovery
in the near future; yet, actually the nadir of the depression
was not reached until a year later, and after that eight
more months passed before the final explosive collapse of
the banking system occurred. It is likely that these prognosticators were led into error, in basing their forecasts on
past cycle patterns, by neglecting to take adequate account
(1) of the general disequilibria produced by the stock market crash, (2) of the disproportion between saving and investment in its effect upon the whole structure of production, and (3) of the banking situation, in contributing to
the continuance of depression.

NEGLECTED FACTORS

In the first place, the depression was as exaggerated
and as protracted as it was because the stock market crash
itself was the most devastating one that the world had
ever witnessed. This was partly because the prior period
of stock market boom was the greatest ever experienced,
and partly because the crash involved a larger number of
people in its destructive effects than had any such previous
disaster. Therefore it is desirable to examine into the rôle
played by the stock market situation, not only in prolonging
the depression, but also in prolonging and intensifying the
boom prior to 1929.

In the second place, the alteration of the structure of
production in the sense of a disproportionate decrease of
investment activity was greater than in any previous depression; this fact in itself goes far toward explaining the
unparalleled extent of the depression. The decline in the
production of producers' goods relative to the decline in the
production of consumers' goods was more pronounced than
ever before, and its repercussions were felt throughout the

whole productive process. Unemployment in the capital goods industries alone was greater than the total unemployment in *all* lines of industry in any depression prior to the recent one; this induced a widening circle of unemployment in other lines of industrial activity and resulted in wholesale loss of purchasing power.

And, in the third place, during no previous collapse was there such a complex entanglement of the banking system with the course of depression. It is scarcely to be denied that this was a factor which contributed, by the destruction of monetary purchasing power, to the length of the recent period of recession. Earlier depressions were usually marked only by a slackening of the *rate* of credit growth, or by actual declines of total bank credit of from 6 to 10 per cent; the decline in total credit outstanding during the recent years amounted to almost 40 per cent for the commercial banks of the country.

But underlying and supplementing all of these factors was a stubbornly persisting lack of equilibrium in the entire economic and price structure. The equilibrium theory is advanced by some as the sole explanation of the depression; the view is held by the authors, however, that this theory is not tenable as an exposition of the *causes* of the depression. Yet it does constitute a large part of the explanation why depression, once started, is as pertinacious as it is, and why industrial revival waits on the restoration of equilibrium conditions. Thus it is seen that this theory is merely one segment of the circle of explanation of the business cycle.

### Percussive Character of Stock Market Crash

The stock market crash itself was the immediately precipitating cause of the depression. While it is true that the peak of constructional activity had definitely been passed, and that general industrial production was beginning to slacken by the time the stock market crash occurred, so that depression doubtless would have ensued eventually, the inevitable decline probably would have been more gradual had it not been for the detonation in Wall Street which rocked the entire industrial strata. Although on first thought it may appear to be incorrect to speak of an external event which marks the beginning of a decline as its "cause," it is nevertheless accurate to say that the stock market crash initiated the depression. While it is the dynamite which "causes" the destruction following an explosion, it is the percussion cap which "causes" the explosion. The whole character of the ensuing depression was colored and shaped by what happened in Wall Street in October, 1929. The pattern of the depression might well have been radically different from what it actually was had it not been preceded by the stock market catastrophe; the decline probably would have been more gradual and hence less severe, and the shattered confidence and demoralized state of mind of the business community no doubt would have been largely lacking if the damaging psychological effects of the stock exchange disaster could have been averted.

The stock market situation had another and prior influence, however. It operated to prolong the boom prior to 1929 and, as the severity of a depression is a function of the extent of the prior boom (though not a precise mathematical one) it indirectly affected the length of the depression. It may be inquired, in view of the stress that has been placed upon the cessation of the increase in credit with its effect upon decreasing investment activity, why the depression did not start sooner than it did. The rate of credit growth began to slacken early in 1928. Total loans and investments of the member banks were greater in October, 1929, than in December, 1928, it is true, and the total for June, 1929, was above that of June, 1928; nonetheless, the *rate* of increase during this period was considerably smaller. Reference to Chart IV on page 136 will show that the flotations of new bond issues began to decline in January of 1928 at the same time that the long-term market rate of interest began to rise. Short-term commercial paper rates were also rising rapidly during most of 1928 and all of 1929. Why, then, in view of these usual indications of a reversal of a boom, did it not come to an end in 1928 instead of toward the end of 1929?

*Stock Market Boom, with Its Fleeting Profits, Sustained Consumer Demand, Delayed and Intensified Disaster*

Clearly the answer is that an industrial recession would have come about in 1928 had it not been, principally, for the stock market boom which was still in full swing, exercising temporarily a dominating influence over wide areas of the economic sphere. And directly connected with the stock market's crescendo, the increased velocity of circulation of bank credit operated as a sustaining influence in prolonging the boom. The velocity of circulation of deposits, as computed by the New York Federal Reserve Bank, rose almost 50 per cent during 1928 and 1929. This increase was in the main a direct outcome of the enhanced activity in the stock market, but at the same time it served to cumulate that activity. For credit must always be considered, not alone as to its absolute amount, but also with respect to its velocity. That is to say, it is *effective credit* which is important, and effective credit is a product of amount and turnover. During the last stage of the boom the rate of increase in the amount of bank credit was declining, but an increase in the velocity of circulation served to more than offset the decline in credit growth, resulting in a steady expansion in the volume of *effective* credit. Thus the stock market boom, with its attendant but ephemeral profits, operated to sustain consumer demand even after investment activity began to slacken, so that the total volume of industrial production was for a time maintained at a relatively high level.

*Stock Market Boom Stimulated by Rapid Retirement of Federal Debt and Mushroom Growth of Investment Trusts*

The stock market boom was also stimulated by two minor contributing factors, the importance of which cannot be measured accurately. First, the retirement of the Federal debt at a rate of over $800,000,000 a year during this period tended to increase the volume of free funds seeking reinvestment. Debt reduction does not of itself *increase* the volume of loanable funds, of course, as the means for retiring the debt are raised by taxation—all that is really involved is a transfer of funds. Debt retirement, however, does serve to shift the demand for securities. As Government bonds were called and paid off, the proceeds were reinvested by the former bondholders, principally in stocks. Second, the striking growth of investment trusts which occurred during 1928 and 1929 helped to drive stock market prices still higher. The investment trusts in the main did not use their funds to acquire new issues of securities; rather they represented a new source of demand for issues outstanding, thereby further forcing up the prices of these old securities.

These new sources of demand for stocks aided in developing a market situation that was especially favorable to the flotation of new stock issues, as against new bond issues. As the price of stocks rose, the yield on stocks declined, so that it became profitable for many corporations to shift their new financing activities from bond issues to capital stock issues. This had the effect of offsetting the tendency toward a decline in total investment activity that normally results from a rising interest rate on long-term bond issues. The shift in popularity from financing through the medium of bond issues to that of stock flotations is indicated in the following table.

TABLE XVIII

NET NEW DOMESTIC CORPORATE FINANCING—REFUNDING EXCLUDED
(In Millions of Dollars)

| TYPE OF FINANCING | 1927 | % | 1928 | % | 1929 | % |
|---|---|---|---|---|---|---|
| Bonds and Notes | 2,962 | 63 | 2,175 | 41 | 1,874 | 23 |
| Short-term Obligations | 221 | 5 | 211 | 4 | 205 | 3 |
| Preferred Stocks | 874 | 19 | 1,149 | 21 | 1,517 | 19 |
| Common Stocks | 600 | 13 | 1,812 | 34 | 4,417 | 55 |
| Total | 4,657 | 100 | 5,347 | 100 | 8,013 | 100 |

Source: *Commercial and Financial Chronicle* (January 18, 1930), Vol. 130, No. 3369, p. 366.

*Stock Prices in Relation to Corporate Earnings*

It has frequently been argued that the stock market boom was justified on the basis of rapidly rising corporate earnings. Some have contended that profits not only were large in absolute amount but that they were increasing at an accelerating rate, and that in view of this consideration the high-level stock prices represented simply the rational discounting of anticipated future earnings. On sober afterthought, however, it appears that the stock market boom was largely a product of bank credit expansion, a mad speculative frenzy which had no rationale whatever. The prices that were bid for stocks in 1929 in most cases could not have been offered without the aid of bank credit (in the form of brokers' loans) to complete the transactions. Tables XXII and XXIII (appearing later in this chapter) show that from 1928 to 1929 Loans on Securities rose from

TABLE XIX

INCOME OF ALL MANUFACTURING CORPORATIONS

Compiled from Statistics of Income, U. S. Treasury Department

(In Millions of Dollars)

| CALEN-DAR OR FISCAL YEAR | CORPORATIONS REPORTING NET INCOME | | | REPORTING NO NET INCOME | | CONSOLIDATED | | |
|---|---|---|---|---|---|---|---|---|
| | Gross Income | Net Income | Income Tax | Gross Income | Deficit | Gross Income | Net Income | % Net on Sales |
| 1916 | $ 14,086 | $ 4,158 | $    81 | $  1,028 | $    221 | $ 15,114 | $ 3,855 | 25.5 |
| 1917 | 40,438 | 5,736 | 1,327 | 1,763 | 177 | 42,201 | 4,232 | 10.0 |
| 1918 | 41,935 | 4,691 | 2,112 | 2,232 | 157 | 44,167 | 2,422 | 5.48 |
| 1919 | 45,705 | 5,219 | 1,359 | 6,585 | 367 | 52,290 | 3,483 | 6.67 |
| 1920 | 45,217 | 4,116 | 945 | 11,432 | 834 | 56,649 | 2,337 | 4.12 |
| 1921 | 24,422 | 1,778 | 352 | 14,020 | 1,899 | 38,442 | D−473 | D−1.23 |
| 1922 | 36,006 | 3,454 | 390 | 8,677 | 813 | 44,683 | 2,251 | 5.04 |
| 1923 | 48,687 | 4,272 | 485 | 7,534 | 701 | 56,221 | 3,086 | 5.48 |
| 1924 | 45,320 | 3,596 | 430 | 8,591 | 832 | 53,911 | 2,334 | 4.33 |
| 1925 | 52,925 | 4,383 | 547 | 7,905 | 682 | 60,830 | 3,154 | 5.18 |
| 1926 | 52,922 | 4,495 | 585 | 9,573 | 787 | 62,495 | 3,124 | 5.01 |
| 1927 | 50,134 | 3,939 | 508 | 13,589 | 851 | 62,723 | 2,580 | 4.05 |
| 1928 | 57,459 | 4,744 | 545 | 9,814 | 834 | 67,273 | 3,366 | 5.00 |
| 1929 | 59,880 | 5,216 | 544 | 12,252 | 810 | 72,132 | 3,862 | 5.36 |
| 1930 | 41,054 | 2,758 | 317 | 19,846 | 1,640 | 60,900 | 801 | 1.31 |
| 15 years | $656,190 | $62,555 | $10,527 | $134,841 | $11,605 | $791,031 | $40,053 | 5.05 |

D—Deficit.

12 per cent of Total Loans and Investments of all banks in the country to 20 per cent, and that the index numbers of Loans on Securities rose from 138 in 1928 to 221 in 1929. Tables XIX and XX, showing the income of all manufacturing corporations filing tax returns with the Treasury Department, indicate that the idea of rapidly increasing corporate profits as the main cause for rapidly rising stock market prices is inadequate. Aggregate profits were large, it is true, and were rising during part of this period; but to attempt to explain the unprecedented increase in share prices solely on the basis of increasing corporate earnings is to neglect the fundamentally causal relationship between rapidly expanding bank credit and rapidly rising stock prices during this period. It is simply a fact that profits were not expanding at all commensurate with the rise in share prices.

TABLE XX

INCOME AND CAPITALIZATION OF ALL MANUFACTURING CORPORATIONS IN THE UNITED STATES

Compiled from Statistics of Income, U. S. Treasury Department

(In Millions of Dollars)

| YEAR | | | END OF YEAR | | | | |
|---|---|---|---|---|---|---|---|
| Calendar Year | Gross Income | Net Income after Tax | Preferred Stock | Common Stock | Surplus Account | Total Net Worth | % Net Income on Net Worth |
| 1924 | $ 53,911 | $ 2,334 | $ 6,766 | $ 16,665 | $ 12,636 | $ 36,067 | 6.37 |
| 1925 | 60,830 | 3,154 | 7,048 | 19,861 | 15,457 | 42,366 | 7.44 |
| 1926 | 62,495 | 3,124 | 7,431 | 23,980 | 14,862 | 46,273 | 6.75 |
| 1927 | 63,723 | 2,580 | 7,359 | 24,195 | 16,496 | 48,050 | 5.37 |
| 1928 | 67,273 | 3,366 | 7,562 | 24,929 | 17,526 | 50,017 | 6.72 |
| 1929 | 72,132 | 3,862 | 7,009 | 26,220 | 19,466 | 52,695 | 7.34 |
| 1930 | 60,900 | 801 | 6,837 | 27,018 | 18,267 | 52,122 | 1.54 |
| 7 years | $441,264 | $19,221 | $50,012 | $162,868 | $114,710 | $327,590 | 5.87 |

Note.—Capitalization figures not available prior to 1924.

Net income of these corporations for the 15 years from 1916 to 1930 constituted an average of but 5.05 per cent of sales; net income for the seven years from 1924 to 1930 represented a return on net worth of but 5.87 per cent. The

profit on sales was higher in 1923 than in 1929, and the return
on net worth was greater in 1925 than in 1929. It should be
stressed that these figures are for *all* manufacturing corporations in the United States, including those corporations
having no net income, and thus show the complete data
with respect to earnings. It is of interest to note that even

CHART V

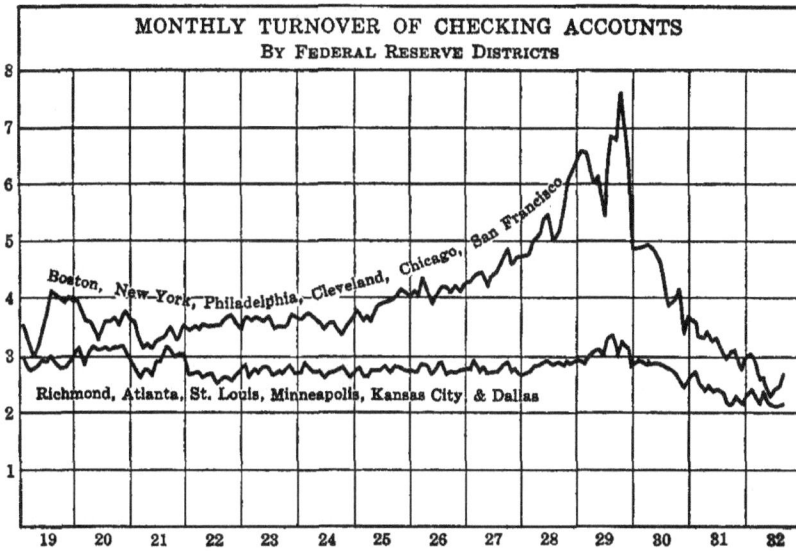

MONTHLY TURNOVER OF CHECKING ACCOUNTS
By Federal Reserve Districts

Source: Cleveland Trust Company *Bulletin* (October 15, 1932), Vol. 13, No. 10.
Reproduced by permission.

during the halcyon days of 1927–1929 deficits were larger
than during any other three-year period from 1916 to 1930,
if the depression years of 1921 and 1930 be left out of account. Professor Clark seems properly to have analyzed
this situation with respect to prospective earnings when he
says:[1]

> Stock prices during the great boom were capitalizing not
> current earnings but future earnings of a sort which any sys-
> tematic analysis should have revealed as beyond all human
> possibility. * * * What was happening was a relative shift of
> demand, in favor of speculative securities, out of all proportion
> to the magnitude of ordinary shifts of this sort, carrying values,

[1] Clark, J. M., *Strategic Factors in Business Cycles*, p. 115.

relative to yields, to points far outside what could be called normal, unless on the basis of an expectation of future increases which no industrial system could maintain.

Colonel Ayres in his Cleveland Trust Company *Bulletin* has shown how the velocity of bank credit rose during the later years of the boom (and collapsed during the depression), as well as its connection with stock market speculation, by segregating velocities according to Federal Reserve districts. The monthly turnover of checking accounts according to Reserve districts is shown by the two curves on Chart V; the upper curve is for those districts in which are located $\frac{11}{12}$ of the stock brokerage offices of the country. The comparative stability of the lower curve is marked; the fact that the pronounced rise in the upper curve began at the time that the stock market boom got well under way, in 1924, speaks for its own importance.

### Bank Credit Directly Underlay Stock Market Advance

The significance of an increasing velocity of circulation of bank credit in stock exchange transactions is that it makes possible a cumulation of speculative profits, and as such profits are realized they may be used to enlarge consumptive expenditures. And, further, to the extent that bank credit is used to finance such speculative activities, realized profits therefrom tend to increase.

If an operator buys, for example, $100,000 worth of stocks with his own available resources (that is, without borrowing) and later sells out for a price of $200,000, a profit of $100,000 is realized. But if the second operator borrows $100,000 to complete the transaction at the price of $200,000, the $100,000 profit realized by the first operator is made possible only by virtue of the extension of $100,000 credit to the second operator. The $100,000 profit for Operator A is nonetheless that much new purchasing power, which he may use either for further speculative activities or spend for additional consumables. If the price of the stock should again double and Operator B sell to Operator C for $400,000, half of which Operator C borrows from his bank, then Operator B profits to the extent of $200,000 as a result of this further extension of credit. To the extent that such transactions become more frequent and additional bank credit is obtained to complete them, greater actual profits are realized and more purchasing power becomes available *during a given time period* for expenditure on consumption goods, or other purposes. It should be apparent that the higher prices for stocks during the boom, and the greater realized profits, were more strictly products of expanding bank credit and a higher velocity for that bank credit, than of any rational discounting of future corporate earning power. Working through the securities market, however, some part of the newly created credit increased consumer demand and thus had an effect upon productive activity.

As soon as the stock market boom collapsed in October, 1929, this artificial and short-lived element in consumer purchasing power evaporated. In this sense, the stock market crash may be considered the immediately generating cause of the ensuing depression. The saturnalia of stock exchange speculation sufficed to carry the New Era boom upward and onward for a time after investment activity began to flag; when the bubble burst, the flood-gates of depression were opened. In what is admittedly a retrospective view, the chief effect of the Federal Reserve expansion of 1927 was to inflate the stock market; little of the new credit found its outlet in commercial loans or investment activity. The Board's expansion policy of 1927 therefore prolonged the boom and forced it to unprecedented heights. All signs seem to have pointed to the beginning of a natural decline early in 1927 which no doubt would have marked the end of the post-War period of expansion; had it not been for intervention by the Federal Reserve Board in that year, it is altogether probable that such a development would have occurred. And had the decline started from the lower level prevailing in 1927 the subsequent depression probably would have been neither so protracted nor so severe.[1]

### CHRONOLOGICAL ASPECTS OF PRODUCTION DECLINE IN RELATION TO STOCK MARKET COLLAPSE

It has been argued by persons inclined to minimize the importance of the Wall Street collapse that production had reached its peak in May or June of 1929 and was already declining when the stock market crash occurred. It is true that the *absolute* peak of industrial production was reached earlier than October, 1929, but the amount of the decline from May (or June) to October was negligible compared with the precipitancy of decline after that date. The *Annalist* Index of Business Activity reached its high point of 110.1 in May of 1929, but in July still stood at 109.9 and by September had declined only to 107.3; by December, however, it had fallen to 92. The Federal Reserve Board's Index of Industrial Production was 126 in June, and in September it stood at 122; by December, it had declined to 101. And to direct attention to a group of industries that constitute an extraordinarily sensitive industrial weathervane, the index of machine tool production reached a peak of 336 in February, 1929, was at 334 in September of that year, but fell to 166 by December. As measured by these three indexes, therefore, the really significant decline in the volume of physical production came after the stock market collapse, rather than before it.

### PROLONGED PROCESS OF INVESTMENT DEFLATION

The major effect of the stock market collapse may be said to have been an investment, or capital, deflation, just

---

[1] " * * * up to 1927 I should have expected that * * * the subsequent depression would be very mild. But, as is well known, in that year an entirely unprecedented action was taken by the American monetary authorities, * * * prolonging the boom for two years beyond what otherwise would have been its natural end. * * * It seems to me that these facts have had a far greater influence on the character of the depression than the developments up to 1927, which from all we know, might instead have led to a comparatively mild depression in and after 1927." Hayek, F. A., "Capital and Industrial Fluctuations," *Econometrica* (April, 1934), Vol. II, No. 2, p. 167.

as the boom was an investment inflation.  An investment deflation, or a deflation of capital values and capital assets, is a much more prolonged process than a commodity, or commercial credit, deflation.  There was a serious deflation of commodity prices, it is true, but it would not have been so pronounced had there not been the accompanying invest-ment deflation to aggravate it.  The industrial system is able to adjust itself to, and to react from, a deflation of commercial credit and a decline in commodity prices much more rapidly and readily if these are not associated with any large deflation of investment credit and of capital values.  The business depression of 1920–1921 was marked by one of the most drastic commodity liquidations on record, yet the entire process of readjustment consumed but about fifteen months.  Although the 1920–1921 depression was one of our more severe ones, measured by the depth of the decline, it was not of long duration because of the fact that there had been no extensive expansion of investment credit and of investment activity accompanying the preceding commercial credit expansion.[1]

## How Shrinkage in Security Values Repressed Production Activity

The stock market crash provided the shock to confidence which definitely and dramatically started the depression on its downward course, revealing to most persons for the first time the inherent instability of the conditions which had prevailed for several years.  The losses suffered in the stock market crash of 1929 affected a greater number of the American people than had any previous collapse; the savings of a lifetime were rudely swept away for great numbers of the rank and file, and many New Era millionaires saw their fortunes vanish almost overnight.  If there is general public participation in a stock market boom, the losses from a

---

[1] "In the case of commercial credit deflation, * * * the economic indigestion is quickly cured.  Excess goods are eliminated from the system, and, after a brief convalescence, normal functioning is again in order."  Bradford, F. A., *Money* (New York: Longmans, Green & Co., rev. ed., 1933), pp. 373, 374.

deflation of that boom fall largely on individuals who are ill-prepared to stand heavy losses; the sharp reduction in consumer purchasing power necessitates a downward revision of the standard of living—for as Keynes remarks,[1] "the public cannot be expected to see their nominal wealth increase by $20,000,000,000 in six months and then lose $26,000,000,000 in three months, and to maintain precisely the same style of life during the second period as during the first." In order to try to save what they had sunk in the stock market, individuals sought to meet the demands of their brokers for more margin, either out of current income which otherwise would have represented consumer purchasing power or out of existing unused savings. But as the decline proceeded, even the owners' original equities (or "margins") were wiped out and the potential purchasing power represented by such savings was swept away. Confronted with the loss of their back-logs of savings, the former speculators sought to retrench all along the line, and the fear of possible unemployment influenced many to refrain from making expenditures which they otherwise would have made. All of this meant a further reduction in retail sales, which soon exercised a further repressive effect on productive activity. Reduced production activity necessarily tended to result in unemployment and decreased demand, and the circle repeated itself in the well-known spiral of deflation.

SHAKEN CONFIDENCE REFLECTED IN DRASTICALLY CUR-
    TAILED CONSTRUCTION NOTABLY IN CAPITAL GOODS
    INDUSTRIES

The shock to confidence wrought by the stock market panic was promptly reflected in the capital market, and the volume of new issues shrank drastically. The new capital flotations in this country dropped 30 per cent from 1929 to 1930, and in the following year declined an addi-

---

[1] *A Treatise on Money*, Vol. II, p. 197.

tional 60 per cent. The *total* of corporate bond issues for the whole year 1932 was less than *half* the average *monthly* figure for 1929. This condition in the capital market was directly associated with a precipitate and extensive decline in the volume of construction and other new capital development. The structure of production was again altered, this time in the sense of a relatively greater *decline* in the production of producers' goods than of consumers' goods. Indeed, the decline in producers' goods production relative to that of consumers' goods was more severe during the recent depression than in any previous one. In other words, a disequilibrium between saving and investment occurred in a form exactly the reverse of that which prevailed during the boom—investment shrank faster than savings declined. After the rapid initial decline in the production of consumers' goods, consumption was maintained at a relatively stable level from the middle of 1930 on, whereas the stream of current income going for saving was constantly dwindling and the *rate* of decline in investment activity was even more pronounced. Such savings as were being made were not utilized by the financial machine to further new investment activity, but were used largely to improve the liquid position of the banks by building up their impaired reserve ratios. The volume of new construction fell to a point lower than that prevailing during the 1920–1921 depression; the per-capita output of durable goods fell to the lowest point during the present century: the volume of pig iron production in *1932* was less than it was in *1892;* and the output of steel in 1932 was the smallest of any year during this century—all of which spell deep and dire depression. For, as has been pointed out in Chapter VI, when investment increases during a boom it stimulates all the processes of production and results in realized profits; conversely, when investment activity declines rapidly during a depression its blighting effects are felt throughout the whole industrial system, and results in losses. When unemployment prevails in the durable goods industries it is well-nigh certain to be accompanied by reduced activity in the consumption goods industries.

Thus it is seen that the investment deflation which first began in the stock and capital markets was soon translated into an investment deflation in the capital goods industries themselves. So long as the decline in the output of producers' goods continued it was to be expected that the depression would persist and deepen.

### IMPACT ON INCOME

The quickest way to have broken the back of depression would have been to direct all possible efforts toward a revival of activity in the capital goods industries. This no doubt would have necessitated reductions in wage rates, at least in the capital goods industries, so that it would have been possible for profits to be made there, instead of the losses that were resulting. Instead, all efforts were directed toward bolstering up consumption, and the maintenance of wage rates was one of the expedients adopted in order to attain that end. The result was simply that, in trying to pay the existing rates of wages and to continue dividend disbursements, corporations and business enterprises generally sustained losses and were compelled to dip into their surpluses to meet their obligations. In making use of surpluses to maintain such current business spending as there was, past saved income was being drawn upon. Yet with losses general over all industry, it was inevitable that the volume of business payments should decline rapidly. This situation is brought out in the table on page 165, showing income produced and distributed for the country as a whole.

The facts of this table are shown graphically in the following chart, which also shows the distribution of the national income going to the various functional groups.

The following table and chart, it is believed, contain the essence of the explanation of the continuance of depression. The short-sighted policy of the Hoover Administration of seeking to maintain wage rates and consumption indicated

TABLE XXI

NATIONAL INCOME, PAID OUT AND DISTRIBUTED
(In Millions of Dollars)

|  | 1929 | 1930 | 1931 | 1932 |
|---|---|---|---|---|
| Income Paid Out | 81,040 | 75,438 | 63,289 | 48,952 |
| Business Savings or Losses | 1,997 | −4,954 | −8,637 | −10,603 |
| Income Produced | 83,037 | 70,484 | 54,652 | 38,349 |

Source: Bulletin 49 of the National Bureau of Economic Research, January 26, 1934.

lack of comprehension of the relations obtaining between wage rates and total wages, and between costs and prices, as determinative of levels of production and consumption; in all fairness, it should be added that the succeeding administration appears to be largely oblivious to the validity of the economic truism that production begets consumption, and that thus far the present Administration has shown but scant inclination to profit in any way from the errors of its predecessors. By consuming more than we have produced we have succeeded only in digging our way deeper into depression; we have tried to recover from depression by spending our way out of it rather than adopting the alternative procedure,—the one which has effected recovery from every past depression,—of saving our way out of it. By the policy of maintaining consumer purchasing power we have had to draw upon our store of past savings, and by so doing we have not only

CHART VI

NATIONAL INCOME
PRODUCED AND DISTRIBUTED

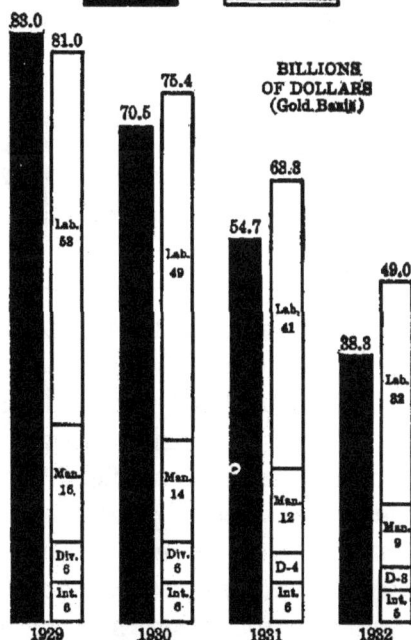

Source: Cleveland Trust Company *Bulletin* (February 15, 1934), Vol. 15, No. 2. Reproduced by permission.

failed to keep up our accustomed rate of capital formation but have actually destroyed past accumulations by neglecting to provide for maintenance, depreciation, and obsolescence. Mr. George O. May, senior partner in the accounting firm of Price, Waterhouse & Company and a member of the Board of Directors of the National Bureau of Economic Research, emphasizes the fact that our policy of maintaining consumption has made use of past savings, as follows:[1]

> It is apparent that a large part of the dividends and interest paid in these years were paid out of capital or out of corporate savings of prior years. It does not seem correct to describe such payments as "income paid out," and the use of this term may have given rise to misconceptions. * * * What the property owners collectively received was largely, if not mainly, the result of their previous thrift—not a part of the current income flow for the depression years. A conclusion substantially different from that presented in Bulletin 49 is reached if the amount of income received by labor is compared with the total income produced for the years from 1929–1932. The figures taken from tables 1 and 2 in Bulletin 49 are as follows:

|  | 1929 | 1930 | 1931 | 1932 |
|---|---|---|---|---|
|  | (Millions of Dollars) | | | |
| Total Income Produced | 83,037 | 70,484 | 54,562 | 38,439 |
| Received by Labor | 52,867 | 48,688 | 41,027 | 31,595 |
| Per Cent of Amount Received by Labor to Total Income Produced | 63.7 | 69.6 | 75.1 | 82.5 |

Mr. May might have added that although total income produced declined 54 per cent from 1929 to 1932, the income received by labor declined only 40 per cent. And here is a brief and conclusive answer to the whole question of the consequences of artificially maintained consumption—*with labor receiving a greater percentage share of the total social product than at any time in recent history, the result was widespread unemployment and stagnation.* The way out is *via* greater production, a larger total social product, and that necessarily follows upon a greater amount of saving being

[1] National City Bank *Letter*, April, 1934, p. 34.

made *and* being converted into investment goods. For "saving," in the sense of merely refraining from possible expenditures for consumers' goods, is not in itself conducive to recovery; indeed, the kind of "thrift" that results only in the piling up of idle bank balances and the hoarding of currency in deposit boxes is strongly conducive to further disastrous deflation. The capitalistic system is "out of joint" either when savings decline sharply or when savings are made but are not converted shortly into capital goods (no less so than when the reverse relationship obtains) and the continuance of the latter condition has meant the continuance of depression.

### ENTANGLEMENT OF BANKS WITH DEPRESSION

The depression had not proceeded far, however, before the banking system became involved in, and with, the processes of deflation. As shown in Chapter V, the banking system had by 1929 developed an illiquid condition which boded ill for the business community in general when the downward spiral should begin. Indeed, the efforts that were made to strengthen the position of the banking system after the decline set in were made in part at the expense of the business community, and in themselves served to hasten the general deflationary movement. When, in an attempt to improve their reserve positions, banks called their "demand" loans and refused to renew maturing commercial loans, much "distress" selling of goods and materials by debtor business concerns necessarily followed. And, as total deposits decrease when loans are paid off, this action on the part of the banks resulted in the destruction of a large amount of purchasing power within the economic system which unquestionably helped to make the decline in commodity prices more precipitate. In other words, there was added pressure placed on the commodity markets, operating to drive prices still lower, from two sources: first, business men were forced to sell their products in order to meet the demands of the banks for payment of their loans, thus increasing the supply of goods coming on the market during a given time-interval, and second, the repayment of loans, through checks drawn by the depositor-borrowers, involved the cancellation of deposits, thus decreasing the total demand in the form of available purchasing power. Total loans and investments in the commercial banks of the country stood at a lower figure at the end of 1932 than during the 1920–1921 depression; commercial loans of all banks in 1932 were less than half of what they had been in 1928, and were 36 per cent less than in 1922; all of the bank credit inflation of 1922 to 1929 was wiped out in the short space of the three years following 1929. Such a wholesale destruction of bank credit was bound to prolong and to intensify the ensuing period of recession.

### Bank Failures Dealt Disruption

Furthermore, an extensive destruction of bank credit brought about largely by bank failures is more damaging than one induced by an orderly liquidation of outstanding bank loans. Business men can ordinarily lessen the disruptive effects of having their loans called for repayment if they have advance notice of that fact. Also, as a measure of economy during depression, they usually seek to reduce their bank indebtedness of their own accord. But when a wave of bank failures sweeps the country, as from 1929 to 1933, it affects most disastrously those who are unprepared to meet the situation. The resulting loss of both business funds and real savings, added to the extinguishment of "created" bank credit when loans were paid off, contributed still further to the stagnation of business activity and to the decline in commodity prices by reducing available purchasing power. There was a rapid deflation of commercial loans and of bank credit during the 1920–1921 depression, but it was not accompanied by widespread bank failures. The number of bank failures in the single year 1931, on the other hand, was greater than the total for *all* the years from 1900 to 1929, and more banks failed in the single month of October,

1931, than in the two years 1920–1921. A very large part of the annihilation of bank credit after 1929 came about in this way. No economic system could withstand such wholesale bank failures and such loss of monetary purchasing power without suffering continued prostration.

The two tables which follow serve to give an idea of what was happening in the banking situation during the course of the depression. It may be observed from Table XXII that in trying to improve their liquidity during the years 1930–1932 the banks increased their investments at the

TABLE XXII

PERCENTAGE DISTRIBUTION OF LOANS AND INVESTMENTS OF ALL BANKS, 1928–1932

(June for Each Year)

| ITEM | 1928 | 1929 | 1930 | 1931 | 1932 |
|---|---|---|---|---|---|
| Loans and Investments | 100 | 100 | 100 | 100 | 100 |
| Loans | 68 | 70 | 69 | 64 | 61 |
|    Commercial Loans | 44 | 33 | 31 | 28 | 26 |
|    Loans on Securities | 12 | 20 | 20 | 17 | 13 |
|    Loans on Real Estate | 11 | 18 | 18 | 18 | 18 |
| Investments | 32 | 30 | 31 | 36 | 39 |
|    In Government Securities | 7 | 7 | 7 | 10 | 14 |
|    In Other Securities | 25 | 23 | 24 | 26 | 25 |

Source: Annual Reports of the Comptroller of the Currency.

TABLE XXIII

INDEX NUMBERS OF LOANS AND INVESTMENTS OF ALL BANKS, 1928–1932

(Base: June, 1922)

| ITEM | 1928 | 1929 | 1930 | 1931 | 1932 || |
|---|---|---|---|---|---|
| Loans and Investments | 145 | 146 | 146 | 138 | 115 |
| Loans | 143 | 150 | 146 | 127 | 100 |
|    Commercial Loans | 137 | 102 | 97 | 83 | 64 |
|    Loans on Securities | 138 | 221 | 223 | 178 | 113 |
|    Loans on Real Estate | 183 | 298 | 299 | 290 | 283 |
| Investments | 150 | 138 | 143 | 160 | 145 |
|    In Government Securities | 119 | 115 | 110 | 164 | 184 |
|    In Other Securities | 162 | 148 | 156 | 159 | 130 |

Source: Annual Reports of the Comptroller of the Currency.

expense of their loans (except loans on real estate), it being considered at that time that investments represented a type of liquid assets which could be realized on at will. Investments constituted 30 per cent of all loans and investments in 1929, but rose to 39 per cent of the total by 1932, an increase of almost one-third. Commercial loans declined from 44 per cent of all loans and investments in 1928 to 26 per cent in 1932; in contrast, investments in Government securities, being looked upon as exceptionally liquid assets, doubled from 1929 to 1932.

Examination of the second table shows that in 1932 total loans and investments were still slightly above what they were in 1922, this being in consequence of the 45 per cent increase in Investments, the 13 per cent increase in Loans on Securities, and the 183 per cent increase in Real Estate Loans. Total Loans stood at the same figure in 1932 as in 1922, but commercial loans were less by 36 per cent. The marked percentage increase in the holdings of Government securities from 1930 to 1932 during the course of the banks' struggle for improved liquidity and for survival should also be noted. It may be remarked further that the figures either for the member banks alone or for the commercial banks alone would show their total loans and investments (and total deposits) to have been less in 1932 than in 1922, as the above figures for "all banks" include the mutual savings banks; there were no failures among the mutual savings banks during the depression, and their loans and investments, and deposits, actually increased from 1929 to 1932.

### THE EQUILIBRIUM THEORY OF THE BUSINESS CYCLE

It remains to complete the theoretical analysis of the business cycle, and of the causes of depression. All of the processes and factors described in the present chapter as being connected with the course of events since 1929—the stock market crash proper, the disproportionality in the structure of production, and the entanglement of the banking system with the several phases of the depression—may be said to have resulted in a general loss of equilibrium throughout the economic system. Thus attention is again focused on the third major division, the equilibrium view, of the eclectic or integrated theory here being developed. Perhaps the chief proponents in this country of the equilibrium theory of business cycles causation are Professor Sprague,[1] Dr. B. M. Anderson, Jr.,[2] and Mr. George E. Roberts,[3] and in England, Professor Henry Clay [4] (now economic consultant to the Bank of England). In the opinion of the writers, to repeat, the equilibrium theory is in and of itself neither a full and sufficient theory of business cycles nor a complete explanation of the causes of the depression. The equilibrium view has validity only as explaining the depression once it has set in—it is descriptive rather than analytical, as it does not show what caused, or started, the depression. And it sheds only faint light on the genesis of the boom which always precedes a depression.

An understanding of the significance of a lack of equilibrium throughout the entire economic system is indispensable, however, in explaining the depth and duration of the depression. The equilibrium view may be said to consist principally of the description of a series of unbalances. The stock market crash itself produced an unbalanced situation which quickly degenerated into depression; the lack of balance between production and consumption, and the disequilibrium between saving and investment, served not only to extend the depression but also to make it more malignant; and the loss of balance in the banking structure together with the consequent demolition of bank credit also aided in prolonging the depression and in making its de-

---

[1] "Major and Minor Trade Fluctuations," in the *Journal of the Royal Statistical Society* (1931), Vol. XCIV, Part IV, pp. 540–549.

[2] "Equilibrium Creates Purchasing Power," the *Chase Economic Bulletin* (June 12, 1931), Vol. XI, No. 3.

[3] The National City Bank *Letter*, various monthly issues since 1929.

[4] "Some Aspects of the World Depression," *Institute of Bankers Journal* (December, 1931, January and February, 1932), Vol. 52, pp. 515–522; Vol. 53, pp. 5–28, and 91–108.

structive effects more pronounced. Of a somewhat different order than the special disequilibriums just mentioned, but of even greater fundamental importance, because it underlay and conditioned these others, was the unbalance found in connection with cost-price relationships, to be dealt with more fully in Chapter IX.

The loss of balance between agriculture and industry— the disparity between the prices the farmer received for the products he sold and the prices he had to pay for the goods he purchased—was another disequilibrating factor tending to prolong the depression, and one worthy of more extensive comment than space limitations permit here. The extent to which the situation had become unbalanced in this respect is indicated by the decline in the ratio of the prices received by the farmer to the prices paid by him from 99 in 1929 to 56 in 1932, and until this ratio was improved it could hardly be expected that lasting recovery would ensue. Nevertheless, it does not follow that recovery would automatically ensue upon restoration of parity in this ratio; other unbalances must also be corrected.

### Equilibrium View Essential

The equilibrium view is an essential part of any cycle theory which essays comprehensiveness. And only a theory which achieves completeness can be accorded full validity as an explanation of the business cycle. Too many so-called theories of the business cycle are what properly should be called "depression" theories; they attempt to account for the beginnings of the decline, but fail to offer any adequate explanation either of the antecedent course of events or of the initiation of the succeeding cycle. Other theories seek to explain the origin of the boom, but stop with that; while still others are concerned to show the relation of the monetary origins of a boom to the subsequent effects upon the structure of production, but fail to carry the analysis on to the depression proper. So far as is known to the writers, no one theory heretofore advanced has attempted to explain why the cycle starts, what gives the boom its special character and driving force, why the boom comes to an end, why the depression persists and deepens, and what conditions are essential for the beginning of the next complete cycle.

The inclusion of the equilibrium theory is necessary to a complete explanation of the whole cycle of boom and depression. It is the third segment, the third phase, of a tripartite theory of the cycle and explanation of the recent depression. It *does* explain the persistence of depression, once under way. So long as unbalance goes uncorrected in the series of relationships just mentioned, recovery will not follow. The *origin* of the cycle may be said to lie in the elasticity of the banking machinery; and for the explanation of the recent cycle and recent depression it lay in the hyperelasticity of the machinery of central banking. The monetary theory, in other words, explains *why*, in a condition of relative equilibrium, the cycle starts—the disequilibrium between the market rate of interest and the natural rate induced by the banking system provides the necessary and sufficient conditions for the upward swing of the cycle. The structural approach contains the essence of the explanation of the *cause* of the oscillations of production—the disequilibrium between investment and saving, the more rapid rate of increase of capital formation made possible by the banking process, is the boom. The equilibrium analysis suffices to explain how depression, once under way as a result of the cessation of the increases of bank credit and of investment, is largely a result of the general disequilibria produced during the prior boom period and continued for a time during the course of the depression. As long as these unbalances go uncorrected, depression *persists*, because the stage is not yet set for the revival of investment activity. All three approaches are necessary for a complete understanding of the full cycle; no one of them standing alone represents a fully developed theory. If any special merit attaches to the foregoing analysis, then, it consists in its fusion of all three of these theories into an integrated and sufficient explanation and analysis of the course and aspects of the recent boom and recent depression. The older monetary theory is not compatible with the actual course of recent economic events; the structural view alone affords no understanding of the originating monetary forces which set the boom in motion; yet, were it not for the persisting lack of equilibrium the depression could be cured by monetary measures, which the experience of the recent years has proved (if it has proved nothing else) cannot be done while disequilibrium prevails. The final chapter (Chapter IX) will attempt to show what conditions are necessary for the restoration of that equilibrium essential for recovery, and may for that reason be considered as representing the concluding portion of the theory of the business cycle here being enounced.

## CHAPTER VIII

# BANKING POLICY AND THE PRICE LEVEL

It was suggested in Chapter II how the War-time disruption of orderly economic activity eventuated in the loss of the industrial balance necessary to the smooth functioning of our national economy. The assertion was there made that the root causes of the recent depression go back to the War—that the War may be considered the remote cause of the depression. It was also brought out in Chapter II and amplified in Chapter V that, working in conjunction with the dislocations caused by the War, the effects of the inauguration of the Federal Reserve System had much to do with bringing about the chaos that prevailed after 1929; and the operation of our central banking system during the post-War years has been designated the proximate cause of the depression.

## MISLEADING BEHAVIOR OF POST-WAR PRICE LEVEL

Among the numerous dislocations engendered by the War, one in particular is deserving of special consideration at this stage of the analysis. Its bearing upon post-War banking policy, and hence upon post-War economic life and upon the depression itself, is of fundamental importance. Reference is had to the behavior, or course, of the price level during the post-War period. It was the one factor which, conceivably more than any other, served to lead astray nearly all prognosticators of the course of economic events during the period leading up to the crash, and after 1929 it was one of the outstanding features of the downward trend of economic activity. The behavior of the price level from 1922 to 1929 also serves to show the fallaciousness of the cruder form of monetary explanation of the business cycle, as, in the view of the adherents of that theory, depression will not ensue if the price level is stable. And the futility of price level stabilization as a goal of credit policy is evidenced by the fact that the end-result of what was probably the greatest price-stabilization experiment in history proved to be, simply, the greatest and worst depression.

There is little question but that the Federal Reserve Board was quite successful in its "management" of the price level, just as there is but little doubt that the depression, in final analysis, was the price paid for that experimentation. Departing from the exposition of a generalized theory of cycles and confining the argument for the present to an analysis of the causes of the recent depression, the price-level-stabilization policies of the Federal Reserve System loom large in the causal category, if indeed they do not occupy first rank in the list of causes serving to explain the great débâcle. Almost all post-War banking developments were conditioned and influenced by Federal Reserve policy aiming at stabilization of the price level. In the light of the events of recent economic history, therefore, and the relation of those events preceding the onset of depression to the ensuing decline, one of the most important single aspects of the American economic situation would appear to have been the course of prices from 1922 onward. The bank credit inflation examined in Chapter V, the distortion of the structure of production made possible by that bank credit expansion described in Chapter VI, and the stock market boom and crash dealt with in Chapter VII, all had their origin in the price-stabilization policy, or managed currency experiment, of the Federal Reserve Board during the years leading up to the depression.

UNJUSTIFIED CRITICISM OF FEDERAL RESERVE BOARD

A disclaimer is entered before proceeding further, however, that this is not merely an attempt to find a scapegoat for the troubles of the last few years. It has been popular to charge the Federal Reserve Board with responsibility for the depression (even by some of the Board's own members), but it appears that much of the criticism leveled against the Board has been motivated largely by unreasoning emotion rather than by calm objective analysis. Lest the following paragraphs should improperly be construed as a general attempt at castigation of the Board, it is urged on the contrary that our purpose is here only to review and to appraise dispassionately the Board's policies and activities in connection with the price situation and its intimate relation to the depression. It is believed, however, that the conclusion is inescapable that the interference on the part of the Board with the "normal" course of economic events in pursuing a policy of price stabilization contributed potently to the generation of the depression. Much of the criticism directed at the Board by others has had to do only with its policy toward the stock market, and particularly its action in 1929; the special concern here is rather with earlier years, and with the relation of Federal Reserve policy to the whole post-War economic situation, of which the stock market situation in 1929 was but one of several results.

### STABLE PRICE LEVEL AND—ENSUING DEPRESSION!

The depression has been explained thus far as the outcome of a central banking inflation, with that inflation translated into a disequilibrium between investment and saving. Supplementing the inflationistic bias inherent in central banking, as an explanation of the course of inflation during the decade of the 'twenties, are measures adopted by the Federal Reserve Board under the delusions of the desirability and the practicability of a stable price level.

So far as is known to the writers, Professor J. M. Clark was the first to point out that even [1]" * * * under perfectly

[1] *The Economics of Overhead Costs* (Chicago: University of Chicago Press, 1923), p. 406. And *cf.* Hayek, *Monetary Theory and the Trade Cycle*, p. 188: "It follows particularly from the point of view of the monetary theory of the Trade Cycle [here set out], that it is by no means justifiable to expect the total disappearance of cyclical fluctuations to accompany a stable price-level * * * "; and see Röpke, W., "Kredit und Konjunktur" (*Jahrbücher für Nationalökonomie und*

steady prices there would still be great booms and depressions in the capital-making industries, and resulting booms and depressions in industry at large." It was the proof of this observation of Clark's as exemplified in the last cycle which was one of the outstanding features that differentiated it from previous ones. Although prices were not perfectly steady, it is true, they were relatively stable for a period of time longer than any prior period involving comparable conditions. Yet depression ensued, in the face of what the advocates of the older form of monetary theory of the business cycle regarded as the *sine qua non* of freedom from depression. Why depression could occur in spite of relative stability of the price level has been set forth in Chapters VI and VII where it was shown that the all-important factor is the way in which increased credit (in the form of producers' credits) enters the economic system and engenders alteration in the structure of production. The relationship of Federal Reserve policy to the stabilized price level, however, is deserving of special consideration. It is necessary at this stage, in other words, to integrate the argument of the preceding chapters with the part played by Federal Reserve injections of credit into the system in the endeavor to bolster the price level.

### Did Federal Reserve Board Deliberately Attempt Price Stabilization?

On first thought, it may not appear an easy task to assess a deliberate policy of price stabilization against the Federal Reserve Board. Most of the Board members have denied the existence of any conscious policy aimed at stabilization, and some have asserted that it was not in their power to stabilize prices, even had they wished to do so. Over against these declarations may be set Professor Commons' observation that the Reserve authorities are prone to belittle their

*Statistik*, 3rd series, Vol. 69), p. 265, quoted by Hayek, *ibid.*, p. 188: " * * * even if a stable price level could be successfully imposed on the capitalist economy the causes making for cyclical fluctuations would not be removed."

influence on prices.[1] This is understandable, in view of the political implications such an admission would carry with it. However, in answer to the question propounded to him at the Stabilization Hearings in 1927:[2] "Do you think that the Federal Reserve Board could, as a matter of fact, stabilize the price level to a greater extent than they have in the past, by giving greater expansion to market operations and restriction or extension of credit facilities?" Governor Strong of the New York Federal Reserve Bank replied, "I personally think that the administration of the Federal Reserve System since the reaction of 1921 has been just as nearly directed as reasonable human wisdom could direct it toward that very object." Five years previously, in 1922, Pierre Jay, also of the New York Federal Reserve Bank, had stated that[3] "the movements of prices would indicate whether the volume of credit was inconsistent with production." George W. Norris, Governor of the Philadelphia Bank, agreed that the Federal Reserve Board authorities[4] "as a body have followed the policy as far as it lay within their power under the existing law, of stabilizing credits to the extent that stabilization of credits might have influenced prices."

A number of authorities on monetary matters whose opinions should be entitled to weight are inclined to recognize price stabilization as one of the objectives of Federal Reserve policy during the years following 1922. Keynes states that[5] "The successful management of the dollar by the Federal Reserve Board from 1923 to 1928 * * * was a triumph for the view that currency management is feasible, * * * ." D. H. Robertson remarks that[6] " * * * a monetary policy consciously aimed at keeping the general price level

[1] *Stabilization Hearings* (69: 1) (Washington: Government Printing Office, 1927), p. 307.
[2] *Ibid.* (69: 2), p. 550.
[3] *Proceedings*, Federal Reserve Board, 1922, Part I, p. 103; quoted by Harris, *Twenty Years of Federal Reserve Policy*, Vol. I, p. 87.
[4] *Hearings on the Strong Bill*, H. R. 7895 (Washington: Government Printing Office, 1927), p. 396.
[5] *A Treatise on Money*, Vol. II, pp. 258–259.
[6] Article on "The Trade Cycle," *Encyclopedia Brittanica*, 14th ed., Vol. 22, p. 354.

approximately stable * * * has apparently been followed
with some success by the Federal Reserve Board in the
United States since 1922." Of the possibility of stabilizing
prices, Joseph Stagg Lawrence says,[1] "It not only can be
done but has been done."

The intention here is not to attempt to develop at length
the argument that the Reserve Board members were consciously endeavoring *solely* to stabilize prices. The significant point is that they were endeavoring to "control" the
banking and credit situation. As Governor Norris points
out, they were embarking upon a conscious policy of "management." Since this policy was directed toward the control
of credits, and since its incidence was largely upon the prevailing domestic situation, it eventuated in the maintenance of a stable price level, as it was virtually certain to do
in view of the lengths to which the control activities extended
and the conscious or unconscious stabilization bias of the
majority of the members of the Board.

That the Board (and the System) was taking unto itself
responsibility for management and control does not seem to
admit of much doubt. The economic life of the United States
for the six years following was to be largely directed and
shaped (far more so than was then realized) in accordance
with the pronunciamento of the now famous *Tenth Annual
Report* of the Federal Reserve Board (1923), described by
Edie as perhaps the most important document of its kind
since the publication in England of the Bullion Report in
1810.[2] The statement of policy there set forth, and reiterated later at various times by members of the Board in

[1] *The Stabilization of Prices* (New York: The Macmillan Company, 1928), p. 125.
[2] Reference in detail to aspects of the 1923 Report would consume too much
space. It must be assumed that the reader is familiar, or at least acquainted, with
that document. Brief reference should be made, however, to one or two significant
statements therein, as well as to certain public statements of some of the Reserve
officials to indicate the prevailing views entertained with respect to controlling
credit conditions by the Reserve System. The tenor of the *Tenth Annual Report*
may be gleaned from the following statements: "Under present conditions * * *
discretion must inevitably play a larger role in central banking administration than
in pre-war days" (p. 38), and, "The objective in Federal reserve discount policy is
the constant exercise of a steadying influence on credit conditions" (p. 9). Dr. Miller
of the Reserve Board made the statement ("Federal Reserve Discount Policy and

their public utterances and to a lesser extent in subsequent Annual Reports of the Board, would almost certainly seem to point to the movement of the price level as a determining influence in the shaping of the control policies of the Board. In a retrospective view, it would seem that such indeed must have been the dominant influence. The very existence of the stable price level which persisted as long as it did, considered in conjunction with the available statistical evidence on Federal Reserve credit operations, would seem well-nigh conclusive proof of that contention. In other words, it is the writers' opinion that we witnessed from 1922 to 1929 the world's greatest laboratory experiment with a *"managed currency" within* the gold standard, involving stabilization of the price level. And, to repeat, the view is advanced that the greater part of our recent troubles was the outcome of that stabilization experiment.

## CURRENCY MANAGEMENT DIFFICULT—BUT NOT NEW

Yet there is nothing genuinely new in currency management as such. Nor is there any direct quarrel with a program of control. The critical point at issue has to do with the choice of objectives and the extent of the control activities; the later part of the present chapter will be devoted to setting forth the writers' views on credit policy, and it will there be shown that the very existence of any such policy necessarily involves management and control. The gold standard prior to the War was a managed standard. That

the Diversion of Credit into Speculative Channels," *Trust Companies* [November, 1925], Vol. XLI, No. 5, p. 590): "Almost from the day of their establishment, the Federal Reserve banks have had to form a larger conception of their functions in the country's credit and economic system to steady credit conditions, to give at all times a firm basis of strength and health to the country's credit organization so far as it lies in the power of the Federal Reserve, and through the wise and intelligent exercise of this function to give steadiness, stability and strength to underlying business conditions." Dr. Burgess of the New York Bank in 1930 wrote ("Guides to Bank of Issue Policy," *Proceedings of the Academy of Political Science* [January, 1930], Vol. XIII, No. 4, p. 511): "In fact, the history of Federal Reserve credit policy in recent years, as we look back on it, shows that the Federal Reserve System has in general exercised restraint at times of excess and has provided the stimulant of easy credit in times of deficiency." It may be observed, parenthetically, that the policy of providing the stimulant has been followed more readily than that of exercising restraint.

it can be managed with considerable success is attested by the fact that England was able to maintain satisfactorily her position as "banker for the world" on the very slender gold she then possessed (the gold reserve of the Bank of England prior to 1913, according to Sir George Paish, never having exceeded $50,000,000 [1]). When the hegemony of world finance passed to the United States during and after the War, and with it the responsibility for international monetary management, there were only a few nations remaining on the gold standard, and the inexperienced or incapable hands in this country essayed to manage a purely domestic gold standard, apparently with but scant regard for the international aspects of the situation. Yet, as will be shown later, this domestic management procedure subsequently had unfortunate international repercussions.

### REDISCOUNT RATE CHANGES AND OPEN-MARKET OPERATIONS AS INSTRUMENTS OF CONTROL

Two changes relating to the tools of management were instituted in the United States during this period, altering the American procedure in some respects from the pre-War system of management in England. One was the less positive use made of rediscount rate changes as a tool of central bank management, and the other was the more positive and extensive use made of open-market operations. Open-market operations had never played a particularly conspicuous rôle in the policies of the Bank of England, short of panic conditions, before the War; the main reliance was placed upon alterations in the rediscount rate. In the experience of this country with a central banking system, the emphasis has been reversed. Comparatively less use has been made of rate changes, and open-market operations have been the chief instrument of Federal Reserve control operations. Explanation may possibly lie in the fact that

---

[1] See Sir George Paish, "Commercial Policy and the Gold Standard," in *Money and Credit in the Recovery Program, Proceedings of the Academy of Political Science* (April, 1934), Vol. XVI, No. 1, p. 84.

almost from the inception of the Reserve System the rediscount rate ruled below the market rate, and thus never attained the effectiveness it enjoyed in England, where the rediscount rate has been traditionally above the market rate; perhaps it was because open-market operations, utilized widely during the period of War financing, represented a seemingly more delicate instrument for experimentation, but one no less effective in the control of the market.[1]

The Reserve Banks can become a positive factor in the money market on their own initiative by influencing the reserve balances of the member banks through open-market operations. In order that an expansion of reserves may follow from a reduction in the rediscount rate, on the contrary, the member banks must aid in the process; they are under no compulsion to increase their reserves by rediscounting merely because the rate is low. Open-market (purchase) operations do force an expansion of reserves, whether or no, and it ordinarily follows that the member banks will expand credit on the basis of these "costless" reserves induced by Federal Reserve action. By embarking upon the initial open-market operations of 1922, the importance and efficacy of which are stressed in the 1923 *Report*, the Board committed itself to a policy of control which continued on into 1928. Even at that later date, unfortunately, the Board refused to recognize its responsibility for the situation which it had created and adopted a "do-nothing" policy for a time sufficiently long to permit a run-away situation to develop.

The Federal Reserve System, in other words, entered upon an active policy of positive control. Banking developments in this country from 1922 onward were almost entirely the consequence of Federal Reserve control operations. Dr. Miller's characterization of the 1927 "boot-strap lifting" experiment as "one of the most costly errors committed by it or any other banking system in the last 75 years" applies

---

[1] *Cf.* Reed, H. L., *Federal Reserve Policy, 1921–1930*, pp. 7–8: "Rate changes are of a positive and emphatic nature * * * and they are not nearly so likely as open-market operations to signify merely cautious experimentation."

with equal force to the experiments of 1922 and 1924.[1]  In the formulation and execution of an essentially inflationistic policy of control, the Board must be charged with a colossal error, the ultimate effect of which was, as Dr. Miller himself admits, the depression.

This, then, constitutes another important link in the chain of reasoning calculated to unravel the causes of the depression.  The execution of the Board's control operations involved inflationistic action if stabilization of the price level was to be achieved, in the sense that it artificially maintained that level and forestalled the inevitable and natural decline which otherwise would have accompanied the post-War expansion of production, and hence explains the bank credit inflation which resulted.

### MOTIVATION OF ADOPTION OF PRICE-STABILIZATION POLICY

This leads to the question of the *raison d'être* of the Board's action: *i.e.*, What motivated the adoption of such a policy of control?  The answer appears to be that the Board was convinced that the price level had fallen far enough after the severe break in 1920–1921, or had fallen to "normal," and hence should be stabilized at that point.  If this notion was held by the Board, it likewise helps to explain the underlying idea of the inflationistic bias.  Normalcy, however, is at best an elusive concept, and one not subject to easy definition; nor is it a simple matter to state what constitutes a normal price level.

### HISTORICAL ANALOGY PROMPTS SKEPTICISM AS TO FULLNESS OF POST-WAR PRICE RECESSION

It is the view of the writers, a *post hoc* view it is true, that the 1921–1922 level of prices still included some part

---

[1] *Cf.* Hayek, *Monetary Theory and the Trade Cycle*, p. 22: "It is probably to this experiment * * * that we owe the exceptional severity and duration of the depression.  We must not forget that for the last six or eight years, monetary policy all over the world has followed the advice of the stabilizers."  Hayek was here referring to the 1927 "experiment"—the writers, as stated, are inclined to assess responsibility against all three experiments, those of 1922 and 1924 as well as that of 1927.

of the rank growth of inflation fostered by ill-conceived war finance, and that a further price recession or deflation was in order before it could be said that a normal price situation had been attained after the War. What would have been a "normal" price level during those years is admittedly hard to say; notwithstanding, it is not reasonable to believe that the index of wholesale commodity prices would plunge 100 points in little over a year and then at once became stable at a point 50 per cent above the level prevailing in 1913.

The basis for this belief lies in historical analogy. After each of the three periods of great war-time inflation in this country—the War of 1812, the Civil War, and the World War—prices eventually fell to a point lower than they had stood at the beginning of the inflation. In view of the course of events in the first two instances, there was ample basis for skepticism that a price level 50 per cent higher than the pre-War level would become a new price norm after the late War. This is not to say that prices necessarily have to recede to their pre-war level following every such period of inflation; the fact remains, however, that they did do so in the preceding cases and hence might have been expected to do so again in this most recent case. And history did repeat itself. But not completely so, for in each of the two earlier periods the pre-war level was reached as the result of a gradual and fairly consistent decline spread over a considerable number of years, whereas in the later instance the price level was artificially stabilized for a time, following an initial drastic decline, and the remainder of the deflation to the 1913 level was postponed until after 1929, with now-familiar disastrous effects.[1]

If "management" was to be the function of the Reserve System—and, it is repeated, there is no complaint against management as such, but rather against the choice of ends and possibly the extent or degree of management—the Board might better have directed its management activities

[1] See below, p. 193 *et seq.*

to preventing "natural" recession from degenerating into headlong deflation. By such a policy it might have been possible to delay the return to the pre-War level of prices (if that level ever did return) to some relatively distant future date. There is nothing inherently bad in a falling price level (in fact, there is much to commend it, as will be elaborated later in this chapter), *provided* the rate of decline is gradual.

Other aspects of the post-War situation also lead to the conclusion that the level of stabilized prices which prevailed from 1922 to 1929 was not a natural nor a normal one, and that the attempts at stabilization were in opposition to powerful influences working for a decline.

### UNPRECEDENTED TECHNICAL PROGRESS INDICATED FALLING PRICES NORMAL

The fact that the period from 1922 to 1929 was one of rapid technical progress need hardly be amplified. As technical progress ordinarily and logically results in enlarged production, however, this development constituted a forceful factor operating to reduce prices. Additional purchasing power had to be injected into the system if the increased output of products was to be taken off the market and if, at the same time, a decline in the price level was to be avoided. But these injections of new credits served also to make more rigid the distorted, unbalanced, economic relationships that had been created during the War. An unbalanced cost-price relationship tended in effect to be solidified by the new emissions of credit. An excellent brief characterization of the situation is found in the following analysis by D. H. Robertson: [1]

> The events of the last 18 months have confirmed rather than shaken me in the belief that the maintenance of an even rate of industrial progress, difficult in any case, will be rendered more difficult still if the world commits itself to the view that, how-

[1] "How Do We Want Gold to Behave?", in *The International Gold Problem* (London: Humphrey Milford, 1932), p. 45. Publication of the Royal Institute of International Affairs.

ever great the improvements in technical efficiency, prices ought never to fall. Looking back, it becomes, I think, more and more arguable that the great American "stabilisation" of 1922–1929 was really a vast attempt to de-stabilise the value of money in terms of human effort by means of a colossal programme of investment in buildings, motor car plants, etc., which succeeded for a surprisingly long period, but which no human ingenuity could have managed to direct indefinitely on sound and balanced lines. It becomes plainer, too, I think, that the disastrous slump in the prices of many foodstuffs and raw materials has been in part, at any rate, a nemesis for ill-considered efforts (greedy in the case of low-cost producers, pathetic and futile in the case of high cost ones) to hold up prices in the face of falling costs. If the business man's psychology jibs at swallowing the moderate price falls dictated by increasing productivity, he renders himself more and not less liable to suffer the catastrophic price falls due to industrial dislocation and crisis—that is my case.

The Federal Reserve Board, then, in its control policies during this period, found itself opposed by two powerful forces operating in the direction of a decline in prices. On the one hand, there was an inescapable tendency toward further deflation to some point below the unnatural plateau of prices attained at the end of the War period; and, on the other hand, the improved technique in production, the application of science to business, which characterized the Second Industrial Revolution was a significant force working for lower prices. In order to effect a stabilization of the price level in the face of these two powerful counterweights it was necessary to force enormous quantities of bank credit into the economic system as an offsetting factor. On this point Robertson makes the further observation which follows:[1]

[1] *Banking Policy and the Price Level*, pp. 54–55. And *cf.* Hayek, *Prices and Production*, pp. 23–24: "Nevertheless, it is perfectly clear that, in order that the supply and demand for real capital should be equalised, the banks must not lend more or less than has been deposited with them as savings. And this means naturally that they must never change the amount of their circulation. At the same time, it is no less clear that, in order that the price level may remain unchanged, the amount of money in circulation must change as the volume of production increases or decreases. The banks could *either* keep the demand for real capital within the limits set by the supply of savings, *or* keep the price level steady; but they cannot perform both functions at once."

Suppose that in a community with a stable population there occurs a general increase in individual productivity. If the bank takes no action there will be a fall in the price level and an increase in the real value of the people's money stocks. * * * By making additional loans of an appropriate pace, the bank can counteract the fall in the price level * * * what is true is that owing to the increase in productivity the bank has been able, without causing a rise in the price-level, to impose upon the public a quantity of Lacking ["forced saving"] whose imposition would have necessitated a rise in the price-level if there had been no increase of productivity.

### PARALLELISM BETWEEN GROWTH OF BANK CREDIT AND PRODUCTIVITY

That the banking system operated directly to counteract the tendency toward a falling price level which should have been regarded as a logical consequence of the increasing productivity of the economic system during the period in question is suggested by an examination of the now-familiar figures for the rate of increase of bank credit and the most authoritative available figures for the rate of increase of productivity. As measured by the physical volume of output per wage-earner (the quotient of the total physical volume of production divided by the number of workers), productivity increased from 1919 to 1927 at the rate of 6.69 per cent per annum.[1] This compares with an increase of bank credit from 1921 to 1929 at a rate slightly in excess of 6 per cent per annum. Although the data do not cover exactly the same years in the two cases, the figures may be considered sufficiently comparable. In other words, in order to offset an increasing productivity of a little more than 6 per cent per annum, the banks had to manufacture credit at approximately the same rate. The result was a comparatively stable price level. In this sense, the creation of bank credit at the rate indicated must be regarded as constituting inflation.[2] It is probable, furthermore, that

[1] *Recent Economic Changes* (New York: McGraw-Hill Book Company, 1929), Table 2, p. 101.

[2] "It is true that our price level was comparatively steady from 1922 to 1929, but that fact is not proof that there was not some price inflation, relative to

the actual increase of productivity would not have been so great had not the introduction and application of technological improvements been speeded up by the rapid growth of bank credit. That is to say, the expansion of bank credit operated to speed up the rate of improvement in productivity through the more rapid creation of improved capital equipment, thereby rendering technological advances effective more quickly. Yet the concurrent effect of increasing the amount of bank credit in circulation was to deprive the public of any immediate benefits of that improving productivity in the form of lower prices.

### ABSENCE OF INVENTORY INFLATION

An alteration in policy on the part of business men served to eliminate one possible source of demand for new credit that was much in evidence whenever easy credit conditions obtained before the War, that is, in the accumulation of stocks of goods in anticipation of a rise of prices. There was no marked increase in demand for goods in the form of expanding inventories, as had been characteristic of previous booms. Business men had learned a severe lesson during the 1920-1921 recession when they were caught with swollen inventories at inflated prices, and did not care to run the risk of another abrupt decline in prices—hence they were loath to accumulate large stocks of goods-on-hand. There

### TABLE XXIV

#### INVENTORIES, ALL REPORTING CORPORATIONS
#### (In Billions of Dollars)

| 1924 | 19.4 |
|------|------|
| 1925 | 19.6 |
| 1926 | 20.9 |
| 1927 | 21.0 |
| 1928 | 20.8 |
| 1929 | 21.0 |

Source: Currie, Lauchlin, "The Failure of Monetary Policy to Prevent the Depression of 1929-1932," *Journal of Political Economy* (April, 1934), Vol. XLII, No. 2, p. 163.

costs. It can be argued that but for credit expansion prices would have fallen, and that they should have done so. It was on such grounds that the Austrian economists predicted the depression." Williams, J. H., in *Gold and Monetary Stabilization*, p. 149.

appears to exist a direct relationship between commercial loans and inventories, since a large part of commercial loans ordinarily are used for the purpose of carrying stocks of finished goods and for materials-in-process. It has already been pointed out that commercial loans for all the member banks were remarkably steady from 1921 to 1929 (Table XIII); the table on page 189 shows that inventories were nearly stationary from 1924 on (figures for prior years not being available).[1]

## EFFECTS OF INFLATION BEST MEASURED WHERE USE OF CREDIT MOST ACTIVE

From yet another point of view, there may also be said to have been inflation during this period. Although wholesale commodity prices were relatively steady, prices in a more inclusive sense *did* rise. That is to say, the emissions of bank credit found expression in a rise of prices *other than* wholesale commodity prices, the index to which most persons are accustomed to refer when considering prices in relation to increased purchasing media. For "credit takes various directions, and the effects of inflation can only be measured best at those points in the business structure where the use of credit has been most active."[2] The "points" where credit played its most active part in affecting prices in the period from 1922 onward are those already referred to—real estate, stocks, and long-term investments. In addition, the new credit found an outlet in the payment of increased wages; for, despite the efforts of Congress to revamp economic theory by legislative fiat in the famous Section 7 of the Clayton Act to the effect that "the labor of a human being is not a commodity or article of commerce," and in the now equally celebrated Section 7a of the National Industrial Recovery Act, wages nevertheless remain a price.

[1] It should be noted that in 1924 the number of corporations reporting was 346,388, and in 1929, 398,815, which fact in itself would account for some part of the increase from 1924 to 1929.

[2] Fraser, H. F., *Great Britain and the Gold Standard* (London: Macmillan & Company, 1933), p. 81.

Wage rates increased at the rate of 2.8 per cent per annum from 1922 to 1927, as compared with 0.5 per cent per annum from 1899 to 1921.[1] And Carl Snyder's Index of the General Price Level, composed of some eleven price series such as real estate prices, security prices, rents, and wage rates, in addition to wholesale prices, rose from 152 in 1922 to 183 in 1929 (on the basis of 1913 as 100), which is at a (compound) rate of 2.7 per cent per annum. If *all* prices are considered, then, it is clear that an inflationary price rise actually did occur in the period following 1922, despite the fact that wholesale commodity prices were relatively stable. Thus the ultimate effect of increasing emissions of bank credit resulting in approximate stabilization of the *wholesale* price level was to cause rising prices in unanticipated quarters.

## WHY STABILIZATION OF PRICE LEVEL IS AN IMPROPER OBJECTIVE OF BANKING POLICY AND AN INADEQUATE GUIDE

This reverts the discussion to the point made in Chapter VI, that much hinges on *how* and *where* the new credit enters the system. When credit is generated through the sale of new bond issues to the banks by entrepreneurs who are engaged in producing new capital goods, it brings about an investment inflation, with the resulting boom characterized by expansion in the investment goods industries, and followed by the inevitable crisis and deflation when the issuance of new credits slackens or ceases. A stable general level of prices in itself means little; it is the disequilibria among particular prices induced by bank credit expansion (or contraction) that is of chief interest and importance for business cycle theory. Hayek is unquestionably right when he says that: [2]

---

[1] *Recent Economic Changes*, pp. 632–633.

[2] *Monetary Theory and the Trade Cycle*, pp. 123–124. Marshall had said somewhat the same thing in his *Economics of Industry* (London: Macmillan & Company, 1879), p. 156: " * * * a manufacturer * * * would not check his production on account of a fall in prices, if the fall affected all things equally * * * . If the price which he got for his goods had fallen by a quarter, and the prices which he had to

General price changes are no essential feature of a monetary theory of the Trade Cycle; *they are not only unessential, but they would be completely irrelevant if only they were completely "general"—that is, if they affected all prices at the same time and in the same proportion.* The point of real interest to Trade Cycle theory is the existence of certain deviations *in individual price-relations* occurring because changes in the volume of money appear at certain individual points. * * * The nature of the changes in the composition of the existing stock of goods, which are affected through monetary changes, depends of course upon the point at which the money is injected into the economic system.

As long as particular prices persist in deviating from a stabilized level, and as long as the level of stabilization itself is made up of an average of fluctuating individual prices, stabilization of the price level is neither adequate nor proper as an objective of or guide for banking and credit policy.[1] The principal shortcoming of price level stabilization as a primary goal of monetary policy is found in the fact that the "freezing" of any one set of prices tends to establish resistances to the readjustments that need to be made continually within the price system if that system is to be kept in balance in the face of a highly dynamic economic setting: stabilization of *all* prices is, of course, quite impossible in any nation other than one having a completely "frozen" economic structure. Nor is an unchanging price level any insurance against depression, as the events of recent monetary history have abundantly proved.

The wholesale price level, then, was artificially supported by the action of the Federal Reserve authorities, and to bring about this artificial support required the emission of an amount of credit vastly in excess of the needs of trade and

pay for labour and raw material had also fallen by a quarter, the trade would be as profitable to him as before the fall. * * * The counters * * * would be less by one quarter, but they would purchase as much of the necessaries, comforts, and luxuries of life as they did before."

[1] "Thus a policy aiming at ultimate stability of the general price-level seems to be neither the 'most natural' nor the 'most effective' policy for the monetary authority to adopt." Robertson, D. H., *Banking Policy and the Price Level*, p. 32. And, "Stable prices is a fetish," Donald K. Kitchin, the London *Times*, June 20, 1933, p. xxiv.

industry. The new excess credit was in considerable measure directed into channels divorced from the normal non-speculative operations of production and commerce, and found expression in the rise of prices in the stock market, in the real estate market, and in wage rates. Federal Reserve control activities, primarily directed at stabilization of the price level, produced the speculative and investment booms, with the attendant disequilibrium between investment and saving, and therefore may be considered a generating cause of our recent plight. Investment inflation ended in depression.

### ARTIFICIAL SUPPORT OF PRICE LEVEL RESULTED IN "RELATIVE" INFLATION

Finally, in yet one other sense there may be said to have been inflation during this period: there was an inflation *relative* to the price level which *might* have prevailed had there not been the managed expansion of credit. If the assumption set out earlier in this chapter, that the level of prices prevailing after the 1920–1921 deflation was still not a "normal" level and that a further down-trend of prices might have been expected, is correct, then it may be said that wholesale commodity prices stabilized at (approximately) the 1922 level represented an inflated price level relative to the normal *trend* of prices.[1] In other words, it may be said that there was a "relative" price inflation, an inflation relative to what probably would have been the normal secular (downward) trend of prices in the absence of credit expansion. Chart VII depicts the course of prices following the three major periods of war inflation in our history, and is based upon an attempt to arrive at a mathematical formulation of the normal decline in prices which follows a war financed by inflationary measures. It shows clearly the gradual and fairly steady return to pre-war

[1] For an expression of the view that a declining secular trend of prices was to be expected after the primary post-War deflation of 1920–1921, see John R. Commons' article on "Price Stabilization" in the *Encyclopedia of the Social Sciences*, Vol. XII, p. 365.

CHART VII

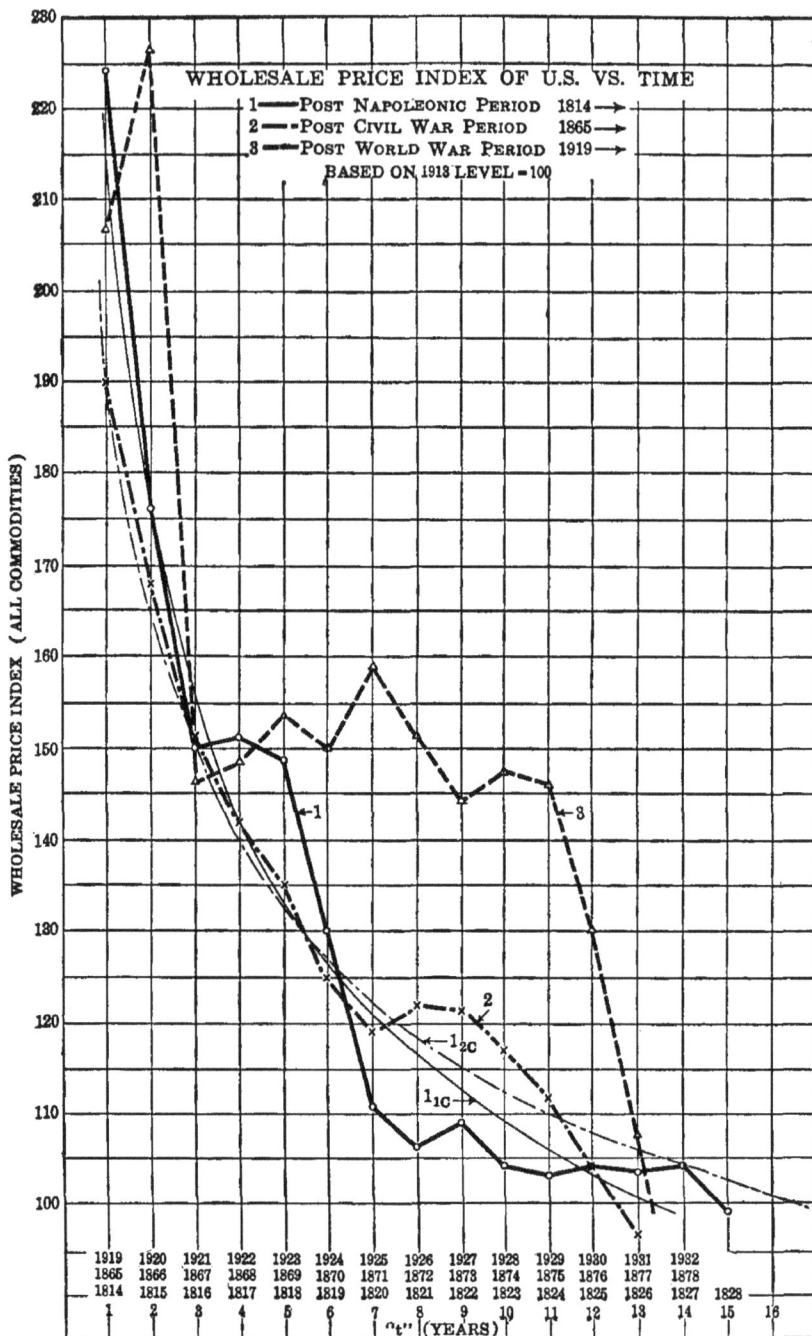

WHOLESALE PRICE INDEX OF U.S. VS. TIME

1 ——— POST NAPOLEONIC PERIOD 1814 →
2 —·— POST CIVIL WAR PERIOD 1865 →
3 ——— POST WORLD WAR PERIOD 1919 →
BASED ON 1913 LEVEL = 100

Source: *The Annalist* (August 26, 1932), Vol. 40, No. 1023, p. 269. Reproduced by permission.

194

levels during the first two periods (the War of 1812 and the Civil War), as contrasted to what has here been characterized as an artificial support, or suspension, of the price level after the World War. The author of this chart states:[1]

> A comparison of the portion of the curve following 1818 in the first period and that following 1923 in the third period shows a very interesting variation. After the year 1818 there was *first* a sharp decline for two years followed by a very easy downward trend for the next eight years; whereas, after 1923 the index numbers *first* eased off very gradually for six years followed by a sharp decline in the last two years. In other words, the portions of the two curves discussed above, [*i.e.*, in Chart VII] are in inverse relation to each other, *and the area enclosed by the apparent parallelogram can very well represent a period of inflation.* [Italics supplied.] The fact asserts itself that the longer the price level is held, the more violent the drop, and that the average time interval for the three periods approximates 13.6 years, compared to 13.7 calculated as a mean [theoretical] value from the first two recession periods.

### Bearing of Cycle Theory upon Control Policy

The decisions of the Federal Reserve Board relative to these questions of policy necessarily must have been predicated upon some theory or theories of the business cycle. And had the Board subscribed to and recognized the importance of a really sound and comprehensive theory of the cycle it is possible that Federal Reserve policies would have been formulated along such different lines as largely to have outflanked the 1929 crash and the ensuing suffering and distress.

---

[1] Eade, Walter F., "Mathematical Analysis of Post-War Price Falls," *The Annalist* (August 26, 1932), Vol. 40, No. 1023, p. 269. And compare the following: "It is safe to assert without qualification that the absolute level of commodity prices is not a reliable indication of the presence or absence of inflation. * * * To begin with, it is necessary to point out that the level of commodity prices is necessarily a relative matter. It is not enough to compare the absolute level of prices without taking into account the long-term trend, which is to say, the level which would exist in the absence of inflation. * * * With the foregoing in mind, the existence of stable commodity prices contemporaneously with marked inflation is readily explained. While prices have been stable or perhaps slowly declining into 1929 in absolute dollar units, they have quite probably been rising relatively to the price-level which would have existed in the absence of inflation." Harwood, E. C., *Cause and Control of the Business Cycle*, pp. 79–83.

For no theory of credit control can be divorced successfully from a theory of the business cycle; and any policy of
credit control will be influenced by the theory of the business
cycle upon which it is based.   This relationship between
theory and policy is neatly stated by Hardy:[1]

> *No analysis of the business situation can be more adequate than
> is the theory of business fluctuations on which it is based.* * * *
> If credit is to be regulated in accordance with the requirements
> of business stability, the administering authorities must have a
> sound and adequate knowledge of the conditions which fore-
> shadow a business boom or a business collapse.   They must
> understand the theory of the business cycle and be masters of
> the art of business forecasting. * * * The assumptions of the
> *Tenth Annual Report* are the assumptions of a certain type of
> cycle theory, which may be characterized briefly as the doctrine
> of over- and under-production. * * * The cause of the fluctua-
> tion is not necessarily to be found in the credit situation, but the
> credit system furnishes the key to its control.   For, if the financ-
> ing of a boom can be prevented, the conditions which engender
> the slump are avoided.

THEORETICAL FOUNDATIONS OF FEDERAL RESERVE POLICY

It appears, however, that the Board took cognizance not
only of the "doctrine of over- and under-production" but
also of the older form of monetary theory of the business
cycle that assigns primary importance to the behavior of
the price level.  "The idea that this [Trade Cycle] theory
must start from the wavelike fluctuations of the price-
level, which are conditioned mainly by monetary causes; the
rise, as well as the fall, of the price-level being brought about
by particular new forces originating on the side of money"[2]
seems to have been at the bottom of the Board's control
policies.   Perhaps it would be more accurate to say that
the Board evidently had some regard for *both* doctrines when
its management policies were taking form.   At any rate, the

---

[1] *Credit Policies of the Federal Reserve System* (Washington: The Brookings Institution, 1932), p. 87. See, also, Commons' article on "Price Stabilization," *op. cit.*,
*supra*, for a further expression of the view that no theory of price stabilization can
be more adequate than the theory of the business cycle upon which it is predicated.

[2] Hayek, F. A., *Monetary Theory and the Trade Cycle*, pp. 121–122.

inference seems clear that, in basing its control assumptions on a spurious theoretical foundation and by acting in accordance with those assumptions, the Board "produced" the investment boom and its inevitable deflation.

### Some International Consequences of "Easy Money" Policy of the United States

It was stated earlier in the present chapter that the Board's policies also had international effects that were of far-reaching import. During the period of the 'twenties when the United States was not only the most powerful commercial and industrial nation in the world, but also was in possession of the major portion of the stock of monetary gold of the world, our domestic developments and conditions were bound to influence the course of economic events in other countries.[1] The Federal Reserve Board in its efforts to inflate purchasing power and to support the price level in this country helped indirectly, and no doubt unwittingly, to arrest the decline of prices in other important commercial nations and thereby served as a directing influence upon general economic conditions abroad.[2]

The credit inflation policies of the Federal Reserve Board, by flooding the local money markets with cheap Reserve credit, facilitated the successful flotation of huge foreign loans in the United States from 1922 to 1928. These foreign loans in turn stimulated an investment inflation abroad, notably in Germany and certain South American countries,

---

[1] "Our United States have become a prodigious power alike for production, for consumption, and in wealth and income of every sort. This is a commonplace; but it is still a little astounding to consider that we produce and consume almost as much of goods (and services) as all the rest of the commercial nations of the world put together. * * * It is therefore, *our* consumption, *our* buying, *our* prosperity, *our* financial conditions, which very largely determine not only our own economic and financial health, but also that of the whole world." Carl Snyder, "Overproduction and Business Cycles," *Proceedings of the Institute of Finance* (Occidental College, 2nd Session, 1931), p. 65.

[2] " * * * our Federal Reserve Board is controlling the gold price level of the entire world." Congressman Strong, in introducing his stabilization bill, H. R. 7895 (1927); and *cf.* Cassel, *The Crisis in the World's Monetary System*, p. 13: "Thus the world's monetary system had arrived at the rather peculiar situation that it was built on a common unit of value, the dollar, which, within wide limits, was determined arbitrarily by the American monetary authorities."

similar to the investment inflation in this country. When the volume of foreign loan flotations in this country declined with the cessation of bank credit expansion during 1928 and 1929, the investment booms in the foreign countries came to an end, and with the decline in investment activity abroad prices in foreign countries began to fall rapidly. And when the stock market crash occurred shortly afterward in this country the attendant destruction of domestic purchasing power reacted on foreign countries in the form of a lessened volume of foreign trade.

As early as June, 1927, the effects of the Federal Reserve Board's domestic credit policies upon the international situation were diagnosed by Professor Bertil Ohlin of Stockholm University as follows: [1]

> The influx and efflux of gold in the United States has thus lost all influence upon the monetary purchasing power and the price level in that country. The question of granting credit is instead determined by what the Federal Reserve Board considers suitable from an economic point of view. This implies nothing less than a revolution in the monetary system not only of the United States but of all countries with a gold standard. The control of the development of the world price level has passed entirely into the hands of the Federal Reserve Board and Governors. * * * The post-war gold standard is * * * [a] kind of "managed currency," in which the control is exercised by the Federal Reserve Board and the boards of the leading Federal Reserve Banks on the basis of considerations which have nothing to do with either gold cover or gold movements, but are dictated chiefly by the possibilities of keeping production going at full pressure.

To the extent that this viewpoint is defensible, it may be logically concluded that the control policies of the Federal Reserve Board were impregnated with responsibility not only for the recent upheavals in the United States, but also, indirectly, for certain aspects of the world-wide depression in trade and industry.[2] The depression was more severe in this

---

[1] *Index*, Svenska Handelsbanken (June, 1927), No. 18, pp. 7 and 9.
[2] *Cf.* Carl Snyder, "Overproduction and Business Cycles," *Proceedings of the Academy of Political Science* (June, 1931), Vol. XIV, No. 3, p. 338: " * * * I believe

country largely because the impact of Federal Reserve control activities was more direct here, and because the inflation of bank credit was greater in the United States (after 1924, at least) than abroad.

Sight should not be lost of the fact, in assessing an appreciable measure of responsibility for recent conditions against the Federal Reserve Board, that the system of central banking constituted the medium through which such errors as were made by the Board were transmitted: responsibility for the depression does not rest solely upon the shoulders of the Board members. The depression was in a proximate sense a product of central bank credit expansion and was far more severe because of the introduction and operation of central banking in this country than it otherwise would have been. The Board's part in the subsequent operation of that central banking system, however, cannot be passed over lightly.

CURRENCY MANAGEMENT THE OFFSPRING OF WAR FINANCE

As Colonel Ayres has said, it is not simply the fact of war itself which causes subsequent depression, but rather the fact that the price advance which accompanies a war financed by inflationistic measures determines the course of economic events in the post-war period.[1] The heightened price level which was an aftermath of war financing made its influence felt upon all subsequent economic activity. Banking policy during the post-War years in this country was directed at stabilization of the price level; as there apparently was a persistent tendency for the price level to decline further from the abnormal height to which war financing had lifted it, in order to effect a temporary stabilization of the commodity price level it became necessary to force such large quantities of new credits into the

there is decisive evidence that it actually was conditions and disturbances in these United States which were largely responsible for this economic disaster [the world depression]. But these conditions appear to have been rather of a monetary and financial character—a saturnalia of speculation * * * "

[1] See p. 36, *supra*.

system that inflation resulted in other important sectors of the price field. Hence this banking policy of "currency management," of which the boom and the ensuing depression were direct consequences, may be said to have been sired by the inflated price level that was in turn the offspring of war finance.

## POLICY OF STABILIZATION OF PRICE LEVEL TENDS TOWARD ITS OWN COLLAPSE

The statement has been made that there is nothing inherently objectionable about banking and credit control or management, as such, but that the authors were in disagreement with the objectives and extent of the control policies as exercised by the Federal Reserve Board during the period from 1922 to 1929. The endeavor has been to show that stabilization of the wholesale price level, or of any one price index, is not a proper objective of banking policy or of credit control, because aberrations continue to occur in the case of particular types of prices when any one index is sought to be stabilized. The remainder of the chapter will be devoted to a consideration of what is held to be a proper and desirable objective, goal, or guide for banking control activities.

Stability of the price level is no adequate safeguard against depression, it is contended, because *any* policy aimed at stabilizing a *single* index is bound to set up countervailing influences elsewhere in the economic system. Although the policy of stabilization may appear to be successful for a time, eventually it will break down, because there is no way of insuring that the agencies of control will be able to make their influence felt at precisely those "points" of strategic importance. As long as economic progress is maintained, resulting in increasing productivity and an expanding total output, there will be an ever-present force working for lower prices. Any amount of credit expansion which will offset that force will find outlets unevenly in sundry compartments of the economic structure; the new credit will have an effect upon the market rate of interest, upon the prices of capital goods, upon real estate, upon security prices, upon wages, or upon all of these, as happened during the late boom. A policy which seeks to direct credit influences at *any* single index, whether it be of prices, either wholesale or retail, or production, or incomes, in the interests of stabilization, will result in unexpected and unforeseen repercussions which may be expected to prove disastrous in the long run.[1]

Furthermore, the fruits of progress and the benefits of improved productivity in the form of lower prices for the products of industry tend to be denied to labor, and to the public in general, by a policy of stabilization, particularly of the commodity price level. Stabilization is, in fact, antithetical to progress; for progress connotes not only technical improvement, but also the diffusion among all classes of the benefits in the form of increased productivity that such improvement makes possible. Therefore it should not be an objective of banking policy to stabilize, or to "freeze," the price level. Instead, the price level should be permitted to fall. In a progressive economy this downward tendency is "normal."

Indeed, in a dynamic economy banking policy should not consciously be aimed at "freezing" *anything*. Any credit policy which has as its object the stabilization of any fluctuating index of economic conditions or economic activity necessarily involves increasing and decreasing the amount of outstanding credit in order to make that control effective. As the index sought to be stabilized rises, credit must be withdrawn; as the index shows a tendency to decline, new credit must be pumped out to forestall that threat. Yet not only is there no assurance that new credit (or the withdrawn credit) will affect *only* the index sought to be stabilized, but there is also no certainty that the timing of the control activities will be proper and well advised.

[1] "In a progressive economy, any attempt to stabilize the wholesale price-index number inevitably generates forces which must destroy stability." Fisher, A. G. B., "Does an Increase in Volume of Production Call for a Corresponding Increase in Volume of Money?" *American Economic Review* (June, 1935), Vol. XXXV, No. 2, p. 210.

## Suggested Guide for Credit Control

A sharply contrasting objective of banking policy, therefore, and the one here advocated, would be the control of the *total amount of credit*, such that the violent inflations and contractions of credit would be eliminated, or at least greatly mitigated, and without special regard for any one index of economic activity. The ideal aim of credit policy is, simply, that the *rate of credit growth should be stabilized*, so that the growth of credit proceeds at the same rate as the growth of population, in the vicinity of one per cent per annum for the United States. The rate of growth of population is undoubtedly the most constant of economic phenomena, one that is well known and predictable for a considerable number of years, and one whose secular trend is subject to verification every ten years by the census figures. As population increases, the amount of circulating media should increase *pari-passu* in order to accommodate in as frictionless a manner as possible the increase in total transactions engaged in by a growing number of people; thus, although the absolute amount of credit would be increasing, the amount relative to the population would not be. This would amount virtually to a constant money supply, and would approach the "neutral money" idea of Wicksell and Hayek; differentia exist between the concept of "neutral" money and the policy here advocated, however, which would consume too much space to point out in detail. All that is proposed here is that the total supply of credit be kept constant, subject to the one qualification of an increasing population; if population increases, credit should increase at the same rate; should the population become stabilized, the total amount of credit should remain unchanged.

Under such a credit policy money, or bank credit, would be able to perform effectively its proper function as a medium of exchange, but would no longer constitute an erratic, independent determinant of economic developments. It should mean the end of "forced saving," and likewise of "windfall profits" in the sense employed by Keynes. Dis-equilibria between investment and saving would disappear, or else be of very short duration; the rate of progress of the economy would be determined exclusively by its rate of real saving. Indeed, the rate of progress itself should be more constant under such a policy, and the extent and rapidity of the changes in the structure of the productive process thereby considerably reduced; production would run more closely in accord with consumption. Adjustments among all the various economic phenomena should under such a stabilized rate of progress proceed more quickly and more surely; frictions and price rigidities should be overcome more readily, and therefore be less significant as disrupting influences.

## OBJECTIVES OF POLICY OF STABILIZING RATE OF CREDIT GROWTH

The specific objectives of such a credit policy are two in number. The first objective is a substantial reduction in the severity and the extent of booms and depressions. If the boom can be prevented—and it cannot readily be seen how a system-wide boom can develop, if the principal contentions of the present analysis are correct, without the aid of rapidly expanding bank credit to create a disequilibrium between investment and saving—there will be no "stacking of the cards" in favor of a subsequent depression. No doubt we still would have some cyclical movement of business activity, but the cycles would be much less pronounced.

The second objective of this credit policy is a price level that would respond readily to increases in productivity resulting from technological advances. A price level changing only as a result of, and in consonance with, increased productivity should be a slowly falling one; and there is much to be said for a gradually declining price level.[1] The

[1] "In the opinion of the writer, there is no reason to suppose that absolute stability of the level of prices, whether wholesale or retail, should be the aim of currency policy. The tendency of increasing productivity should be in the direction of falling prices; and provided that prices do not fall at a rate greater than productivity increases, there is no reason to fear that industrial depression or unemploy-

rate of increase of the physical volume of production is a relatively constant economic phenomenon over long periods of time, barring periods of rapid emissions of bank credit and of deep depression. It is also an economic constant about which considerable knowledge now exists, and this knowledge is being extended each year.[1] Almost fifty years ago Alfred Marshall advocated a gradually falling price level in his evidence before the Gold and Silver Commission Inquiry, from which the following excerpts are taken:[2]

> * * * I think that one wants very much stronger statistical evidence than one has yet to prove that a fall of prices diminishes perceptibly and in the long run the total productiveness of industry. Supposing that it does not diminish considerably the total productiveness of industry, then its effect is, I think, on the whole good; because it certainly tends to cause a distribution of wealth better than that which we should otherwise have * * * when prices are falling, manufacturers are put on their mettle and exert themselves to the utmost to invent improved methods and to avail themselves of the improvements made by others * * * I doubt whether the influence exerted in this direction [in the direction of discouragement of enterprise by a slow and gradual fall] is very great. On the other hand, during such a fall a powerful friction tends to prevent money wages in most trades from falling as fast as prices; and this tends almost imperceptibly to establish a higher standard of living among the working classes, and to diminish the inequalities of wealth. * * * in fact I think it is not clearly established that a rise of prices is on the whole to be preferred to a fall.

### Objections to Falling Price Level Examined

One objection to a falling price level which will immediately come to many minds is that large and undeserved benefits will accrue to the *rentiers*, the fixed-interest-receiving class, because when loans are repaid the lender will receive

ment will follow." Gregory, T. E., article on "Money" in the *Encyclopedia of the Social Sciences*, Vol. X, p. 612; and see Hayek, *Prices and Production*, p. 89: "It would appear rather that the fall of prices proportionate to the increase in productivity, which necessarily follows when, the amount of money remaining the same, production increases, is not only entirely harmless, but is in fact the only means of avoiding misdirections of production."

[1] Mainly in consequence of the exceedingly valuable studies of Carl Snyder.

[2] Alfred Marshall, *Official Papers*, p. 20 and pp. 91–92, and p. 19. And see the excellent article dealing with this whole subject by A. G. B. Fisher, *op. cit.*

back a greater amount of purchasing power at the lower price level than he loaned at the former higher one. This will at the same time prove detrimental to the borrower, it is frequently argued, because he will have to pay back a greater amount of purchasing power than he borrowed; there is, in other words, an unearned increase in purchasing power for the lender which represents an equally undeserved hardship for the borrower. In answer to this objection it may be asserted that in the case of relatively short loans, five to ten years, say, the price-fall would not be great enough to result in any considerable advantaging of the lender or disadvantaging of the borrower; and in the case of longer-term loans, say forty to sixty years, the fall in the rate of interest which normally accompanies a secular fall in the price level will in large part offset any nominal improvement in the capitalist's status. For a 6-per-cent loan repaid forty years in the future may have to be reinvested at 4 per cent, or even less. A sum of money loaned or invested in bonds, if substantial in amount, is ordinarily reinvested when repaid, rather than used subsequently for the purchase of consumption goods by the capitalist. Thus seeming gains and losses tend to cancel out in the long run; the seeming advantage accruing to the lender by virtue of the return of a larger amount of purchasing power is offset by the reduction in the interest rate if he reinvests, and the hardship on the borrower occasioned by the necessity of repaying in terms of more valuable dollars is counterbalanced by the more favorable terms on which he can obtain a new loan.

It is true that the interest payments during the years the bond is outstanding, if not reinvested, do represent an increase of purchasing power for the bondholder. But in this connection Sir Josiah Stamp points to a significant counterconsideration: [1]

> What is desired is rather that the unit of purchasing power shall represent a consistent unit of human effort, and if that effort has more bountiful results, justice in distribution of the

[1] *Papers on Gold and the Price Level* (London: P. S. King & Son, 1932), p. 30.

total product will be met if the proportions between people are not radically changed. In this sense it is not unfair that the bond holder who has lent the equivalent of two pairs of boots should receive when repaid forty years later, the equivalent of three pairs, if his claim on current production represents no higher proportion of the national product.

Yet at the same time that the price level was falling gradually in response to conditions of improving productivity, money wages would tend to remain stable. "For under such conditions, even though money wages are not reduced, a rising real wage-bill to employers does not mean a rising real labor-cost per unit of goods produced." [1] Stable money wages with increasing productivity would mean rising "real wages"; in this way the laboring classes would receive a constantly rising "real income," and in a manner calculated to minimize labor disputes and industrial conflict. The benefits of the improved productivity would accrue directly to the laborer equally as much as to the capitalist, and inequalities of wealth and income, as Marshall suggests, would tend to be diminished. Furthermore, the increase in the real productivity of labor would in the long run be conducive to the shortening of hours of work, and this without the necessity of any legislative fiat promulgated with only scant regard for its implications and ultimate consequences. Labor would be enabled to obtain its fair share of an enlarging total product of industry; "real wages" would rise; and with rising real incomes would come a rise in the standard of living, including more leisure in which to enjoy the enhanced income.

*Falling Prices Place Premium on Industrial Efficiency*

Still a further benefit accruing to society as a whole from a gradually declining price level would be the more certain

---

[1] Robertson, D. H., "The Monetary Doctrines of Messrs. Foster and Catchings," *Quarterly Journal of Economics* (May, 1929), Vol. XLIII, No. 3, p. 484. And see Hawtrey, R. G., *Trade Depression and the Way Out* (London: Longmans, Green & Co., 1933), p. 100: "To the argument that the collapse of the price level is not due to monetary causes, but is merely the natural consequence of the increased productivity made possible by technological progress, the answer is simple. In so far as the fall of prices is due to improved methods of production, *no* reduction of wages is required for the maintenance of equilibrium."

elimination of the unfit—only the most efficient entrepreneurs would be able to continue to produce with the
price level falling, and the less efficient would more speedily
be weeded out. The same might be true of some entire
industries as well as of individual entrepreneurs. A premium
would be placed upon industrial efficiency and rational
management. "Pure" profits under such a situation would
tend to approach the vanishing point. Even inefficient
producers can make profits on a rising price level, which is
one reason for the deep-rooted popular bias in favor of inflation. Rising prices and easy profits, however, generally
stimulate the launching of new enterprises that are able to
justify their existence only so long as prices continue to
advance. The shrinking of business failures to a minimum
at the same time that prices are rising is usually a storm
signal for the economic system in the not-so-distant future.
And the government is almost always, in the subsequent
depression, importuned to "take care of" those rash ad-
venturers who (with more credit than sense at their disposal) had rushed into those industries where soberer business judgment indicated the treading was not good.

### STABILIZATION OF RATE OF CREDIT GROWTH WOULD TEND TOWARD EQUILIBRATION OF INVESTMENT AND SAVING

In support of a policy of credit control aimed at stabilizing
nothing other than the rate of credit growth, additional
arguments could be offered and further evidence adduced in
favor of a gradually falling price level conditioned by technical advances and the resulting enhancement of productivity. Suffice it to emphasize in conclusion at this point,
however, that the major benefit which should accrue from
a banking policy directed toward stabilizing the per-capita
rate of credit growth would be an equilibration of investment
and saving, hence tending to eliminate, or at least to smooth,
the business cycle. If the use of the banking machinery for
the purpose of arbitrarily manufacturing new producers'
credits can be rigidly controlled, so that the rate of credit

growth is kept both constant and slight, deviations of the market rate of interest should prove very small and of short duration: there should be a tendency toward an equilibration of the natural and the market rates of interest, thereby eliminating the one condition most potent in creating a disequilibrium of investment and saving. There should be a sufficiently prompt adjustment of the market rate to the natural rate so that any chance disequilibrium between the two would not persist long enough for appreciable disequilibrium between investment and saving to emerge. The rate of increase of investment would depend upon, and be directly limited by, the rate of saving; money (meaning bank money, or credit) would be used to facilitate the transformation of real savings into real capital equipment, and not to induce "forced saving." If these disequilibria were cured, although wave-like movements of business activity might still persist, the amplitude of such movements should be severely reduced; the peaks and troughs of the waves need no longer be described as "booms" and "depressions"— there would be only self-correcting wavelets.

### VELOCITY CHANGES AS A FACTOR AFFECTING BANK CREDIT OR MANAGEMENT

One final possible objection remains to be touched upon. It is still contended by some that the velocity of circulation of credit is an independent force working for cyclical variations in trade and prices. We have already adverted to Carl Snyder's studies showing that the rate of increase of trade over long periods of time is virtually a constant. And reference to Chart V will show that the velocity of circulation for cities outside of New York changes within rather narrow limits. It is Snyder's further contention that velocity is also virtually a constant, at least in the absence of cyclical variations in trade.[1] But Snyder holds, as do we also, that

[1] Snyder, Carl, "The Problem of Monetary and Economic Stability," *Quarterly Journal of Economics* (February, 1935), Vol. XLIX, No. 2, pp. 186–187, and 189: "Then in 1924 a renewed attempt [was made] at statistical proof of the Newcomb equation and a new formulation of that equation in the light of the newly found gen-

it is the wide variations in the volume of credit which produce the cyclical movements in business activity: if our contention that a constant credit supply would eliminate the disequilibrium between investment and saving is sound, then the swings in velocity would tend toward minima. For, as we have argued, if investment and saving are in equilibrium, then production and consumption, and all economic activity, will be in equilibrium. Under such conditions, there seems little reason to expect alterations in the velocity of circulation of an extent sufficiently appreciable to generate independent cyclical movements by themselves. Any changes in velocity which might develop would affect only *trade*, as such, and not constructional and investment activity. Velocity changes, it is here argued, originate in the violent swings in investment activity to which we have been accustomed in the past, and transmit themselves to trade and the consumers' goods industries. Therefore, if this originating influence can be eliminated by bringing investment and saving into consonance with each other, the possibility of any wide swings in the velocity of circulation of credit should also be eliminated.

Conceding, however, that during the period when the credit control policy here being advocated is in process of realization there might be some rather marked changes in the velocity of circulation (particularly in consideration of the present low level of deposits turnover), there is no objection to attempts being made to mitigate any influence which velocity might exert in the direction of preventing the fulfillment of the objectives of that credit policy. As we have indicated, we are not opposed to the utilization of some degree of management within narrow limits. That the

eral synchronism of velocity and trade; that is, for ordinary times, at least, the equation of $\frac{MV}{T} = P$, reduces to a simple equilibrium of M and P, allowing always for the very steady, secular or long-time growth of Trade * * * for if it be true that deposit velocity and trade activity tend generally to correspond (with some infrequent exceptions), then it is clear that neither the variations in velocity nor in trade activity are normally a factor in the determination of the price level. The only factors involved then would be the volume of the medium of exchange that is, in our day, so largely bank credit, and the long-time *trend* of trade growth."

Federal Reserve Board will continue to employ discretion and judgment, in a word "management," is to be expected. If it becomes necessary, in view of the judgment of the Board, to offset any seemingly independent cyclical influences produced by changes in the velocity of circulation of credit, then we feel that the Board should be free to exercise its own wisdom and discretion in attempting to correct this and other more or less similar disturbing influences. We believe, however, that such corrective action in the direction of expanding or contracting credit in order to offset velocity changes should at no time be extensive. Even small departures from a constant rate of credit growth should no doubt have rather rapid countervailing effects upon the velocity factor, and the more so as the policy of stabilization of the rate of credit growth becomes more effective in the future. It should not be necessary, in other words, to change the total supply of credit to the extent of 4, 6, or 10 per cent within a given year to correct an antecedent change in velocity.

It may be inquired how such a banking policy could be realized in practice. The agency for control and the tools of administration of such control already exist. All that would be necessary would be the adoption of such a policy and adherence to it. Mistakes might be made in the early years of its application, but they should become progressively fewer and less serious. The Federal Reserve Board, with its control over member bank reserves through the rediscount rate and open-market operations, is already in large measure adequately implemented for the task of regulating the supply of credit; and with the control over member bank reserve ratios embodied in the Banking Act of 1935 a further instrument of control is made available to the Board, of which advantage has already been taken by the Board in increasing member bank reserve requirements on August 15, 1936.

## CHAPTER IX

# THE ECONOMIC IMPLICATIONS OF RECOVERY

Thus far our inquiry has been directed primarily to events prior to 1933. The statistical material presented has purposely not been extended beyond December, 1932. The Banking Panic of 1933 and the inauguration of the so-called New Deal economic policies may be considered as marking the termination of the secondary post-War business cycle. Our major interest is with the causes and aspects of that cycle, not with either the New Deal program or the current recovery. A host of volumes treating of the Government's recovery program has appeared since 1933; it is not our desire merely to add to that list. Rather, it is just because so many of the books of the last few years which have dealt with recovery display so little understanding of the causes of the Great Depression that an analysis of those causes is in order. Also, the fact that many Governmental policies aimed at promoting recovery reflect inadequate appreciation of the fundamental causes of the last cycle is added justification for the concentration of major attention upon the depression and the events leading up to it. If no lessons have been learned from the last depression, then eventually the evils of depression may be but worse compounded. With the necessity for regulating "the coming boom" already a subject for comment, and with a racing stock market again confronting us, a sober backward glance at the causes of the last boom can scarcely be amiss.

Diagnosis without prescription, however, admittedly is of little therapeutic value. It is not enough to direct attention to the phases of the last cycle and to the causes of the last depression, to the exclusion of the causes and the conditions for recovery as such. An explanation of the causes of the Great Depression will not of itself point the way to a satisfactory and enduring recovery. The diagnosis inherent in that explanation should, nevertheless, indicate the line of treatment to be followed if the economic system is to be relieved of its depression illness; recovery measures should take account of the causes and nature of depressions, and of business cycles generally. If, therefore, the theory of the business cycle and the explanation of the Great Depression herein developed are accurate, an adequate recovery program should be related thereto. It should be equally self-evident that recovery measures which are based upon those theories of the business cycle whose essential falsity we have already emphasized may end by producing even more far-reaching disaster. Foolhardy procedures which are divorced from economic realities, or whose economic implications are not understood by their promoters, do not perforce become sanctified and wise merely by designating them as "action"; tilting at windmills does not draw water.

We turn at this point, then, to a brief examination of certain aspects of the current recovery, and to the task of indicating, at somewhat greater length, certain conditions which we believe it is imperative should be present to assure a better balanced and more lasting recovery. That the United States is at this time experiencing a marked degree of recovery is now apparent to any well-informed observer of the contemporary economic scene. Proposals of alternative policies, or criticisms of the deficiencies of the present recovery program, therefore run the risk not only of being unwelcome but also court the danger of increasing "out-of-dateness" as the pace of recovery may quicken. Why discuss the causes and conditions of recovery when Recovery is here? To say "what should have been done," or to propose "what must be done" even now, if difficulties for the future are to be averted, will no doubt appear to many as merely Cassandra-like croakings. But when a recovery program, which, while it may appear effective, depends for its efficacy upon much the same kind of "cheap money" inflation which our analysis has shown was the main cause of the Great

Depression, then the present recovery must ultimately prove as illusory as the New Era of the 'twenties; and it is the duty of economists to pierce the veil of illusion.

Although, as just stated, we have at long last turned the corner from depression to recovery, it is nevertheless true that many unpleasant reminders of depression are still with us. To those who take a realistic view of the current situation, its paradoxes must at least give cause for wonderment. Certainly the recovery movement to the date of this writing is a peculiar one: it is shot through with anomalies. With the estimates ranging from as little as 8 million to as great as 12 million unemployed, with governmental relief rolls still at high levels, and with the United States ranking sixth among the nations of the world in degree of recovery from the depths of depression, there very obviously is something wrong, somewhere. The paradox of rising profits accompanied by increased and extra dividends for many corporations while the earnings of capital in many important industries is still negative, the anomaly of rising wage rates for men in employment in some industries at a time when widespread unemployment still prevails, and the phenomena of higher tax rates, higher governmental income, and greater Treasury deficits than have been witnessed in any peacetime period in our history, all demand explanation. The pleasing prospect of a runaway bull market in the Stock Exchange should not again be permitted to delude us into an ostrich-like attitude toward other sectors of the economic field.

The fact would seem to be that the authorities who are undertaking the "management" of the current recovery, and congratulating themselves that prosperity is returning because they "planned it so," are utterly oblivious of the fact that recovery is being engineered largely by the same means which produced the last boom—and depression. With this difference: whereas the banking system during the 'twenties was producing an investment credit inflation by extending credit to business men and corporations, Government is now assuming the rôle of inducing new deposit currency in the banking system and thereby producing a consumption credit inflation. The Federal Government, instead of private corporations, is issuing the bonds which the banks are now purchasing, thereby inflating the deposit currency structure all over again. These "created" funds are in this instance being used principally to finance consumption expenditures through relief disbursements, make-work projects, and the like. This newly created Bank Money, in circulating through the economic system, is ultimately finding its way into corporate treasuries in the form of newly created profits and into individuals' bank accounts as newly created monetary income. The profits are again being used to finance new capital development, and the enhanced income of individuals is helping to promote the stock market boom. Thus the inflationary procedure of the current cycle reverses somewhat that of previous ones, when the new credit first entered the system through the capital goods industries and from there filtered through the economic system to the consumption goods field and to the stock market. Perhaps the boom will thereby be a little slower in gaining headway than previous ones; but the point to be noted is that the two procedures are in essence the same: they both depend upon an inflation of bank credit at a rate faster than the rate of increase of physical production. And the fact to be emphasized is that the current inflation tends to conceal and to preserve the fundamental disequilibria which so prolonged the Great Depression and which we are now carrying over therefrom without having once squarely faced the problem of correcting them. It is doubtful whether any given amount of inflation will cure these disequilibria. When the inevitable depression succeeds such an artificially created boom as is now being engendered, we may no doubt expect the "managers" of the recovery, judging by their published and spoken utterances, to assess blame for that depression almost anywhere but where it rightfully will belong.

For these reasons, it is at this point desirable to gain a closer but brief view of the chief means by which recovery is being effected. The underlying philosophy of the Administration's attempts at recovery rests in the under-consumption theory of depressions. The familiar "prime the pump" argument is but an expression of this idea: all that is necessary, it is argued, is that new monetary purchasing power be generated in the economic system, and the pump of production will again function. This neglects the fact that if the pump were in good working order, priming would be unnecessary, and that if the pump is not in order, then it were better to find out why it is not. For if its continued functioning is dependent only upon continued priming, then the priming deserves to be termed by its proper name, inflation; and as soon as the priming ceases, so will the pumping.

Now, whence comes this new purchasing power? The explanation is simple, but significant. It carries us back to familiar ground already traversed in previous chapters. We have pointed out that when the banks purchase new bond issues, they thereby increase bank deposits, just as when they increase their loans. In the one case, corporate credit is being monetized by the banking machinery; in the other case, it is the Government's credit which is being monetized; in *both* cases, new monetary purchasing power is being created in the form of deposit currency. Specifically, when the Government issues ten billion dollars in Government bonds and sells them to the banks, the banks in purchasing these bonds give the Government new deposit credit on their books to the extent of ten billion dollars. Against this ten-billion-dollar deposit credit the Government may now write checks to pay relief recipients, WPA workers, bonuses for not raising wheat or cotton, or any of the many disbursements now being assumed by the Government.

It is illuminating to follow the course of these checks as they circulate throughout the economic and financial systems. They are turned over by the original recipients to their landlords, to their grocers, or used to pay old debts; or they are used to buy new shoes, new automobiles, or for amusements. These secondary recipients commonly deposit the checks in *their* banks. We now find that these individuals, collectively, are possessed of ten billion dollars of bank deposits that they did not have before; instead of the newly created deposits standing to the credit of the Government on the banks' books, a like amount now stands to the credit of business concerns, corporations, and individuals. There is thus an *increase* of ten billion dollars in the total of bank deposits. We might follow this new deposit currency through several more circuits, but the process should by now be familiar. The important thing to note is that the Government, in its policy of financing relief and recovery by issuing bonds which are purchased principally by the banks, is aiding in the creation of new deposits in the banking system, which begin by being a credit to the Government's account and continue as credits to individuals and corporations. For one thing is certain: these newly created deposits are not self-liquidating in character; once ten billion dollars in new deposits has been created in this fashion, that amount of deposits continues in the banking system so long as the deficit borrowing continues and the bonds are not retired.[1]

## No Easy Road to Recovery from Depression

There is, unfortunately, no broad, smooth, "royal road" to Recovery. Instead, we are almost always confronted with the somber prospect of being obliged to double back over virtually the same paths by which we descended to the trough of depression if the recovery is to have a solid foundation. It is usually necessary to retrace our steps until we arrive at a condition in some respects similar to that prevailing at the inception of the previous boom; ill-advised attempts to "short-cut" that route are foredoomed to fall

---

[1] Or unless the bonds are sold by the banks to the public, who pay for the bonds by writing checks against deposits.

short of their mark. It is gross folly to expect genuine and balanced recovery to flow from conditions and measures which maintain the disequilibria which characterize depression.

The discussion which follows, therefore, has general applicability to recovery from any depression—past, recent, or future—originally generated by monetary means. Although making use of the analysis of the causes of the recent depression as set forth in earlier chapters, the proposals which follow merely utilize the processes which in the main have been followed in effecting recovery from all past depressions. As the original impulsion for the last boom came from the monetary side during a period of relative equilibrium, producing an alteration in the structure of production which terminated in general disequilibrium for the whole economy, it is first necessary to restore at least some semblance of that original equilibrium so that new capital development once more becomes possible and genuinely profitable. Had attempts at recovery since 1929 aimed simply at the restoration of equilibrium in the economic system, it is most unlikely that the "spottiness" of the present recovery would be so marked.

The pressing need is still to restore a measurable state of economic balance within the system, rather than to restore superprosperity. Prosperity of the 1927–1929 sort can wait; indeed, it may even be hoped that that particular brand of prosperity never returns. What is now essential is to put men back to work—in a word, *to produce;* and the restoration of employment, and production, are dependent upon equilibrium. At the same time, it is imperative to eliminate the inflationary uncertainties inherent in the continued unbalanced budgets and deficit borrowing that constitute ominous threats to the future stability both of the currency and the credit of the Federal Government, and also to discontinue the damage to the public morale inherent in our Americanized system of the dole under the thinly disguised name of relief work.

SAVING VERSUS SPENDING OUR WAY TO PROSPERITY

Although the fundamental causes of depression are footed in the inherently inflationistic character of the banking machinery, it by no means follows that monetary influences are the sole cause for continuance of depression, nor that the only way of escape is *via* the monetary route.[1] The severity and duration of the recent depression are attributable to the third of the links in the chain of causation elaborated above, the loss of equilibrium. The fact that general disequilibrium has persisted, particularly that between costs and prices, is the reason why so little new investment has been made for a number of years; and because investment activity is still at a low ebb, unemployment has continued.[2] To recover from depression it is necessary that the capital-goods industries should revive and that investment activity should again proceed under its own power. In other words, we must *save* our way out of depression, we must increase the real savings that make the creation of real capital possible, instead of spending our way to recovery by cumulating governmental deficits which concentrate attention on consumption as has now been done for five years.[3] But in order for real savings to be forthcoming (or to be used) to finance new investment it is first essential that at least relative equilibrium be restored.

[1] "We are required to assume that if it is true that trade fluctuations are primarily monetary phenomena, therefore the only way we can get out of the muddle is by the Central Banks taking action. It may very well be that the main reasons for fluctuation in the volume of trade and for the existence of the cycle are to be found in the mismanagement of the credit system by Central or Commercial Banks. I do not think that it follows that you can therefore show that the proper method of overcoming the depression is by means of Central Bank action." Gregory, T. E., in his discussion of O. M. W. Sprague's paper on "Major and Minor Trade Fluctuations," in the *Journal of the Royal Statistical Society* (1931), Vol. XCIV, Part IV, p. 549.

[2] "I find the explanation of the current business losses, of the reduction of output, and of the unemployment which necessarily ensues on this not in the high level of investment which was proceeding up to the spring of 1929, but in the subsequent cessation of this investment. I see no hope of a recovery except in a revival of the high level of investment." Keynes, J. M., "An Economic Analysis of Unemployment," in *Unemployment as a World Problem*, p. 12.

[3] "It is not necessary here to repeat all the arguments in support of the view that, during this depression no less than in all previous ones, intensive saving is an essential condition for an increased output of capital goods. * * * It is now gen-

## EQUILIBRIUM BEGETS PURCHASING POWER

Dean A. B. Adams is correct, it is believed, in holding that each cycle tends to terminate in equilibrium [1]—which is but another way of saying that recovery cannot make real progress until an equilibrium condition obtains. During the Great Depression, however, virtually every conceivable action was taken to postpone the termination date of the last cycle and to prolong the lack of equilibrium in existence at the time the slump set in. There seems little evidence that this problem has yet been seriously faced or that the necessity for facing it is yet widely appreciated. Until the problem is recognized, it seems doubtful that the character of the recovery can prove altogether satisfactory to its sponsors.

The focal point of attack in the restoration of equilibrium is the cost-price relationship. The most significant disequilibrium still persisting is that between costs, prices, and profits. The level of prices is a given datum, however, a *fait accompli*. There is, as a matter of fact, no good reason why recovery could not proceed from a low level of prices; but there are, on the other hand, serious flaws in the doctrine that recovery is impossible until prices have risen to some mythical level. Most of the positive action aiming at recovery so far has sought to correct the disparity between prices and costs by raising the price level up to the cost level by means of credit expansion, rather than by increasing the real volume of purchasing power by enlarging production employment irrespective of the price level. There is no necessary objection to an enlarged volume of credit, as will

erally agreed that the main function of any policy that aims at combatting the crisis is to create possibilities for increased production in the means-of-production group, in which unemployment is most serious. * * * There is manifestly no surplus of money awaiting long-term investment; if there were the Stock Exchange and the investment market would present quite a different aspect. Within the extremely contracted field of savings there is now, during the depression, a *relatively* large supply of short-term credit awaiting short-term investment in the banks, * * * but there is in particular a lack of *that type of credit* that is a *sine qua non* of an increase in the long-run production of fresh capital goods." Johan Åkermann, *Economic Forecast and Realty, 1928-1932*, p. 19.

[1] Adams, A. B., *Economics of Business Cycles* (New York: McGraw-Hill Book Co., Inc., 1925).

be explained shortly; there is, however, ample cause for dissent from the idea that worth-while recovery can be effected solely by monetary means, as well as for disagreement with the view that the timing of the expansion of credit is a matter of but slight importance. To engineer a price rise by inflationary measures without first correcting the more important maladjustments inherited from the past boom, while it may generate a temporary recovery or even a boom, is tantamount to "freezing" those maladjustments at their depression level and thus preventing a more genuine and lasting recovery. It should be pointed out, further, that to carry those maladjustments over to the depression which ensues when the present inflationary price-raising experiment comes to an end is but to court possible worse disaster at that time. We have already shown that the prosperity of the 'twenties, fed by bank credit inflation, concealed disequilibria which we carried over from the 1920–1921 depression; the recovery of the 'thirties, likewise financed by bank credit inflation, conceals maladjustments which were not corrected during the Great Depression. The absolute level of prices, it must be repeated, is not so important as the relationships between particular prices and particular cost margins. It seems much less hazardous for long-run stability, therefore, to effect the needed adjustments between costs and prices by reducing costs rather than by forcing prices up by means of inflationary credit expansion.

## COST REDUCTION, EARNINGS ON CAPITAL, AND THE STANDARD OF LIVING

But the question of cost reduction, unfortunately, is inextricably mixed up with those larger questions of wage levels and purchasing power, of ideas of social justice and the standard of living, and can be dissociated from political implications only with great difficulty. These are issues which almost always arouse controversial misunderstandings, because rooted in popular misconceptions of the real relationships between costs and prices, between wages and purchasing power. Nevertheless, popular prejudices and specious rationalizations should not be permitted to obscure the logical conclusion that what is needed, if relative equilibrium is again to appear and if the recovery is to be more than an ephemeral one, is a reduction of certain wage rates which are out of line with the accomplished reduction in prices and the cost of living. "The present plan is a war against unemployment and its success is purely a matter of fairly simple organization to overcome the existing disequilibrium between commodity prices and money costs of production." [1] "It will of course appear nonsensical to those who hold that the cure for unemployment is to be found in raising wages and so increasing consumption and the demand for consumption goods. Of course, if wages could be raised without making any other change whatever, that argument would be plausible." [2]

The objection will doubtless be raised that, even though cost reduction may be the only sure way out of the dilemma, there may be possibilities of lowering costs other than by reduction of wage rates, and that cost reduction should not be achieved exclusively at the expense of the wage-earner. Why should not Capital, in other words, be made to bear some part of the burden? It may be answered, in the first place, that the wage contract is the most flexible of the contracts involved in the processes of production: the terms of employment are rarely definite in time, nor of long duration. Secondly, Capital during the depression experienced larger cuts than is generally appreciated, in the way of conversions, reorganizations, and scaling down of interest payments, not to mention bankruptcies, for many classes of bonds, and in the form of reduced or passed dividends for many stocks. Furthermore, conversions of bonds bearing high rates of interest to lower schedules have been proceeding in 1935 and 1936 at a prodigious pace. Such dividend schedules as

---

[1] Graham, F. D., *The Abolition of Unemployment*, p. 89.
[2] Beveridge, Sir W. H., *Unemployment: A Problem of Industry*, p. 89.

were maintained during the depression in most cases were cared for out of past-accumulated surpluses, net earnings to capital in general being realized only in the last year or two. Thirdly, employers generally during the depression effected cost-saving economies in other directions to the limit of their abilities; indeed, in many instances it was only by virtue of savings in overhead costs and by postponement of repairs and replacements that production was possible at all. But the consequences of the policy of refraining from providing for obsolescence and depreciation proved to be that the capital-goods industries suffered the more severely and that unemployment was thereby more widespread. Lastly, it should be noted that although the *contract* of employment is highly flexible, the wage rate itself proved to be one of the most inflexible of the many rigidities in evidence during the depression: an attempt to appraise the significance of this fact leads into the questions of real wages as contrasted with money wages, of wage rates as compared with total wages, and of total wages and total effective purchasing power.

*The Common and Current Misunderstanding of Relations between Monetary Wage Rates and "Real" Purchasing Power*

What is hoped to be accomplished by a reduction of wage rates is *an increase of aggregate purchasing power*. To many persons, unfortunately, this may seem to be a paradoxical statement. For the greatest confusion has reigned on the subject of wages and purchasing power throughout the depression, during the years of hyper-prosperity when the doctrine of high wages was at its zenith, and now. All too many writers who discuss wages and purchasing power point to the fact that the indexes of weekly earnings are below their pre-depression levels, and hence argue that wages have already been reduced as much as labor can stand; and they are quite correct in contending that total purchasing power has been reduced because weekly earnings have declined. They neglect, however, to call attention to the fact that there was no great reduction of wage *rates* during the depression, and they refuse to see any connection between the rigidity of wage rates (the *hourly rate* as contrasted with the daily or weekly wage payment)—making it necessary to resort to part-time working schedules, share-work schemes, and other similar uneconomic programs—and the reduction in weekly earnings.

The arguments in opposition to the reduction of wage rates (as a means of increasing total purchasing power during a period of widespread unemployment) rest on the confusion of wage rates and total wage income, and indicate an inability (or unwillingness) to understand the difference between money wages and "real wages." Perhaps a more accurate statement would be that the real nature of wages is obscured by the monetary label which attaches to them.[1] All arguments opposing reductions in monetary wage rates during a period when unemployment prevails reveal a lack of comprehension of the interrelations among wage rates, unit costs, prices, and volume of employment. They seek to stress the purchasing power of wages as an influence upon consumption without recognizing that wages enter prominently into costs for the producers and into prices for the consumers. It is contended that as wage rates are reduced, purchasing power is also diminished; with a lower level of wages, costs, and prices, it is frequently argued, the incomes of the wage-earners will still be insufficient to generate an increase in demand for consumers' goods, and all that will result from a reduction of wage rates is a lower standard of

---

[1] "The tendency upon the part of labor to estimate wages solely in terms of dollars frequently leads to serious economic error. The real significance of the wage labor receives is not the dollar in hand but rather what the dollar will buy. Wages are always comparative. Cheap money means dear commodities; dear money means cheap commodities." *The Labor Banker*, issued by the Brotherhood Investment Company, an organization affiliated with the Brotherhood of Locomotive Engineers: quoted in the National City Bank *Letter*, October, 1932, p. 159. And *cf.* Pigou, A. C.: "To a great extent people—employers and employed alike—think in money. Our income is [stated in terms of] our money income, and it requires an effort to realize that, provided the price of the things we buy with money has halved, we are really no worse off with a money income that is also halved." *The Theory of Unemployment* (London: Macmillan & Company, 1933), p. 294.

living.    Hence the reduction of costs through wage rate reductions is said to lead inevitably to an endless spiral of deflation, with falling prices being followed by further wage reductions, and so on, resulting in ever-greater unemployment and ending in complete collapse.

Such theories look only on one side of the account.  They view money wages as original purchasing power, coming from out of the blue.  They fail to take into consideration the fact that the incomes of individuals are for the most part made up of, *i.e.*, are identical with, the expenditures by business enterprises; abstention from expenditure by business concerns results directly and indirectly in the loss of income both for other business concerns and for individuals, for [1] " * * * most of the dollars which they [individuals] receive come to them because business enterprises have been willing to buy services and commodities for them."   And the reason entrepreneurs are willing to buy labor services in exchange for a price (wages) is because they are able, in view of the relations of costs and prices, to market their products at a profit, or because they *think* they can do so.  When the money price of wages is such as to induce entrepreneurs to go on producing, employment is steady.  Money is simply a convenient means for exchanging goods and services, a convenient way of expressing the purchasing power which is ultimately bottomed in the exchange of goods and services.

Furthermore, opponents of a policy of wage rate reductions as a recovery measure persist in confusing the issue by stressing the purported relationship between wage rates and the standard of living.  Either they erroneously infer that those arguing for a reduction of wage *rates* are plying a campaign for the reduction of *wages*, or else they designedly imply that a reduction of wage rates will automatically lead to a lowered standard of living.  They do this by confusing, either by intention or from ignorance, a reduction of wage *rates* with a reduction of *wages*.  As a matter of fact, the primary objective of the sincere proponents of a policy of

[1] Sumner Slichter, *Towards Stability*, p. 4.

wage rate reductions is the increasing of aggregate wages. There is no direct connection between the hourly rate and the standard of living; the standard of living, on the other hand, is a function of the total wage income and the cost of living. A program of reduction of wage rates, which brings costs into line with prices so that entrepreneurs are induced to embark upon greater productive operations, will put unemployed workers back onto jobs, will expand the aggregate of wage payments, and will enhance the total volume of consumer purchasing power. For surely it is futile to talk of a sacrosanct standard of living when eight million people are unemployed. *Whose* standard of living is contemplated? Only those in employment? A "standard" necessarily connotes an average, and it is the average of the whole population (employed as well as unemployed) which is involved in the computation of a standard of living. The brutal truth is that the standard of life for the American people has fallen drastically since 1929 for the simple reason that the policy of maintaining high wage rates has resulted in reduced employment and decreased production of the goods and services that constitute "real income."

If all workers were employed, it is possible that a reduction of wage rates would bring a reduction of total purchasing power, because in that situation total wage payments would also be reduced.[1]    But given a situation where, say, only half the employable population has work but wage rates are maintained at the level which prevailed when the unemployment set in, purchasing power is reduced by half, for [2] "an unemployed laborer has no purchasing power at all, however high may be the wage rate he would get if he had a job." If, now, wage rates are reduced by 30 per cent, so that it becomes profitable in view of the new relationship between costs and prices to employ 100 per cent of the workers again, purchasing power is increased by 40 per cent

---

[1] This would not *necessarily* follow, however, if prices and the cost of living declined proportionately.

[2] Jacob Viner, *Balanced Deflation, Inflation, or More Depression* (The Day and Hour Series, the University of Minnesota, No. 3, 1933), p. 11.

(from 50 per cent to 70 per cent of the original figure), even though it stands at 30 per cent less than the level prevailing during the previous period of full employment. But if prices and the cost of living are also 30 per cent lower than in the first period of full employment there is no relative reduction of purchasing power whatever—"real wages" are the same in each instance.

### REDUCING WAGE RATES WOULD LEAD TO INCREASED WAGES—AN ILLUSTRATION

What, it may be asked, will induce entrepreneurs to increase their aggregate costs by embarking upon the larger spending programs involved in hiring back that half of the population which was unemployed, with no assurance of an increase in prices? The answer involves an obvious but very important point—namely, that the reduction of wage rates enables the manufacturer to reduce his *unit costs* materially, and this follows because his income is increased more than proportionately to the increase in his total costs, including overhead and labor costs. This point is seldom adequately stressed by the proponents of a policy of wage rate reduction, and is commonly neglected altogether by the opponents of such a policy; it will perhaps be made more clear by the following illustration, admittedly unrealistic in some of its assumptions (as all specific examples of general propositions are apt to be), but sufficiently close to the real state of affairs in the business world to clarify the principle involved.

Assume (Case I) an economic system with 10,000,000 men employed at $1 a day working 6 days a week, or an aggregate weekly wage of $60,000,000 (it is convenient to use a daily wage rate instead of an hourly one to simplify the calculation; it does not vitiate the illustration if it be assumed that the number of hours worked *per day* at the $1 wage does not change throughout). Add an assumed $30,000,000 for overhead and other costs and weekly total cost is $90,000,000. If the 10,000,000 workers produce 60,000,000 units of product during a week, the cost per unit is $1.50. If the product sells for $1.50 the entrepreneurs just break even (it is also convenient to leave the question of profit out of consideration, and to assume that the entrepreneurs are content to go on producing at full capacity if they neither gain nor lose).

Let us now assume that this situation is altered (Case II): The price of the product falls (for reasons beyond the control of the entrepreneurs, as happens during any depression) by 30 per cent, to $1.05 per unit. At this price the entrepreneurs see fit, let us say, to discharge 30 per cent of the workers; overhead costs are reduced 30 per cent; and a 5-day week is inaugurated (a very realistic assumption during this depression!) for the remaining 7,000,000 workers in employment, but their daily wage rate remains at $1. [1] The total wage bill is now $35,000,000 per week, overhead costs are $21,000,000, and total weekly costs are $56,000,000. But if those workers now in employment produce at their same daily rate per man, the number of units of output is now 35,000,000 weekly and the cost per unit is no longer $1.50, but $1.60; unit costs have *risen* with a reduced volume of output, and a loss of 55 cents per unit is experienced at the price of $1.05. [2]   It is apparent, furthermore, that this situation cannot continue for long, because such heavy losses will "wipe out" more and more employers and in consequence unemployment will grow progressively.

Now assume further (Case III) that the daily wage rate is reduced 30 per cent. At a 70-cent daily rate the 3,000,000 unemployed are rehired and the full 10,000,000 again work 6 days a week for a weekly wage of $4.20 per man, or a total weekly wage of $42,000,000 as against the $35,000,000 weekly wage in Case II. If overhead costs remain at $21,-

---

[1] In the interest of simplification, no figures for marginal returns per unit of costs are introduced in the above illustration. As the figures stand, they may seem to indicate that marginal productivity per man per day is $1.05, and therefore that additional men might profitably be employed at a wage of $1.00 per day. This conclusion is not intended, of course; the discrepancy in the figures arises out of the fact that no account is taken of the cost of materials and other variable costs, and this again in order to simplify as much as possible.

[2] Unit costs *need not* rise *above* the previous figure, in actuality; but they almost certainly will stand at some point above selling price.

000,000, total costs per week are now $63,000,000. But as weekly output is again 60,000,000 units, the cost per unit falls to $1.05. Since the price is (assumed to remain at) $1.05, an exact equivalence of costs and prices is attained once more; instead of a 55-cent loss per unit, the entrepreneurs again break even. And this situation provides for full re-employment and an increase in aggregate purchasing power of $7,000,000 weekly, or 20 per cent, over Case II.

It is of course true that the 7,000,000 men now working 6 days a week at the $4.20 wage are situated less favorably than when they were working 5 days for $5.00; however, as was pointed out above, their former advantage was necessarily of a temporary and highly precarious nature. Moreover, it is surely self-evident that general social and economic welfare is enhanced greatly by having the full 10,000,000 employed, even at the reduced daily and weekly rate. And the 7,000,000 are no worse off in Case III than they were in Case I, because the $4.20 wage will buy as much "real income" at a $1.05 unit price as did the $6 wage at a price of $1.50 per unit.

Oversimplified as it admittedly is, the above illustration goes to the heart of the matter of wage rates and wages, or "real" wages and "real" purchasing power. The business man's calculations and activities are ultimately bottomed on the relation between his unit costs and his unit selling prices. As his unit costs fall, he is motivated to increase output; doing so, he will hire more workers, even if his *total* costs go up. As soon as he rehires workers, however, he automatically starts to circulating the additional purchasing power that is needed to take the increased output off the market. For as Professor Slichter has well stated, the income of consumers depends directly, and largely, upon the volume of business spending: [1] "This means that the fluctuations in consumer incomes, which produce fluctuations in consumer spending, are the *result* of changes which have *already* occurred in business spending. Consequently, the explana-

[1] Slichter, *op. cit.*, p. 4.

tion of fluctuations in the total volume of spending must be sought, not in spending by consumers, but in spending by business enterprises."

## The Fallaciousness of the Doctrine that High Wage Rates Are Synonymous with Full Purchasing Power

Perhaps no single action taken during the depression had more to do with its prolongation than that of former President Hoover, acting under a mistaken notion as to the real nature of wages and deluded by the doctrine of high purchasing power (possibly a pardonable delusion, in view of its widespread popularity), when he asked employers in November of 1929 to maintain their wage rates (unless it was the instituting of the NRA—but it is probable there would have been no NRA, nor New Deal either, had it not been for the Hoover experiment of November, 1929). Professor Viner's judgment on Mr. Hoover's action in this connection, as well as his views on the subject of wage rates and purchasing power in general, are in point: [1]

> President Hoover would have rendered a service instead of a disservice to labor if instead of pledging employers to maintain wage rates he had obtained from them a pledge to maintain their total employment, with freedom to reduce wages as circumstances made necessary. * * * ALL THAT IS GUARANTEED BY WAGE RATES HIGHER THAN EMPLOYERS CAN AFFORD TO PAY AND STILL GIVE EMPLOYMENT TO THE AVAILABLE SUPPLY OF LABOR IS UNEMPLOYMENT. * * * LARGE PAYROLLS DO MEAN HIGH PURCHASING POWER, BUT HIGH WAGES MAY AND OFTEN DO REDUCE RATHER THAN INCREASE THE SIZE OF THE TOTAL PAYROLL. * * * It would be very nice if simply by doubling or tripling all wage rates overnight, we could end the depression, but its effect would be rather to make unemployment complete instead of partial.

## Wage Rates, Depression and Recovery— 1920–1921 and 1929–1936

In previous depressions wage rates were generally reduced rather drastically, and with comparative rapidity. And

[1] *Balanced Deflation, Inflation, or More Depression,* p. 12.

recovery from past depressions proceeded from the time when a comparative equilibrium of wage costs and prices was again achieved. The rigidity of wage rates during the Great Depression, on the other hand, is one of the outstanding features which differentiates it from previous ones. An examination of the index of wage rates in manufacturing industries will suffice to indicate the rapidity and extent of the reduction accomplished during the 1920–1921 depression. In the third quarter of 1920 (the quarter in which the depression set in) the index number of wage rates stood at 245 (using 1914 as the base year); during the fourth quarter of 1920 the index did not change; but during the respective quarters of 1921 the wage-rate index declined successively to 229, 217, 205, and 192. Prices in the meantime declined from a high of 247 in the second quarter of 1920 to approximately 140 in the third quarter of 1921. The following table, by contrast, indicates the slowness with which wage rates gave way during the recent depression. It shows that wage rates in manufacturing industries after three years of this depression were as high as they were at the end of 1921; yet the price level was below the 1913 level and the cost of living was only 28 per cent above the 1913 level. Wage rates declined in one year, from the third quarter of 1920 to the fourth quarter of 1921, by 22 per cent; from the third quarter of 1929 to the third quarter of 1931, two full years, wage rates declined but 4 per cent, and there was no change at all during the first year of the Great Depression.

TABLE XXV

WAGE RATES IN MANUFACTURING INDUSTRIES
(1914 = 100)

| YEAR | MANUFACTURING WAGE RATES, HOURLY | | | |
|---|---|---|---|---|
| | Quarter I | Quarter II | Quarter III | Quarter IV |
| 1929 | | | 239 | 240 |
| 1930 | 240 | 240 | 240 | 236 |
| 1931 | 233 | 231 | 229 | 221 |
| 1932 | 213 | 205 | 196 | 190 |

Source: The National Industrial Conference Board.

Mention has already been made of one charge frequently made against a policy of wage rate reduction, namely, that it is inevitably deflationary, leading to a sequence of falling prices followed by falling wage rates which in turn result in further price declines, the whole process cumulating unemployment and ending in complete prostration. This indictment might deserve some measure of serious consideration if it were not made with complete disregard for existing disparities between prices and wages, were it not that price deflation is an accomplished fact without a corresponding reduction in wage rates. Furthermore, this argument neglects to consider that there is *some* point at which falling wage rates will catch up with falling prices; *at* that point, prices will cease to decline because of the greater demand engendered by increased employment made profitable at the new (equilibrium) level of costs and prices. The above table aids in refuting the contention that wage rate reductions can only result in a cumulative further fall of prices. The most rapid decline in prices occurred during the first two years of depression when wage rates were reduced but little; and, on the other hand, the period of the most marked reduction in wage rates was also the period when the decline in prices slackened.[1]   The reduction of wage rates from the third quarter of 1929 to the third quarter of 1931 was but 4 per cent, and during these two years prices fell precipitately; from the third quarter of 1931 to the third quarter of 1932 wage rates were reduced 14 per cent, and in this twelve-month the decline in prices slowed down markedly; and beginning in the third quarter of 1932 there was a positive recovery in business activity.   The maintenance of wage

[1] *Cf.*, in this connection, Åkermann's *Economic Forecast and Reality, 1928–1932*, p. 22: "The time-factor connecting the fall of the price level with that of the wage level really calls for special inquiry, but even without it we can at any rate draw attention to the fact that during the present depression the price level fell most heavily during the first two years (1929–1931), when the wage level was maintained virtually unaltered, whereas the first three quarters of 1932 witnessed a tendency towards stabilization of the price level combined with a heavy all-round reduction of the wage level. *If it were true that a reduction of the wage level would cause a simultaneous and corresponding fall in prices, there would of course be no way of accounting for this fact.*"

rates at 90 per cent above the 1914 level (at the end of 1932) would not have worked havoc if prices and the cost of living had also been 90 per cent above the 1914 level. The fact remains, however, that prices in 1932 were below the 1914 level and the cost of living was but slightly above the 1914 level. Hence there existed an uneconomic level of real wages, and the inevitable result of a level of real wages that is too high is unemployment.[1]

But what, it may be asked, is the justification of this long discussion about the necessity of reductions in wage rates? The answer is that it is purposed to establish conclusively the nature of this requisite step on the road to recovery.

### RESTORATION OF EQUILIBRIUM BETWEEN NATURAL AND MARKET RATES OF INTEREST

It is essential to reduce wage rates so as to restore the equilibrium between costs and prices in order that there may emerge at least a reasonable prospect of profits to induce business concerns to expand production and increase employment. This directs attention once more to the realized rate of return to capital and its relation to the market rate of interest. It has been shown that when there is a disequilibrium between the natural and market rates of interest in favor of the former, new investment becomes profitable; it has been indicated that the market rate is the more

---

[1] "Under the present social system real wage rates cannot be raised beyond a point without inducing unemployment. Apart from improvements in methods of production and so on, it is impossible both to maintain existing money wages when commodity prices are falling and to raise them parallel to commodity prices when these are rising except at the cost of a large number of people being unable to find work. Since January, 1930, the Board of Trade index of general commodity prices has fallen some 20 per cent; the cost of living index some 14 per cent; and the index of money wages 5 per cent. During this period of heavy depression there has thus taken place a substantial rise in the rate of real wages for persons in employment. I think that we should be frank about this matter. It is, in my opinion, beyond question that this state of things is responsible for the high level of unemployment. Maybe this is an unpopular doctrine. If so it is the more the duty of economists to announce it." Pigou, A. C., in a letter to the London *Times*, August 4, 1933, p. vi; and *cf.* Beveridge, W. H., *Unemployment: A Problem of Industry*, p. 371: " * * * as a matter of theory, the continuance in any country of a substantial volume of unemployment which cannot be explained by specific maladjustments of place, quality, and time, is in itself proof that the price being asked for labor as wages is too high for the conditions of the market; demand for and supply of labor are not finding their appropriate price for meeting."

variable of the two rates of interest; and it has been further shown that under some circumstances the market rate may be artificially depressed below the natural rate by the liberal issuance of bank credit which is inflationary in its effects.

It is possible, however, to achieve the same end by raising the "natural" or "productivity" rate, that is, by making the currently anticipated return at important investment margins a profitable one by lowering wages and other "direct" costs. When losses are being sustained generally over a wide range of industry, the marginal productivity rate of capital approaches zero; but by reducing variable costs, losses may be converted into profits and the anticipated rate of return to capital at new investment margins increased. It is therefore necessary to bring about a re-emergence of those conditions where the expected rate of return to capital is in excess of the cost paid for loanable funds: the market rate of interest conceivably may stand at zero, but if the average return to capital is represented by positive losses and all that will result from borrowing is more losses, loanable funds will not be employed to finance new productive activity.

Stated bluntly, it is desirable to bring about a redistribution of the national dividend, to the temporary detriment of certain classes of (employed) labor, and in favor of the capitalist-entrepreneur in the form of profits which will stimulate investment activity and restore employment in the capital-goods industries. The important "structural" disequilibrium still persisting is that between consumption and saving, between the production of producers' goods and the production of consumers' goods, and this disequilibrium must be corrected before anything like normalcy can be expected to return. When the output of consumption goods declines by some 15 per cent while that of production goods falls 50 per cent and more, it is obviously essential to bring about a greater degree of correspondence between the two in order to restore the balanced relations which are necessary for the orderly progress of production. This restoration of balance can be effected by reducing wage rates, by bringing variable costs into such relation with prices that profits are no longer impossible of attainment, so that entrepreneurs again have a rational basis for making use of loanable funds.[1] A further consideration that makes important the rehabilitation of profits is that profits in large part are used to finance repairs and replacements, in order to take care of depreciation and obsolescence. It has already been pointed out that a large share of total saving is corporate saving, which is converted into investment goods directly through the process of "plowing back earnings" into plant improvements, new machinery, and the like, without the intermediation of the capital market. Not all business spending, in other words, is directly involved with the output of finished goods; some of it normally goes to the producers of capital equipment in order to maintain the existing machinery of production in good working order. When profits are not being made, when business income is negative, then maintenance, repairs, and replacement are postponed, with the effect of continuing unemployment in the capital industries.

### ACCELERATED ACTIVITY IN PRODUCTION OF DURABLE GOODS A KEY TO EMPLOYMENT AND RECOVERY

The great unsolved problem of the recovery movement is that of stimulating investment activity, whether through the reinvesting of business earnings in maintenance and in new equipment or through the conversion of the savings of the public into new investment goods by resort to the capital market. The greatest unemployment still prevailing is that among the makers of durable goods. Colonel Leonard Ayres in the Cleveland Trust Company *Bulletin* for January,

---

[1] "A redistribution of the present proceeds of industry, such that more would accrue to him [the entrepreneur], would not reduce the *existing* volume of purchasing power, but would induce him, by additional orders for raw material, plant and labour, to expand the volume of output and employment. * * * The mere fact that unemployment was falling would restore to the industries producing consumption goods part of the demand which they might temporarily have lost." Gregory, T. E., *Gold, Unemployment and Capitalism*, p. 39.

1934, estimates that of a total of almost 14 million persons without jobs at the peak of unemployment in March, 1933, 6½ million were from the durable goods industries, nearly 6 million were from the "service" industries, and only 1½ million were from the consumption goods industries.[1] Investment activity, in a word, is the tail that wags the industrial dog.

It is in the capital-goods industries, and in the construction industry in particular, that the greatest rigidity of wage rates appears. And it is precisely for this reason, in large part, that the construction industry and other durable goods industries are still depressed. The construction industry has been traditionally one of the most important in the country. In 1920 there were 2,467,500 employees in the building trades, as compared with 1,108,000 employed on steam railroads, 1,019,000 in mining, and less than a million in textiles; the iron and steel industry (essentially a capital-goods industry itself) with 3,107,000 workers, alone exceeded construction in number of employees.[2] The construction industry normally employs almost 18 per cent of those in non-agricultural pursuits, and from ten to eleven million people are estimated as being directly dependent upon construction for a living.[3] The industry's wage bill in 1926 was larger than that of any other industry, totaling approximately $3,000 million, in comparison with the $658 million wage bill of the motor vehicle industry.[4] It is estimated that in 1926 the volume of construction in the United States aggregated more than $7 billion in value; this may be compared with the figure of $6.5 billion gross operating revenues for the steam railroads, and with a value of $3.4 billion for the motor vehicles produced in 1925.[5]

[1] "The central fact about the great depression as we enter its fifth year is that there are nearly five million providers of services out of work because more than five million producers of durable goods are unemployed. These unemployed people in the durable goods industries are the controlling factor in our depression problem, and the whole program for increasing consumer purchasing power promises little help for them." Cleveland Trust Company *Bulletin,* December 15, 1933.

[2] Article on the Construction Industry in the *Encyclopedia of the Social Sciences,* Vol. IV, pp. 265–266.

[3] *Ibid.*   [4] *Ibid.*   [5] *Ibid.*

The construction industry, however, is financed to a large extent by savings forthcoming from persons and business units outside the industry. The situation differs from the case of the consumption goods industries, where the workers in a sense constitute (at least a large part of) the market for their own output; the purchasers of the output of the construction industry are the savers and other business concerns, whose incomes are not directly dependent upon personal employment *in that industry*. But the greater part of the incomes of the workers in the construction industry is spent for consumers' goods, so that revival of construction activity automatically increases demand, hence profits, hence employment, in the consumption goods industries. Logically, therefore, the cycle of revival starts in the construction industry (and other capital-goods industries), for increased constructional activity sets in motion a whole series of repercussions in allied and related lines which bring with them the return of high-level consumption.

### DESIRABILITY OF LOWER PRICES IN CAPITAL-GOODS INDUSTRIES DICTATES LOWERED WAGE RATES THEREIN

Unquestionably one of the pressing problems involved in the restoration of general equilibrium is that of regaining balanced relations between the prices of capital goods and the prices of other goods. It is in the capital-goods industries that the smallest relative decline in prices has occurred. This is but natural, however, in view of the relatively slight decline in wage rates that has taken place in those industries, and in consideration of the fact that labor costs constitute a greater proportion of total costs in the construction and durable goods industries in general than in the case of other industries. A survey conducted by the New York *Herald* in 1921 showed that labor received 85 cents of every dollar of cost in steel making, and 85 cents in building construction;[1] what the respective proportions may be today

[1] See Jordan, David F., *Practical Business Forecasting* (New York: Prentice-Hall, Inc., 1927), p. 239.

is difficult to ascertain, but estimates commonly place the percentage of labor costs in these industries in the neighborhood of 65 cents of each dollar. Thus prices for capital goods are high because wage rates in those industries are high; and it is imperative that the prices of capital goods approach the level of raw material and other prices before capital development can again proceed in any great volume.[1]

At this point it is desirable to drop the simplifying assumption used in the illustration of pages 226–228, above, that no change occurs in prices with a reduction of wage rates. For, actually, if wage rates decline in the industries producing durable goods the prices of such goods will tend to decline likewise, and as the prices of capital goods fall, savings and corporate surpluses will be used increasingly to finance new capital development or replacements, instead of lying idle in the banks or being used to purchase Government bonds to finance relief, as now. And as the demand for capital equipment revives, employment in the industries making capital goods will increase, setting in operation the reverberations in the consumption and other industries alluded to above. Therefore, instead of a program of universal wage rate reductions taking no account of the disequilibria prevailing among certain prices, there appears to be sound practical justification for the advocating of concentration of reductions of wage rates in the construction and other durable goods industries for the specific purpose of lowering the prices of capital goods.

Index numbers of wage rates in some of the principal building trades, based upon wage scales in effect in 1913 as 100, calculated from figures given in the *Monthly Labor Review*, are shown in the following table.

[1] "It is not simply a problem of how to raise prices. It is a problem of how to raise some prices and how to hold down, and even depress, other prices. For what is needed is to close the gaps which the depression has opened, and that means not only raising farm and raw materials prices, but holding down retail prices, and pushing down prices entering into capital equipment. For the prices of capital goods are still inordinately high as compared with other goods." Walter Lippmann, in the New York *Herald Tribune*, November 10, 1933.

TABLE XXVI

WAGE RATES IN THE BUILDING INDUSTRY
(1913 = 100)

| OCCUPATION | JULY, 1932 |
|---|---|
| Bricklayers | 193.7 |
| Building Laborers | 323.1 |
| Carpenters | 201.4 |
| Cement Finishers | 205.5 |
| Inside Wiremen | 237.2 |
| Painters | 248.0 |
| Plasterers | 200.2 |
| Plumbers | 201.8 |
| Stonecutters | 208.7 |
| Structural-iron Workers | 206.8 |

It will be seen that notwithstanding the reductions in wage scales made between 1929 and 1932, average rates in the above-named trades were still more than 100 per cent above the 1913 level. Here, then, is one of the key logs in the wage-jam which must be extricated before investment activity can effect any measurable recovery.

The wage and price policies of the United States Steel Corporation during the 1920–1921 depression, and during the Great Depression, offer an interesting comparison. Steel plays so prominent a rôle in all construction activity, and in the production of virtually all durable goods, as has already been pointed out, that the course of steel prices throws much light on the low state of activity in the capital-goods industries. In February of 1920 wages in the Steel Corporation were 46 cents an hour, up 130 per cent from 1914. On May 16, 1921, Steel's wages were reduced to 37 cents an hour, and on the 29th of August, slightly more than a year after the beginning of depression, to 30 cents an hour. This represents a reduction of 35 per cent from February, 1920, to September, 1921. The price of steel billets in February, 1920, was $60 a ton; in May, 1921, the price was $37 a ton; and on the first day of September, 1921, the price was set at $29 a ton, down 52 per cent in 19 months.[1] The low

---

[1] *Survey of Current Business*, January, 1922, pp. 11 and 43.

point in steel prices and wage rates in the Steel Corporation coincided almost exactly with the beginning of recovery from that depression; and following almost immediately upon the last cut in prices and wage rates, employment in the Steel Corporation began to increase.

By 1924, Steel's wages had risen from the depression low of 30 cents an hour to 50 cents (incidentally showing that a reduction of wage rates is not necessarily even semi-permanent). This rate was continued until September, 1931, when a 10 per cent reduction was put into effect, bringing the hourly rate to a point but 1 cent less than the 1920 peak of 46 cents, and still 50 per cent higher than the rate in effect in September, 1921. This reduction, two full years after the onset of the Great Depression, was the only one effected by the Steel Corporation; and since the inauguration of the New Deal, wage rates have actually risen above the 1929 peak. The price of steel billets, in contrast with the 1920–1921 experience, averaged $32.67 a ton for 1929 and $26.52 a ton for 1932. This represents a decline of 18 per cent in three years, and is below the 1921 price, but it is approximately 30 per cent above the price of steel billets in 1914.

Herein is found one of the foremost explanations why construction activity has been around 30 per cent of the 1923 average, why the railroads have not been buying steel rails, why the production of freight cars declined 99½ per cent during the depression, and why the index of machine tool production stood at 13 in February of 1933 as contrasted with 336 in February of 1929. How much less hope is there for any other than an evanescent recovery in the face of a situation in which wage rates in the steel industry are higher in 1936 than in 1929 and the new prices are also above the 1929 level! Of what use is governmental insurance of housing construction when a compilation of the Dow Service Daily Building Reports of New York show that a residence which cost $5,000 before the depression and whose cost had finally fallen to $2,560 in 1933, had its cost back to $4,675 in 1934, due to "the bulk effect of the codes"; [1] and most of the building code prices and wage rates are still being maintained.

### EXPANSION OF BANK CREDIT, EXPANSION OF BUSINESS—A QUESTION OF ORDER

A further step on the road to recovery involves a larger use of business credit. If a condition of equilibrium can again be attained, through the process of reducing the proportion of the national dividend now going to labor (which is simply too high a proportion to permit the employment of *all* labor) in favor of capital, so that the anticipated rate of return to capital is once more equal to or above the market rate, there will again emerge that possibility of profit which is necessary to new investment activity. If and when new investment activity promises a profit, the situation in the capital market will alter: new bond issues to finance new construction can be floated more readily, and the current supply of real savings will be translated into new capital equipment, instead of being hoarded, or piling up as excess reserves in the banking system, or going into Government securities in a search for liquidity, or being used to finance a speculative stock exchange boom in old securities. That is to say, current savings and idle or hoarded bank deposits will be used to purchase new issues, and the injection of these bank deposits into the system *via* the investment and capital markets in the form of actively circulating reproductive credit will provide the necessary means to finance the new construction and capital-goods production. Furthermore, banks will again become purchasers of corporate issues instead of Government bonds, thereby providing additional new monetary purchasing power to corporate users thereof. The greater general activity fostered by greater production in the durable goods industries will also tend to call forth a greater amount of commercial credit in the form of working capital, and recovery should proceed along better balanced lines. [2]

---

[1] The National City Bank *Letter*, May, 1934, p. 72.

[2] " * * * it is not difficult to see further that once given the emergence of profits to the average entrepreneur, a series of repercussions in the field of credit-creation

In connection with this question of the timing of credit-creation the writers' recommendation differs from the widely held view that we should lift ourselves from depression by an inflationistic price-raising procedure (as we are now doing)—that bank credit should first expand and that production will then follow.  There is no quarrel regarding the desirability of higher prices for some classes of goods, but there is disagreement with the view which holds that monetary and credit manipulation *alone* will suffice to cure the unbalances left over from the depression.  Recovery is always accompanied by increasing prices in many lines because of the greater demand engendered by increased employment, and there is no objection to such a rise of prices.  But there is nothing inconsistent in holding that such a natural price rise is desirable coincidentally with rejection of the idea that the rise in prices should come first, brought about solely by artificial, inflationistic measures, regardless of what happens to employment.  An inflationary policy aimed at lifting the level of prices to the so-called 1926 level, or *any* particular level, but without correcting fundamental disequilibria, is undesirable and provocative of subsequent disaster.

A "NATURAL," AS OPPOSED TO A FORCED, RISE IN PRICES

There is a highly important distinction to be made between a rise in prices which comes about because business men expand their production and use additional bank credit in the process, and those price increases which take place in anticipation of inflation or as a result of positive inflationistic action irrespective of whether or not the errors of the past period of inflation have been corrected.  In other words,

are likely to take place, which will remove the danger (if any) that the expansion of production and employment will be checked by insufficiency of purchasing power. For entrepreneurs are more willing to borrow, and bankers more willing to lend, in a period when profits are emerging than in a period when industry as a whole is sustaining losses. It may be argued, therefore, that the adjustment of costs to prices is the necessary preliminary to the inception of monetary processes which will initiate an upward movement of prices, and thus assist such adjustment in those portions of the field of production where it has not already taken place." Gregory, T. E., *Gold, Unemployment and Capitalism*, p. 40.

what may be called a natural rise of prices, induced by the greater demands for goods that result from the employment of a greater number of workmen, is quite different from a price rise engineered entirely by forced expansion of bank credit, devaluation delusions, "doing something for silver," or other inflationistic measures. As a matter of fact we have witnessed for four years and more a policy of deficit borrowing which has forced Government bonds on the banks and has created new credits to such an extent that the demand deposits of the member banks of the Federal Reserve System are now higher than they were in 1929 ($16,324 million on June 29, 1929, $19,161 million on March 4, 1936); and for almost five years we have experienced excessively low rates of interest for short-term capital coincidentally with unprecedented excess reserves in the banking system; both conditions indicate that the basic immediate need is not for more credit, but rather that conditions in the investment market are still such that extensive long-term investment is not being made.[1]

The view of the writers is, then, that the emissions of bank credit should follow, not precede, a restoration of equilibrium which as yet has not been achieved. If the situation is regarded apart from political and other incidental considerations, it would even appear preferable that recovery should be attained without resorting to any further expansion of bank credit. If the necessary new investment activity could be financed by current real savings and by the utilization of idle funds now in the banking system awaiting investment, the possibility of another inordinate boom would be mitigated. The total volume of bank deposits now in

[1] "Clearly a mere offer of cheap money does not suffice; banks at times of depression may go on offering cheap money for months or even years together before any recovery happens." Beveridge, W. H., *Unemployment: A Problem of Industry*, p. 331; and see Robertson, D. H., *Banking Policy and the Price Level*, p. 81: " * * * while there is always *some* rate of money interest which will check an eager borrower, there may be *no* rate of money interest in excess of zero which will stimulate an unwilling one"; also see p. 79, *ibid.*: " * * * those theorists are right who have found the cause of 'crises' in a 'deficiency of capital.' But what is deficient is not *money*, otherwise the situation could be cured, as all experience shows it cannot, by continued inflation."

existence is in excess of the 1920 total ($51,335 millions of deposits [exclusive of interbank deposits] on June 30, 1936, as against $37,721 million in June, 1920), yet the price level and the cost of living are both below the levels prevailing in 1920–1921. Between December 30, 1933, and December 31, 1935, total deposits (exclusive of interbank deposits) increased by $10,459 million, or at the rate of $100 million a week.[1] What is to be desired is a greater *use* of bank credit now in existence rather than a greater absolute volume of credit. The present volume of bank credit or bank deposits conceivably might be doubled or tripled, but if this resulted only in piling up deposit balances in the banks there would not necessarily ensue any permanently stimulating effect upon prices or the volume of production and trade. Indeed, the very existence of the present huge excess reserves in the banking system, together with the current relatively low deposits turnover, indicate that business men and bankers do not consider conditions propitious for a further expansion of bank credit. Some of these newly created bank deposits undoubtedly represent hoarded monetary savings; and if they do, so long as the existing imbalances in the capital-goods industries continue, employment in those industries will not increase materially. What is necessary is a revival of activity in the new-issues market, a greater use of these unused bank balances to purchase corporate new issues, thereby stimulating new investment activity.

The crux of the argument here developed at length is neatly summed up in a single paragraph of Mr. R. H. Brand's Addendum to the Macmillan Report (p. 211):

> As a result of the great fall of prices without an equivalent reduction of costs, production all over the world is resulting in losses instead of profits. It is sometimes argued that a reduction of costs (in particular wage costs) will do nothing to alter this

[1] "As measured by the volume of purchasing power in the form of demand deposits in our banks, we recently have been inflating at an average weekly rate some six times as great as we did in the commodity price inflation of 1914–1920 and in the stock price inflation of 1921–1929." Ralph West Robey, "Fiscal Policy and Credit Control," *Proceedings of the Academy of Political Science* (May, 1936), Vol. XVII, No. 1, p. 12.

situation, because the reduction of costs is a reduction of incomes, and involves therefore a destruction of purchasing power. But costs do not represent the whole of the incomes derived from production and still less do wage costs. These incomes include *profits*, and it is upon profits being normal that the whole activity of private enterprise depends. The first impact of a reduction of costs is felt in an increase of profits or a substitution of profits for losses. A re-distribution of the present proceeds of industry so that more of the proceeds would accrue to the shareholder and entrepreneur would not reduce the existing volume of purchasing power, but would induce entrepreneurs, by additional orders for raw material, plant and labour, to expand the volume of employment and thus should lead rather to an increase than a decrease of purchasing power. So long as enterprise promises a loss rather than a profit, no one will borrow and the normal process by which money is generated through the lending operations of the banks is interrupted. But a reduction of costs would alter the outlook, borrowers would come forward and money would become available to pay the additional incomes arising from the additional production.

## The Price Level and the Debt Level

One other question relating to the matter of prices and costs merits separate consideration. It is argued by those who hold that it is necessary to raise prices to the 1929 level (or the 1926 level) that there must be an adjustment of the price level to the debt level: that at the lower level of prices the debt burden constitutes too large a charge upon the national income and results in inequity between debtor and creditor. That is to say, the view is held in many quarters that an adjustment by means of a fall of costs rather than by means of a rise of prices is objectionable because it would still leave the debt burden too high in terms of prices. But if, by an adjustment of costs and prices, there results increasing employment and enhanced output, the real burden represented by debt charges upon output as a whole becomes smaller. A burden of fixed debt charges which, in consequence of a low level of output, constitutes a third of the national dividend, becomes, when output is doubled, only a sixth of that dividend (assuming new debts would not be created as fast as production expanded, and also disregarding entirely the alleviation of the debt burden which would come from a natural rise of prices accompanying an increase of productive output).

Secondly, there is no proof that the whole of the existing burden of debt was created at the high level of prices prevailing from, say, 1927 to 1929. It seems probable, rather, that the price level now prevailing would more accurately represent the average at which the bulk of existing indebtedness was contracted. And finally, it must be borne in mind that the refunding of old debt obligations (which has been proceeding during 1935–1936 at a tremendously accelerated rate) during a period of low interest rates will serve to reduce progressively the burdensomeness of the debt overhead. All in all, it would seem that the debt-burden bugaboo is less terrorizing and much less significant than many persons have believed it to be.

## CONCLUSION

It will be objected, perhaps, that the foregoing recommendations for recovery are more easily prescribed than carried out. Nevertheless, despite the dangers attendant upon prediction in economic affairs which are so largely influenced by political considerations and actions, it seems a safe enough assertion that unless certain wage rates and certain prices are reduced, unless there be restored a more "economic" balance between costs and prices, we must look forward to a long period such as that referred to by Sir William Beveridge, the continuance in this country of a substantial volume of unemployment which will in itself be proof that the price being asked for labor as wages is too high for the conditions of the market. For, "It is a well-known generalisation of Economics that a wage which is held above the equilibrium level necessarily involves unemployment * * * . The history of England since the War is one long vindication of its accuracy." [1]  May it be hoped that the history of the United States after 1929 will not longer continue to be a further vindication of it.

[1] Robbins, Lionel, *An Essay on the Nature and Significance of Economic Science* (London: Macmillan & Company, 1935), p. 146.

# BIBLIOGRAPHY

## LIST OF ABBREVIATIONS USED

| | |
|---|---|
| *A.E.R.* | The American Economic Review. |
| *Annals.* | The Annals of the American Academy of Political and Social Science. |
| *Ec.* | Economica. |
| *E.J.* | The Economic Journal. |
| *Econ.* | Econometrica. |
| *I.L.R.* | International Labour Review. |
| *J.A.S.A.* | The Journal of the American Statistical Association. |
| *J.I.B.* | The Journal of the Institute of Bankers. |
| *J.P.E.* | The Journal of Political Economy. |
| *Proc. Acad. Pol. Sci.* | The Proceedings of the Academy of Political Science. |
| *Q.J.E.* | The Quarterly Journal of Economics. |
| *R.E.S.* | The Review of Economic Statistics. |
| *S.K.Q.R.* | Skandinaviska Kreditaktiebolaget Quarterly Report. |
| *Index.* | Svenska Handelsbanken Index. |

# BIBLIOGRAPHY

## I. OFFICIAL PUBLICATIONS

UNITED STATES:

Commission of Gold and Silver Inquiry. United States Senate. *European Currency and Finance.* Serial 9, Vol. I, 1925.

69 Cong., 1 Sess. *Stabilization.* Hearings on H.R. 7895, Committee on Banking and Currency, 1927.

70 Cong., 1 Sess. *Brokers' Loans.* Hearings on Sen. Res. 113, Committee on Banking and Currency, 1928.

70 Cong., 1 Sess. *Stabilization.* Hearings on H.R. 11806, Committee on Banking and Currency, 1928.

70 Cong., 3 Sess. *Operation of the National and Federal Reserve Banking Systems.* Hearings on Sen. Res. 71, Committee on Banking and Currency, 1931.

72 Cong., 1 Sess. *Stabilization of Commodity Prices.* Hearings on H.R. 10517, Committee on Banking and Currency, 1932.

GREAT BRITAIN:

*Final Report of the Royal Commission Appointed to Inquire into the Depression of Trade and Industry. Cmd.* 4893, 1887.

*First Interim Report of the Committee on Currency and Foreign Exchanges after the War.* (The Cunliffe Report.) *Cmd.* 9182, 1918.

*Report of the Committee on Finance and Industry.* (The Macmillan Report.) *Cmd.* 3897, 1931.

LEAGUE OF NATIONS:

*Currencies after the War.* A survey of conditions in various countries. London, 1920.

*Commercial Banks, 1925–1933.* Pub. 2. A. 5, Geneva, 1934.

*Memorandum on Commercial Banks, 1913–1929.* Pub. 2. A. 26, Geneva, 1930.

*Course and Phases of the World Economic Depression.* Pub. 2. A. 21, Geneva, 1931.

*Interim Report of the Gold Delegation of the Financial Committee.* Pub. 2. A. 26, Geneva, 1930.

*Second Interim Report of the Gold Delegation of the Financial Committee.* Pub. 2. A. 2, Geneva, 1931.

*Report of the Gold Delegation of the Financial Committee.* Pub. 2. A. 12, Geneva, 1932.

*Selected Documents Submitted to the Gold Delegation of the Financial Committee.* Pub. 2. A. 34, Geneva, 1930.

*Selected Documents on the Distribution of Gold Submitted to the Gold Delegation of the Financial Committee.* Pub. 2. A. 7, Geneva, 1931.

*World Economic Survey, 1931/1932* (1932/1933, 1933/1934). Geneva, 1932 (1933, 1934).

*World Production and Prices, 1925–1932.* Pub. 2. A. 12, Geneva, 1933.

## II. BOOKS

ADAMS, A. B., *Economics of Business Cycles.* McGraw-Hill Book Co., New York, 1925.
*Our Economic Revolution.* University of Oklahoma Press, Norman, 1933.
*Profits, Progress and Prosperity.* McGraw-Hill Book Co., New York, 1927.
*The Trend of Business, 1922–1932.* Harper & Bros., New York, 1932.

ÅKERMANN, JOHAN, *Economic Forecast and Reality, 1928–1932.* Svenska Bokhandeln, Stockholm, 1932.
*Economic Progress and Economic Crises.* Macmillan & Co., London, 1932.
*Some Lessons of the World Depression.* Nordiska Bokhandeln, Stockholm, 1931.

ALDRICH, WINTHROP W., *The Causes of the Present Depression and Possible Remedies.* Chase National Bank, New York, 1933.

ANGELL, J. W., *The Theory of International Prices.* Harvard University Press, Cambridge, 1926.

AYRES, LEONARD P., *The Chief Causes of This and Other Depressions.* Cleveland Trust Company, Cleveland, 1935.
*The Economics of Recovery.* The Macmillan Co., New York, 1933.

BELLERBY, J. R., *Monetary Stability.* The Macmillan Co., New York, 1925.
*The Control of Credit.* P. S. King & Son, London, 1923.

BERRIDGE, W. A., *Purchasing Power of the Consumer.* A. W. Shaw & Co., Chicago and New York, 1925.

BEVERIDGE, SIR W. H., *Causes and Cures of Unemployment.* Longmans, Green & Co., London, 1931.
*Unemployment: A Problem of Industry (1909 and 1930).* Longmans, Green & Co., New York, 1931.

BOGEN, JULES I., and NADLER, MARCUS, *The Banking Crisis: The End of an Epoch.* Dodd, Mead & Co., New York, 1933.

BROWN, HARRIS, SCHUMPETER, et al., *The Economics of the Recovery Program*. McGraw-Hill Book Co., New York, 1934.

BURGESS, W. RANDOLPH, *The Reserve Banks and the Money Markets*. Harper & Bros., New York, 1927.

BURNS, A. F., *Production Trends in the United States Since 1870*. National Bureau of Economic Research, New York, 1934.

BURTON, T. E., *Financial Crises*. D. Appleton & Co., New York, 1903.

CASSEL, GUSTAV, *Post-War Monetary Stabilization*. Columbia University Press, New York, 1928.
*The Crisis in the World's Monetary System*. Oxford University Press, New York, 1932.
*The Theory of Social Economy*. Harcourt, Brace & Co., New York, 1932, 2nd ed.

CLARK, J. M., *Strategic Factors in Business Cycles*. National Bureau of Economic Research, New York, 1934.
*Studies in the Economics of Overhead Costs*. University of Chicago Press, Chicago, 1924.

CLAY, HENRY, *The Post-War Unemployment Problem*. Macmillan & Co., London, 1929.

COLE, G. D. H. (ED.), *Studies in Capital and Investment*. V. Gollancz, London, 1935.
*What Everybody Wants to Know About Money*. A. Knopf, New York, 1933.

CURRIE, LAUCHLIN, *The Supply and Control of Money in the United States*. Harvard University Press, Cambridge, 1935.

DOUGLAS, PAUL H., *Controlling Depressions*. W. W. Norton & Co., New York, 1935.

DUNKMAN, W. E., *Qualitative Credit Control*. Columbia University Press, New York, 1933.

DURBIN, E. F. M., *Purchasing Power and Trade Depression*. J. Cape, London, 1933.
*The Problem of Credit Policy*. John Wiley & Sons, New York, 1935.

EDIE, L. D., *Money, Bank Credit and Prices*. Harper & Bros., New York, 1928.
*The Banks and Prosperity*. Harper & Bros., New York, 1931.
*The Stabilization of Business*. The Macmillan Co., New York, 1923.
"The Future of the Gold Standard." In *Gold and Monetary Stabilization*. Chicago University Press, Chicago, 1932.

EINZIG, P., *The World Economic Crisis, 1929–1931*. Macmillan & Co., London, 1931.
*World Finance, 1914–1935*. The Macmillan Co., New York, 1935.

ELLIS, HOWARD S., *German Monetary Theory, 1905–1933.* Harvard University Press, Cambridge, 1934.

ELY, R. T., *Hard Times: The Way In and the Way Out.* The Macmillan Co., New York, 1931.

FISHER, IRVING, *Booms and Depressions: Some First Principles.* Adelphi Co., New York, 1932.
*Purchasing Power of Money.* The Macmillan Co., New York, 1913.
*Stable Money: A History of the Movement.* Adelphi Co., New York, 1934.
*Stabilizing the Dollar.* The Macmillan Co., New York, 1920.
*The Rate of Interest.* The Macmillan Co., New York, 1907.
*The Theory of Interest.* The Macmillan Co., New York, 1931.

FOSTER, W. T., and CATCHINGS, W., *Money.* Houghton Mifflin Co., Boston and New York, 1923.
*Profits.* Houghton Mifflin Co., Boston and New York, 1925.

FRASER, H. F., *Great Britain and the Gold Standard.* Macmillan & Co., London, 1933.

GAYER, A. D., *Monetary Policy and Economic Stabilization.* The Macmillan Co., New York, 1935.

GOLDSCHMIDT, R. W., *The Changing Structure of American Banking.* Geo. Routledge & Sons, London, 1933.

GRAVES, L. M., *The Great Depression and Beyond.* Brookmire Economic Service, New York, 1932.

GREGORY, T. E., *Foreign Exchange Before, During, and After the War.* Oxford University Press, New York, 1925, 3rd ed.
*Gold, Unemployment and Capitalism.* P. S. King & Son, London, 1933.
*The Gold Standard and Its Future.* Dutton & Co., New York, 1935, 3rd ed.

HABERLER, GOTTFRIED, "Money and the Business Cycle" in *Gold and Monetary Stabilization.* University of Chicago Press, Chicago, 1932.

HANSEN, A. H., *Business Cycle Theory: Its Development and Present Status.* Ginn & Co., Boston and New York, 1927.
*Cycles of Prosperity and Depression.* University of Wisconsin Press, Madison, 1921.
*Economic Stabilization in an Unbalanced World.* Houghton Mifflin Co., Boston and New York, 1932.

HARDY, C. O., *Credit Policies of the Federal Reserve System.* The Brookings Institution, Washington, 1932.
*The Warren-Pearson Price Theory.* The Brookings Institution, Washington, 1935.

HARRIS, S. E., *Twenty Years of Federal Reserve Policy*. Including an Extended Discussion of the Monetary Crisis, 1927–1933. Harvard University Press, Cambridge, 1933.

HARWOOD, E. C., *Cause and Control of the Business Cycle*. Financial Publishing Co., Boston, 1932.

HAWTREY, R. G., *Currency and Credit*. Longmans, Green & Co., New York, 1919.
*Good and Bad Trade*. Constable & Co., London, 1913.
*Monetary Reconstruction*. Longmans, Green & Co., New York, 1923.
*The Art of Central Banking*. Longmans, Green & Co., New York, 1932.
*The Gold Standard in Theory and Practice*. Longmans, Green & Co., New York, 1933, 3rd ed.
*Trade and Credit*. Longmans, Green & Co., New York, 1928.
*Trade Depression and the Way Out*. Longmans, Green & Co., New York, 1933.

HAYEK, F. A., *Monetary Theory and the Trade Cycle*. Harcourt, Brace & Co., New York, 1933.
*Prices and Production*. Geo. Routledge & Sons, London, 1935, 2nd ed.

HOBSON, J. A., *The Economics of Unemployment*. Allen & Unwin, London, 1922.
*The Industrial System*. Longmans, Green & Co., London, 1909.

HOLLANDER, J. H., *Want and Plenty*. Houghton Mifflin Co., Boston and New York, 1932.
*War Borrowing*. The Macmillan Co., New York, 1919.

HUBBARD, J. B., *The Banks, the Budget and Business*. The Macmillan Co., New York, 1934.

HULL, G. H., *Industrial Depressions*. F. A. Stokes & Co., New York, 1911.

ISLES, K. S., *Wages Policy and the Price Level*. P. S. King & Son, London, 1934.

JOHANNSEN, N., *A Neglected Point in Connection with Crises*. Bankers' Publishing Co., New York, 1908.
*Business Depressions, Their Cause*. Published by the Author, Stapleton, New York, 1925.

KEMMERER, E. W., *Kemmerer on Money*. The John C. Winston Co., Philadelphia and Chicago, 1934, 2nd ed.

KEYNES, J. M., "An Economic Analysis of Unemployment." In *Unemployment as a World-Problem*. University of Chicago Press, Chicago, 1931.
*The General Theory of Employment Interest and Money*. Harcourt, Brace & Co., New York, 1936.
*A Treatise on Money*. Harcourt, Brace & Co., New York, 1930, 2 vols.

*Essays in Persuasion.* Macmillan & Co., London, 1931.

*Monetary Reform.* Harcourt, Brace & Co., New York, 1924.

*The Means to Prosperity.* Harcourt, Brace & Co., New York, 1933.

KJELLSTROM, E. T. H., *Managed Money: The Experience of Sweden.* Columbia University Press, New York, 1934.

KNIGHT, F. H., *Risk, Uncertainty and Profit.* Houghton Mifflin Co., Boston and New York, 1921.

KUZNETS, S., *Cyclical Fluctuations.* Greenberg, Inc., New York, 1926.

LAUGHLIN, J. L., *A New Exposition of Money, Credit and Prices.* University of Chicago Press, Chicago, 1931, 2 vols.

LAVINGTON, F., *The Trade Cycle.* P. S. King & Son, London, 1922.

LAWRENCE, J. S., *The Stabilization of Prices.* The Macmillan Co., New York, 1928.

LAYTON, SIR W. T., *The Economic Situation of Great Britain.* London General Press, London, 1931.

LAYTON, SIR W. T., and CROWTHER, GEOFFREY, *An Introduction to the Study of Prices.* Macmillan & Co., London, 1935.

LLOYD, E. M. H., *Stabilization.* Allen & Unwin, London, 1923.

McCRACKEN, H. L., *Value Theory and Business Cycles.* Falcon Press, New York, 1933.

MACDONALD, WM., *The Menace of Recovery.* The Macmillan Co., New York, 1934.

MACFIE, A. L., *Theories of the Trade Cycle.* Macmillan & Co., London, 1934.

MACGREGOR, D. H., *Enterprise, Purpose and Profit.* Clarendon Press, Oxford, 1934.

MACIVER, R. M. (Chmn.), *Economic Reconstruction.* Columbia University Press, New York, 1934.

MARSHALL, ALFRED, *Money, Credit and Prices.* Macmillan & Co., London, 1923.

*Official Papers.* The Macmillan Co., New York, 1926.

*Principles of Economics.* Macmillan & Co., London, 1920, 8th ed.

MILL, JOHN STUART, *Principles of Political Economy.* (1848) Longmans, Green & Co., London, 1923, Ashley Edition.

MILLS, F. C., *Economic Tendencies in the United States.* National Bureau of Economic Research, New York, 1932.

*The Behavior of Prices.* National Bureau of Economic Research, New York, 1927.

VON MISES, L., *The Theory of Money and Credit.* Harcourt, Brace & Co., New York, 1935.

MITCHELL, W. C., *Business Cycles*. University of California Press, Berkeley, 1913.

*Business Cycles: The Problem and Its Setting*. National Bureau of Economic Research, New York, 1927.

(Chmn.) *Recent Social Trends in the United States*. Report of the President's Research Committee on Social Trends. McGraw-Hill Book Co., New York, 1933, 2 vols.

MITCHELL, W. C., and THORP, W. L., *Business Annals*. National Bureau of Economic Research, New York, 1926.

MLYNARSKI, FELIKS, *The Functioning of the Gold Standard*. A Memorandum Submitted to the Gold Delegation of the Financial Committee of the League of Nations. League of Nations, Geneva, Pub. F. 979. II. A. 25. 1931.

MOULTON, H. G., *Income and Economic Progress*. The Brookings Institution, Washington, 1935.

*The Formation of Capital*. The Brookings Institution, Washington, 1935.

PASLOVSKY, LEO, *Current Monetary Issues*. The Brookings Institution, Washington, 1933.

PATTERSON, E. M., *The World's Economic Dilemma*. McGraw-Hill Book Co., New York, 1930.

PHILLIPS, C. A., *Bank Credit*. The Macmillan Co., New York, 1920.

PIGOU, A. C., *Industrial Fluctuations*. Macmillan & Co., London, 1929, 2nd ed.

*The Economy and Finance of the War*. J. M. Dent & Sons, London, 1916.

*The Political Economy of War*. Macmillan & Co., London, 1921.

*The Theory of Unemployment*. Macmillan & Co., London, 1933.

*Unemployment*. Henry Holt & Co., New York, 1913.

PIQUET, HOWARD, *An Outline of New Deal Legislation*. McGraw-Hill Book Co., New York, 1934.

RANKIN, MARY T., *Monetary Opinions and Policy, 1924–1934*. P. S. King & Son, London, 1935.

REED, H. L., *Federal Reserve Policy, 1921–1930*. McGraw-Hill Book Co., New York, 1930.

*The Commodity Dollar*. Farrar and Rinehart, New York, 1934.

RICARDO, DAVID, *Principles of Political Economy and Taxation*. (1817) G. Bell & Sons, London, 1922, Gonner Edition.

RIEFLER, W. W., *Money Rates and Money Markets in the United States*. Harper & Bros., New York, 1930.

ROBBINS, LIONEL, *The Great Depression*. The Macmillan Co., New York, 1934.

ROBERTSON, D. H., *A Study of Industrial Fluctuations.* P. S. King & Son, London, 1915.

*Banking Policy and the Price Level.* P. S. King & Son, London, 1929, 2nd ed.

*Money.* Harcourt, Brace & Co., New York, 1929, 2nd ed.

ROBINSON, GEORGE BUCHAN, *Monetary Mischief.* Columbia University Press, New York, 1935.

ROGERS, J. H., *America Weighs Her Gold.* Yale University Press, New Haven, 1931.

SALTER, STAMP, KEYNES, et al., *The World's Economic Crisis and the Way of Escape.* The Century Co., New York, 1932.

SALTER, SIR ARTHUR, *Recovery: The Second Effort.* D. Appleton & Co., New York, 1931, rev. ed.

SHAW, W. A., *The Theory and Principles of Central Banking.* Isaac Pitman & Son, London, 1930.

SIMPSON, H. D., *Purchasing Power and Prosperity.* The Foundation Press, Chicago, 1936.

SLICHTER, SUMNER, *Towards Stability.* Henry Holt & Co., New York, 1934.

SPAHR, WALTER E., *The Federal Reserve System and the Control of Credit.* The Macmillan Co., New York, 1931.

*The Monetary Theories of Warren and Pearson.* Farrar and Rinehart, New York, 1934.

SPRAGUE, O. M. W., *Recovery and Common Sense.* Houghton Mifflin Co., Boston and New York, 1934.

STAFFORD, JACK, *Essays on Monetary Management.* P. S. King & Son, London, 1933.

STAMP, SIR JOSIAH, *Papers on Gold and the Price Level.* P. S. King & Son, London, 1931.

*The Financial Aftermath of War.* C. Scribner's Sons, New York, 1932.

TEBBUTT, A. R., *The Behavior of Consumption in Depression.* Harvard University Bureau of Business Research, Boston, 1933.

THORNTON, HENRY, *An Enquiry into the Nature and Effects of the Paper Credit of Great Britain.* Hatchard, London, 1802. Reprinted, McCulloch, J. R. (Ed.), *Scarce and Valuable Tracts on Paper Currency and Banking.* Published by Lord Overstone, London, 1857.

VINER, JACOB, "International Aspects of the Gold Standard." *In Gold and Monetary Stabilization.* University of Chicago Press, Chicago, 1932.

*Balanced Deflation, Inflation, or More Depression.* The Day and Hour Series of the University of Minnesota, No. 3, University of Minnesota Press, Minneapolis, 1933.

WAGEMAN, ERNST, *Economic Rhythm.* McGraw-Hill Book Co., New York, 1930.

WARREN, G. F., and PEARSON, F. A., *Gold and Prices.* John Wiley & Sons, New York, 1935.
*Prices.* John Wiley & Sons, New York, 1933.

WATKINS, L. L., *Bankers' Balances.* A. W. Shaw & Co., Chicago and New York, 1929.

WELLS, D. A., *Recent Economic Changes.* D. Appleton & Co., New York, 1889.

WERNETTE, J. P., *Money, Business and Prices.* P. S. King & Son, London, 1933.

WEYFORTH, W. O., *The Federal Reserve Board.* A Study of Federal Reserve Structure and Credit Control. Johns Hopkins Press, Baltimore, 1933.

WHITNEY, CAROLINE, *Experiments in Credit Control: The Federal Reserve System.* Columbia University Press, New York, 1934.

WICKSELL, KNUT, *Interest and Prices.* Macmillan & Co., London, 1936.
*Lectures on Political Economy,* Vol. I. The Macmillan Co., New York, 1934.
*Lectures on Political Economy,* Vol. II. Geo. Routledge & Sons, London, 1935.
*Über Wert, Kapital und Rente.* (1893) Reprinted as No. 15 of the Series of Reprints of Scarce Tracts in Economics. London School of Economics, 1933.

WITHERS, HARTLEY, *Bankers and Credit.* E. Nash & Grayson, London, 1924.
*International Finance.* Dutton & Co., New York, 1916.
*Our Money and the State.* J. Murray, London, 1917.
*The Business of Finance.* Dutton & Co., New York, 1918.
*War and Lombard Street.* J. Murray, London, 1917.
*War-Time Financial Problems.* J. Murray, London, 1919.

WILLIAMS, J. H., "Monetary Stabilization and the Gold Standard." In *Gold and Monetary Stabilization.* University of Chicago Press, Chicago, 1932.

WILLIS, H. P., "Federal Reserve Policy in Depression." In *Ibid.*

WILLIS, H. P., and CHAPMAN, J. M., *The Banking Situation: American Post-War Problems and Developments.* Columbia University Press, New York, 1934.

*The Economics of Inflation.* Columbia University Press, New York, 1935.

WILLIS, H. P., CHAPMAN, J. M., and ROBEY, R. W., *Contemporary Banking.* Harper & Bros., New York, 1933.

WRIGHT, QUINCY (ED.), *Gold and Monetary Stabilization.* Lectures on the Harris Foundation, 1932. University of Chicago Press, Chicago, 1932.

*Unemployment as a World-Problem.* Lectures on the Harris Foundation, 1931. University of Chicago Press, Chicago, 1931.

YOUNG, ALLYN A., *An Analysis of Bank Statistics for the United States.* Harvard University Press, Cambridge, 1928.

*Economic Problems, New and Old.* Houghton Mifflin Co., Boston and New York, 1927.


## III. ARTICLES IN JOURNALS AND PERIODICALS

ANDERSON, B. M., JR., "Money and Credit in Booms, Crises and Depressions." *The Annalist,* May 3, 1935, Vol. 45, No. 1163.

"An Analysis of the Money Market." *Chase Economic Bulletin,* June 4, 1928, Vol. 8, No. 1.

"Bank Expansion versus Savings." *Ibid.,* June 25, 1928, Vol. 8, No. 2.

"Bank Money and the Capital Supply." *Ibid.,* November 8, 1926, Vol. 6, No. 3.

"Cheap Money, Gold and Federal Reserve Policy." *Ibid.,* August 4, 1924, Vol. 4, No. 3.

"Commodity Price Stabilization a False Goal of Central Bank Policy." *Ibid.,* May 8, 1929, Vol. 9, No. 3.

"The Gold Standard versus 'A Managed Currency.'" *Ibid.,* March 23, 1925, Vol. 5, No. 1.

ANGELL, J. W., "Gold, Banks and the New Deal." *Political Science Quarterly,* December, 1934, Vol. XLIX, No. 4.

"Monetary Theory and Monetary Policy." *Q.J.E.,* February, 1925, Vol. XXXIX, No. 2.

"Money, Prices, and Production: Some Fundamental Concepts." *Ibid.,* November, 1933, Vol. XLVIII, No. 1.

"The 100 Per Cent Reserve Plan." *Ibid.,* November, 1935, Vol. L, No. 1.

ANGELL, J. W., and FICEK, K. F., "The Expansion of Bank Credit." *J.P.E.,* February and April, 1933, Vol. XLI, Nos. 1 and 2.

BALOGH, THOMAS, "Absorption of Credit by the Stock Exchange." *A.E.R.,* December, 1930, Vol. XX, No. 4.

BANCROFT, HUGH, "Fighting Economic Law—Wage Scales and Purchasing Power." *Barron's,* January 25, 1932, Vol. XII, No. 4.

"Wage Cuts a Cure for Depression." *Ibid.*, October 19, 1931, Vol. XI, No. 42.

BELL, J. W., "Recent Changes in the Character of Bank Liabilities and the Problem of Bank Reserves." *A.E.R. Supplement*, March, 1932, Vol. XXII, No. 1.

BICKERDIKE, C. F., "A Non-Monetary Cause of Fluctuations in Employment." *E.J.*, September, 1914, Vol. XXIV, No. 95.

"Individual and Social Interests in Relation to Saving." *Ibid.*, September, 1924, Vol. XXXIV, No. 135.

"Saving and the Monetary System." *Ibid.*, September, 1925, Vol. XXXV, No. 139.

BOBER, W. C., "Disparities in Price Levels the Root Cause of the Stagnation in Building." *The Annalist*, January 18, 1935, Vol. 45, No. 1148.

BODE, KARL, and HABERLER, GOTTFRIED, "Monetary Equilibrium and the Price Level in a Progressive Economy." *Ec.*, February, 1935, Vol. II (NS), No. 5.

BONN, M. J., "Some Causes and Some Problems of the Present Crisis." *J.I.B.*, October, 1931, Vol. LII, Part VII.

BOUNIATIAN, MENTOR, "Economic Depression and Its Causes." *I.L.R.*, July, 1934, Vol. XXX, No. 1.

"Technical Progress and Unemployment." *Ibid.*, March, 1933, Vol. XXVII, No. 3.

BRADFORD, F. A., "Social Aspects of Commercial Banking Theory." *A.E.R.*, June, 1933, Vol. XXIII, No. 2.

BURGESS, W. RANDOLPH, "Guides to Bank of Issue Policy." *Proc. Acad. Pol. Sci.*, November, 1929, Vol. XIII, No. 4.

"The Mechanism of Federal Reserve Policy." *American Bankers' Association Journal*, February, 1926, Vol. XVIII, No. 8.

"The Open Market Operations of the Federal Reserve System." *Acceptance Bulletin*, December, 1928, Vol. 10, No. 12.

BURNS, A. F., "The Quantity Theory and Price Stabilization." *A.E.R.*, December, 1929, Vol. XIX, No. 4.

CAILLOUX, JOSEPH, "Gold Movements and Price Fluctuations." *The Banker*, March, 1930, Vol. XIII, No. 50.

CANNAN, EDWIN, "Bank Deposits." *Ec.*, January, 1921, Vol. I, No. 1.

CARVER, T. N., "A Suggestion for a Theory of Industrial Depressions." *Q.J.E.*, May, 1903, Vol. XVII, No. 3.

CASSEL, GUSTAV, "Causes of the Fall of Prices." The London *Times'* "Annual Financial and Commercial Review," February 19, 1931.

"The Functions of Central Banks." Lloyds Bank *Monthly Review*, March, 1930, Vol. I (NS), No. 1.

"The Monetary Character of the Present Crisis." *J.I.B.*, June, 1931, Vol. LII, Part VI.

"The Rate of Interest, the Bank Rate, and the Stabilization of Prices." *Q.J.E.*, August, 1928, Vol. XLII, No. 4.

"Discount Policy and Stock Exchange Speculation." *S.K.Q.R.*, October, 1928.

"Disturbances in the World Economy Owing to Relative Changes in Prices." *Ibid.*, July, 1931.

"Does the Stock Exchange Absorb Capital?" *Ibid.*, April, 1929.

"Fallacies Regarding the Lack of Purchasing Power." *Ibid.*, April, 1935.

"Managed Currency." *Ibid.*, January, 1934.

"The Central Banks and the Control of the Supply of Money." *Ibid.*, October, 1930.

"The Connection Between the Discount Rate and the Level of Prices." *Ibid.*, October, 1927.

"The Dislocation of Prices and Its Consequences." *Ibid.*, April, 1927.

"The Influence of Bank Policy on the Level of Prices." *Ibid.*, April, 1931.

"The Influence of the United States on the World Price Level." *Ibid.*, January, 1928.

"The Problem of Business Cycles." *Ibid.*, January, 1933.

CHANDLER, H. A. E., "International Aspects of Federal Reserve Policy." *A.E.R. Supplement*, March, 1926, Vol. XVI, No. 1.

CLARK, J. M., "Business Acceleration and the Law of Demand: A Technical Factor in Economic Cycles." *J.P.E.*, March, 1917, Vol. 25, No. 3.

"Economics and the National Recovery Administration." *A.E.R.*, March, 1934, Vol. XXIV, No. 1.

CLAY, HENRY, "Some Aspects of the World Depression." *J.I.B.*, December, 1931, and January and February, 1932, Vol. LII, Part IX, and Vol. LIII, Parts I and II.

COMMONS, J. R., McCRACKEN, H. L., and ZEUCH, W. E., "Secular Trends and Business Cycles: A Classification of Theories." *R.E.S.*, October, 1922, Vol. IV, No. 4.

CONKLIN, W. D., "Building Costs in the Business Cycle." *J.P.E.*, June, 1935, Vol. XLIII, No. 3.

CRICK, F. W., "The Genesis of Bank Deposits." *Ec.*, June, 1927, Vol. VII, No. 20.

CUMBERLAND, W. W., "Economic Causes and Consequences of Stock Market Inflation and Deflation." *Proceedings of the Institute of Finance*, 2nd Session, 1931, Occidental College.

CURRIE, LAUCHLIN, "The Decline of the Commercial Loan." *Q.J.E.*, August, 1931, Vol. XLV, No. 4.
"The Failure of Monetary Policy to Prevent the Depression of 1929–1932." *J.P.E.*, April, 1934, Vol. XLII, No. 2.
"Treatment of Credit in Contemporary Monetary Theory." *Ibid.*, February, 1933, Vol. XLI, No. 1.

DANIELS, G. W., "Spending and Investing." *The Manchester School*, 1934, Vol. V, No. 2.

EADE, W. F., "Mathematical Analysis of Post-War Price Falls." *The Annalist*, August 26, 1932, Vol. 40, No. 1023.

EDIE, L. D., "Gold Economies and Stable Prices." *J.P.E.*, February, 1929, Vol. 37, No. 1.
"Post-War Fluctuations in Wholesale Commodity Prices." *A.E.R. Supplement*, March, 1928, Vol. XVIII, No. 1.
"The Relation of Credit to Commodity Prices." *Proceedings of the Institute of Finance*, 2nd Session, 1931, Occidental College.

EGLE, W., "Money and Production." *J.P.E.*, June, 1935, Vol. XLIII, No. 3.

EITEMAN, W. J., "Speculation, Bank Liquidity and Commodity Prices." *A.E.R.*, December, 1934, Vol. XXIV, No. 4.

ENGLAND, MINNIE T., "Analysis of the Crisis Cycle." *J.P.E.*, October, 1913, Vol. XXI, No. 8.
"Economic Crises." *Ibid.*, April, 1913, Vol. XXI, No. 4.

FETTER, FRANK A., "Interest Theories and Price Movements." *A.E.R. Supplement*, March, 1927, Vol. XVII, No. 1.

FICEK, K. F., "Some Aspects of the Monetary Situation: Problems of the Federal Reserve System." *The Annalist*, August 2, 1935, Vol. 46, No. 1176.

FISHER, A. G. B., "The Significance of Stable Prices in a Progressive Economy." *The Economic Record Supplement*, March, 1935, Vol. XI.
"Volume of Production and Volume of Money." *A.E.R.*, June, 1935, Vol. XXV, No. 2.

FISHER, IRVING, "A Statistical Relation Between Unemployment and Price Changes." *I.L.R.*, June, 1926, Vol. XIII, No. 6.
"Our Unstable Dollar and the So-Called Business Cycle." *J.A.S.A.*, June, 1925, Vol. XX, No. 149.

FRANK, L. K., "A Theory of Business Cycles." *Q.J.E.*, August, 1923, Vol. XXXVII, No. 4.

FRIDAY, DAVID, "The Formation of Capital: Measurement and Relation to Economic Activity." *A.E.R. Supplement*, March, 1933, Vol. XXIII, No. 1

GIBSON, A. H., "Why Gold Must Be Restored as the World Economic Controller." *The Bankers', Insurance Managers', and Agents' Magazine,* October and November, 1933, Vol. CXXXVI, Nos. 1075 and 1076.

GIFFORD, C. H. P., "The Concept of the Length and Period of Production." *E.J.,* December, 1933, Vol. XLIII, No. 172.

GOLDSTEIN, A., "Federal Reserve Aid to Foreign Banks." *Review of Economic Studies,* February, 1935, Vol. II, No. 2.

GREGORY, T. E., "Currency Stabilization and Business Recovery." *Mysore Economic Journal,* August and September, 1935, Vol. 21, Nos. 8 and 9.

"Expansionist Theories of Currency and Banking Policy." *J.I.B.,* January and February, 1935, Vol. LVI, Parts I and II.

"The Practical Working of the Federal Reserve Banking System of the United States." *Ibid.,* December, 1929, January and February, 1930, Vol. L, Part IX, and Vol. LI, Parts I and II.

"The Economic Significance of 'Gold Maldistribution.'" *The Manchester School,* 1931, Vol. II, No. 1.

"The Gold Problem." *World Trade,* July, 1929, Vol. I, No. 3.

"The Gold Standard: Phases in a Diverse History." The London *Times'* "Gold Supplement," June 20, 1933.

"The Price Level and the Rate of Interest." *Index,* May, 1930, Vol. V, No. 53.

"The Theory of Central Banking." Lloyds Bank *Monthly Review,* April, 1930, Vol. I (NS), No. 2.

"Twelve Months of American Dollar Policy." *Ec.,* May, 1934, Vol. I (NS), No. 2.

"What Can Central Banks Really Do?" *A.E.R.,* March, 1925, Vol. XV, No. 1.

HANEY, LEWIS H., "The Price System in Relation to Unemployment, Depression and Inflation." *The Annalist,* May 3, 1935, Vol. 45, No. 1163.

HANSEN, A. H., "Capital Goods and the Restoration of Purchasing Power." *Proc. Acad. Pol. Sci.,* April, 1934, Vol. XVI, No. 1.

"Certain Aspects of Demand in Relation to the Business Cycle." *A.E.R.,* March, 1924, Vol. XIV, No. 1.

"The Theory of Technological Progress and the Dislocation of Employment." *A.E.R. Supplement,* March, 1932, Vol. XXII, No. 1.

HANSEN, A. H., BODDY, F. M., and LANGUM, J. K., "Recent Trends in Business-Cycle Literature." *The Review of Economic Statistics,* May, 1936, Vol. XVIII, No. 2.

HANSEN, A. H., and TOUT, HERBERT, "Investment and Saving in Business Cycle Theory." *Econ.,* April, 1933, Vol. I, No. 2.

HARDY, C. O., "Gold and Credit." *Annals*, January, 1933, Vol. 165.
"Savings, Investment and the Control of Prices." *J.P.E.*, June, 1931, Vol. 39, No. 3.

HARRIS, S. E., "The Federal Reserve Act and Federal Reserve Policies." *Q.J.E.*, May, 1931, Vol. XLV, No. 3.

HARROD, R. F., "The Expansion of Credit in an Advancing Community." *Ec.*, August, 1934, Vol. I (NS), No. 3.

HART, A. G., "The 'Chicago Plan' of Banking Reform—A Proposal for Making Monetary Management Effective in the United States." *Review of Economic Studies*, February, 1935, Vol. II, No. 2.

HARTZELL, ELMER, "Time Deposits." *Harvard Business Review*, October, 1934, Vol. XIII, No. 1.

HARWOOD, E. C., "Deterioration of the American Bank Portfolio—A Ratio Analysis, 1920–1928." *The Annalist*, August 2, 1929, Vol. 34, No. 863.

HAWTREY, R. G., "Monetary Analysis and the Investment Market." *E.J.*, December, 1934, Vol. XLIV, No. 176.
"The Monetary Theory of the Trade Cycle and Its Statistical Test." *Q.J.E.*, May, 1927, Vol. XLI, No. 3.

HAYEK, F. A., "A Note on the Development of the Doctrine of 'Forced Saving.'" *Q.J.E.*, November, 1932, Vol. XLVII, No. 1.
"On the Relationship Between Investment and Output." *E.J.*, June, 1934, Vol. XLIV, No. 174.
"Capital and Industrial Fluctuations." *Econ.*, April, 1934, Vol. II, No. 2.
"Reflections on the Pure Theory of Money of Mr. J. M. Keynes." *Ec.*, August, 1931, and February, 1932, Vol. XI, No. 33, and Vol. XII, No. 35.
"The Maintenance of Capital." *Ibid.*, August, 1935, Vol. II (NS), No. 7.
"The 'Paradox' of Saving." *Ibid.*, May, 1931, Vol. XI, No. 32.

HILL, MARTIN, "The Period of Production and Industrial Fluctuations." *E.J.*, December, 1933, Vol. XLIII, No. 172.

HOLLANDER, J. H., "Do Government Loans Cause Inflation?" *Annals*, November, 1917, Vol. LXXV, Whole No. 164.

HOOVER, CALVIN B., "Brokers' Loans and Bank Deposits." *J.P.E.*, December, 1929, Vol. 37, No. 6.

HUTTON, GRAHAM, "Recovery and the Rate of Interest." Lloyds Bank *Monthly Review*, February, 1935, Vol. 6 (NS), No. 60.

JEVONS, H. S., "Banking and the Price Level." *The Manchester School*, 1931, Vol. II, No. 1.

KALDOR, NICHOLAS, "A Case Against Technical Progress?" *Ec.*, May, 1932, Vol. XII, No. 36.

KEMMERER, E. W., "Controlled Inflation." *A.E.R. Supplement*, March, 1934, Vol. XXIV, No. 1.

"Inflation." *A.E.R.*, June, 1918, Vol. VIII, No. 2.

KEYNES, J. M., "Member Bank Reserves in the United States." *E.J.*, March, 1932, Vol. XLII, No. 165.

"The Pure Theory of Money: A Reply to Dr. Hayek." *Ec.*, November, 1931, Vol. XI, No. 34.

KING, W. I., "Recent Monetary Experiments and Their Effect Upon the Theory of Money and Prices." *J.A.S.A.*, June, 1935, Vol. XXX, No. 190.

"Unemployment and Wage Rates." *The Annalist*, May 3, 1935, Vol. 45, No. 1163.

KISCH, C. H., "Central Banking: Recent Developments." *The Banker*, August, 1928, Vol. VII, No. 31.

"Recent Developments in Central Banking." *Ibid.*, May, 1930, Vol. XIV, No. 52.

KNIGHT, F. H., "Capital, Time and the Interest Rate." *Ec.*, August, 1934, Vol. I (NS), No. 3.

"Professor Hayek and the Theory of Investment." *E.J.*, March, 1935, Vol. XLV, No. 177.

KREPS, T. J., "Dividends, Interest, Profits, Wages, 1923–1935." *Q.J.E.*, August, 1935, Vol. XLIX, No. 4.

KUZNETS, S., "Monetary Business Cycle Theory in Germany." *J.P.E.*, April, 1930, Vol. 38, No. 2.

"Equilibrium Economics and Business Cycle Theory." *Q.J.E.*, May, 1930, Vol. XLIV, No. 3.

LEDERER, EMIL, "Technological Progress and Unemployment." *I.L.R.*, July, 1933, Vol. XXVIII, No. 1.

LEFFINGWELL, R. C., "Treasury Methods of Financing the War in Relation to Inflation." *Proc. Acad. Pol. Sci.*, June, 1920, Vol. IX, No. 1.

MACHLUP, FRITZ, "The Liquidity of Short-term Capital." *Ec.*, February, 1932, Vol. XII, No. 35.

MACKENROTH, G., "Period of Production, Durability, and the Rate of Interest in the Economic Equilibrium." *J.P.E.*, December, 1930, Vol. 38, No. 6.

MARTIN, P. W., "Overproduction and Underconsumption: A Remedy." *I.L.R.*, July, 1926, Vol. XIV, No. 1.

MEANS, G. C., "Price Inflexibility and the Requirements of a Stabilizing Monetary Policy." *J.A.S.A.*, June, 1935, Vol. XXX, No. 190.

MILLER, A. C., "Federal Reserve Policy." *A.E.R.*, June, 1921, Vol. XI, No. 2.

"Responsibility for Federal Reserve Policies: 1927–1929." *Ibid.*, September, 1935, Vol. XXV, No. 3.

"War Finance and Inflation." *Annals*, November, 1917, Vol. LXXV, Whole No. 164.

MILLS, F. C., "Price Aspects of Monetary Problems." *Proc. Acad. Pol. Sci.*, April, 1934, Vol. XVI, No. 1.

MITCHELL, W. C., "The International Pattern in Business Cycles." *Bulletin de l'Institut International de Statistique*, 1935, Vol. 28.

MITCHELL, W. F., "Interest Cost and the Business Cycle." *A.E.R.*, June, 1926, Vol. XVI, No. 2.

"Interest Rates as Factors in the Business Cycle." *A.E.R. Supplement*, March, 1928, Vol. XVIII, No. 1.

MONROE, A. E., "Investment and Saving: A Genetic Analysis." *Q.J.E.*, August, 1929, Vol. XLIII, No. 4.

MOULTON, H. G., "Commercial Banking and Capital Formation." *J.P.E.*, May, June, July, November, 1918, Vol. XXVI, Nos. 5, 6, 7, 9.

"The Relation of Credit and Prices to Business Recovery." *Proc. Acad. Pol. Sci.*, April, 1934, Vol. XVI, No. 1.

NEISSER, HANS, "General Overproduction: A Study of Say's Law of Markets." *J.P.E.*, August, 1934, Vol. XLII, No. 4.

"Monetary Expansion and the Structure of Production." *Social Research*, November, 1934, Vol. I, No. 4.

NORTON, J. E., "Bank Rate and the Money-Market in the United States." *E.J.*, December, 1921, Vol. XXXI, No. 124.

NOYES, C. REINOLD, "Stable Prices vs. Stable Exchanges." *Econ.*, April, 1935, Vol. III, No. 2.

"The Gold Inflation in the United States, 1921–1929." *A.E.R.*, June, 1930, Vol. XX, No. 2.

OAKWOOD, JOHN, "How High Wages Destroy Buying Power." *Barron's*, February 29, 1932, Vol. XII, No. 9.

"Wage Cuts and Economic Realities." *Ibid.*, June 29, 1931, Vol. XI, No. 26.

"Wage Proposals and Economic Realities." *Ibid.*, July 27, 1931, Vol. XI, No. 30.

OHLIN, BERTIL, "Central Bank Policy and Stock Exchange Prices." *Index*, July, 1928, No. 31.

"Gold Movements and Deflation in 1925–1927." *Ibid.*, December, 1927, No. 24.

"Gold Policy and the Distribution of the World's Gold." *Ibid.*, February, 1929. No. 38.

"The Inadequacy of Price Stabilization." *Ibid.*, December, 1933, Vol. VIII, No. 96.

"Knut Wicksell." *E.J.*, September, 1926, Vol. XXXVI, No. 143.

PAISH, SIR GEORGE, "Commercial Policy and the Gold Standard." *Proc. Acad. Pol. Sci.*, April, 1934, Vol. XVI, No. 1.

"Prices Should Not Be Stabilized—The Fundamental Aspects of the Trade Depression." *Barron's*, January 5, 1931, Vol. XI, No. 1.

PERSONS, C. E., "Credit Expansion, 1920 to 1929, and Its Lessons." *Q.J.E.*, November, 1930, Vol. XLV, No. 1.

PERSONS, WARREN M., "Bank Loans and the Business Cycle." *R.E.S.*, February, 1921, Vol. III, No. 2.

"Cyclical Fluctuations of the Ratio of Bank Loans to Deposits." *Ibid.*, October, 1924, Vol. VI, No. 4.

"The Basis for Credit Expansion under the Federal Reserve System." *Ibid.*, January, 1920, Vol. II, No. 1.

"Theories of Business Fluctuations." *Q.J.E.*, November, 1926, Vol. XLI, No. 1.

PHINNEY, J. T., "Gold Production and the Price Level: The Cassel Three Per Cent Estimate." *Q.J.E.*, August, 1933, Vol. XLVII, No. 4.

PIGOU, A. C., "Inflation." *E.J.*, December, 1917, Vol. XXVII, No. 108.

"The Monetary Theory of the Trade Cycle." *Ibid.*, June, 1929, Vol. XXXIX, No. 154.

PRIBRAM, KARL, "Equilibrium Concept and Business Cycle Statistics." *Bulletin de l'Institut International de Statistique*, 1935, Vol. 28.

RAMSBOTTOM, E. C., "The Course of Wage Rates in the United Kingdom, 1921-1934." *Journal of the Royal Statistical Society*, 1935, Vol. XCVIII, Part IV.

REED, H. L., "Federal Reserve Policy and Brokers' Loans." *A.E.R. Supplement*, March, 1929, Vol. XIX, No. 1.

"The Stabilization Doctrines of Carl Snyder." *Q.J.E.*, August, 1935, Vol. XLIX, No. 4.

RICHARDSON, J. H., "The Doctrine of High Wages." *I.L.R.*, December, 1929, Vol. XX, No. 6.

ROBBINS, LIONEL, "Consumption and the Trade Cycle." *Ec.*, November, 1932, Vol. XII, No. 38.

"Paper Systems: Some Disadvantages Considered." The London *Times'* "Gold Supplement," June 20, 1933.

"The Economic Crisis of 1930: The Gold Question." The London *Times'* "Annual Financial and Commercial Review," February 10, 1931.

"The Ottawa Resolutions on Finance and the Future of Monetary Policy." Lloyds Bank *Monthly Review*, October, 1932, Vol. 3 (NS), No. 32.

ROBERTS, GEORGE E., "Speculation, Gold and Bank Policy." *R.E.S.*, November, 1929, Vol. XI, No. 4.

"The Responsibility for Credit Inflation." *Proc. Acad. Pol. Sci.*, November, 1929, Vol. XIII, No. 4.

ROBERTSON, D. H., "A Note on the Theory of Money." *Ec.*, August, 1933, Vol. XIII, No. 41.

"Theories of Banking Policy." *Ibid.*, June, 1928, Vol. VIII, No. 23.

"Industrial Fluctuations and the Natural Rate of Interest." *E.J.*, December, 1934, Vol. XLIV, No. 176.

"Saving and Hoarding." *Ibid.*, September, 1933, Vol. XLIII, No. 171.

ROBEY, R. W., "The Progress of Inflation and 'Freezing' of Assets in the National Banks." *The Annalist*, February 27, 1931, Vol. 37, No. 945.

"Fiscal Policy and Credit Control." *Proc. Acad. Pol. Sci.*, May, 1936, Vol. XVII, No. 1.

RÖPKE, W., "Trends in German Business Cycle Theory." *E.J.*, September, 1933, Vol. XLIII, No. 171.

RORTY, MALCOLM, "The Necessity for Wage Reductions in the Present Crisis." *Proc. Acad. Pol. Sci.*, January, 1932, Vol. XIV, No. 4.

SCHUMPETER, J. A., "A Theorist's Comment on the Current Business Cycle." *J.A.S.A. Supplement*, March, 1935, Vol. XXX, No. 189A.

"The Explanation of the Business Cycle." *Ec.*, December, 1927, Vol. VII, No. 27.

"The Present World Depression: A Tentative Diagnosis." *A.E.R. Supplement*, March, 1931, Vol. XXI, No. 1.

SHACKLE, G. L. S., "Some Notes on Monetary Theories of the Trade Cycle." *Review of Economic Studies*, October, 1933, Vol. I, No. 1.

SHAFER, JOSEPH E., "An Explanation of the Business Cycle." *A.E.R.*, December, 1928, Vol. XVIII, No. 4.

SLICHTER, SUMNER, "The Economics of Public Works." *A.E.R. Supplement*, March, 1934, Vol. XXIV, No. 1.

SNYDER, CARL, "Commodity Prices versus The General Price Level." *A.E.R.*, September, 1934, Vol. XXIV, No. 3.

"On the Structure and Inertia of Prices." *Ibid.*, June, 1934, Vol. XXIV, No. 2.

"The Influence of the Interest Rate on the Business Cycle." *Ibid.*, December, 1925, Vol. XV, No. 4.

"The World-Wide Depression of 1930." *A.E.R. Supplement*, March, 1931, Vol. XXI. No. 1.

"The Problem of Monetary and Economic Stability." *Q.J.E.*, February, 1935, Vol. XLIX, No. 2.

"Over-Production, Excess Capacity and Business Cycles." *Proceedings of the Institute of Finance*, 2nd Session, 1931, Occidental College.

"New Measures of the Relations of Credit and Trade." *Proc. Acad. Pol. Sci.*, November, 1929, Vol. XIII, No. 4.

"Overproduction and Business Cycles." *Ibid.*, June, 1931, Vol. XIV, No. 3.

"Concerning Economic Disequilibria and Maladjustments." *Bulletin de l'Institut International de Statistique*, 1935, Vol. 28.

"The Debt Theory of Depressions." *Ibid.*, 1935, Vol. 28.

SOUTER, R. W., "Equilibrium Economics and Business Cycle Theory." *Q.J.E.*, November, 1930, Vol. XLV, No. 1.

SPAHR, WALTER E., "Currency Inflation: Its Nature and Implications." *A.E.R.*, June, 1934, Vol. XXIV, No. 2.

"Bank Failures in the United States." *A.E.R. Supplement*, March, 1932, Vol. XXII, No. 1.

SPRAGUE, O. M. W., "Price Stabilization." *A.E.R.*, March, 1929, Vol. XIX, No. 1.

"The Discount Policy of the Federal Reserve System." *Ibid.*, March, 1921, Vol. XI, No. 1.

"Major and Minor Trade Fluctuations." *Journal of the Royal Statistical Society*, 1931, Vol. XCIV, Part IV.

"The Relationship between Loans and Taxes in War Finance." *Annals*, November, 1917, Vol. LXXV, Whole No. 164.

STAFFORD, JACK, "Saving and Investment." *The Manchester School*, 1931, Vol. II, No. 1.

"The Equilibrium Rate of Interest." *E.J.*, June, 1935, Vol. XLV, No. 178.

"The Relation of Banking Technique to Economic Equilibrium." *Ibid.*, 1932, Vol. III, No. 2.

STRAKOSCH, SIR HENRY, "The Crisis: A Memorandum." Supplement to *The Economist* of January 9, 1932, Vol. CXIV, No. 4611.

THEISS, E., "Dynamics of Saving and Investment." *Econ.*, April, 1935, Vol. III, No. 2.

"Quantitative Theory of Industrial Fluctuations Caused by the Capitalistic Technique of Production." *J.P.E.*, June, 1933, Vol. XLI, No. 3.

TUCKER, R. S., "Price Fluctuations and the Gold Supply." *Ibid.*, August, 1934, Vol. XLII, No. 4.

WALKER, E. R., "Saving and Investment in Monetary Theory." *The Economic Record*, December, 1933, Vol. IX, No. 17.

"Structural Changes and Cyclical Variations." *The Economic Record Supplement*, March, 1935, Vol. XI.

WATKINS, G. P., "Economics of Saving." *A.E.R.*, March, 1933, Vol. XXIII, No. 1.

WATKINS, M. W., "Commercial Banking and Capital Formation." *J.P.E.*, July, 1919, Vol. XXVII, No. 7.

WHITAKER, A. C., "Federal Reserve Position and Policies." *A.E.R. Supplement*, March, 1930, Vol. XX, No. 1.

WICKSELL, KNUT, "The Influence of the Rate of Interest on Prices." *E.J.*, June, 1907, Vol. XVII, No. 66.

WILLIAMS, J. H., "The World's Economic Dilemma—Internal *versus* External Monetary Stabilization." *Proc. Acad. Pol. Sci.*, April, 1934, Vol. XVI, No. 1.

WILLIS, H. P., "The Probable Trend of Rate of Interest and Investment." *A.E.R. Supplement*, March, 1923, Vol. XIII, No. 1.

"The Failure of the Federal Reserve." *North American Review*, May, 1929, Vol. CCXXVII, No. 5.

"Who Caused the Panic of 1929?" *Ibid.*, February, 1930, Vol. CCXXIX, No. 2.

"American Banking and the Panic of 1929." *The Banker*, December, 1929, Vol. XII, No. 47.

"A Crisis in American Banking." *Ibid.*, November, 1929, Vol. XII, No. 46.

"A Turning Point in American Banking." *Ibid.*, December, 1928, Vol. VIII, No. 35.

"The Federal Reserve System and Inflation." *Proc. Acad. Pol. Sci.*, June, 1920, Vol. IX, No. 1.

"The Present Relationship between Credit and Prices." *Ibid.*, January, 1925, Vol. XI, No. 2.

WITHERS, HARTLEY, "Causes of the Panic." The London *Times'* "Annual Financial and Commercial Review," February 9, 1932.

WORKING, HOLBROOK, "Bank Deposits as a Forecaster of the General Price Level." *R.E.S.*, July, 1926, Vol. VIII, No. 3.

YOUNG, ALLYN A., "The Trend of Prices." *A.E.R. Supplement*, March, 1923, Vol. XIII, No. 1.

YOUNG, RALPH A., "The United States and Gold." *Annals*, January, 1933, Vol. 165.

## IV. OTHER PUBLICATIONS

*Availability of Bank Credit, The*, National Industrial Conference Board. New York, 1932.

*Banking Situation in the United States, The,* National Industrial Conference Board. New York, 1932.

*Business Cycles and Unemployment,* Report and Recommendations of a Committee of the President's Conference on Unemployment. McGraw-Hill Book Co., New York, 1923.

*Future of Monetary Policy, The,* A Publication of the Royal Institute of International Affairs. Oxford University Press, London, 1935.

*International Gold Problem, The: Collected Papers,* A Publication of the Royal Institute of International Affairs. Oxford University Press, New York, 1931.

*Monetary Policy and the Depression,* A Publication of the Royal Institute of International Affairs. Oxford University Press, New York, 1933.

*Recent Economic Changes in the United States,* Report of the Committee on Recent Economic Changes of the President's Conference on Unemployment. McGraw-Hill Book Co., New York, 1929, 2 vols.

*Recent Social Trends in the United States,* Report of the President's Research Committee on Social Trends. McGraw-Hill Book Co., New York, 1933, 2 vols.

*Social and Economic Reconstruction in the United States,* International Labour Office. Geneva, 1934.

DONALDSON, JOHN (ED.), *Gold: A World Problem.* The Academy of Political and Social Science, *The Annals,* January, 1933, Vol. 165.

MOON, PARKER T. (ED.), *Business, Speculation and Money.* Academy of Political Science, *Proceedings,* November, 1929, Vol. XIII, No. 4.

*Can Prices, Production and Employment Be Effectively Regulated? Ibid.,* January, 1932, Vol. XIV, No. 4.

*Depression and Revival. Ibid.,* June, 1931, Vol. XIV, No. 3.

*Inflation and High Prices. Ibid.,* June, 1920, Vol. IX, No. 1.

*The Crisis in World Finance and Trade. Ibid.,* May, 1932, Vol. XV, No. 1.

*Stabilizing Business. Ibid.,* July, 1927, Vol. XII, No. 3.

*Steps Toward Recovery. Ibid.,* January, 1933, Vol. XV, No. 2.

PATTERSON, E. M. (ED.), *Financing the War.* Academy of Political and Social Science, *The Annals,* November, 1917, Vol. LXXV, Whole No. 164.

# INDEX

Adams, A. B., 72, 219

Agriculture, 172

Åkermann, Johan, 64, 72, 124, 147, 219, 231

Anderson, B. M., 82, 95, 171

Anticipated profits, 131

Ayres, Leonard P., 35, 36, 158, 199, 234

Bank credit, extent of use, 21, relation to use of gold, 47, credit expansion and direct saving contrasted, 98–100, affected by rising reserve ratio of Federal Reserve Banks, 101–102, relation to stock market advance, 158, factor of velocity changes, 208, 210, order of business and credit expansion, 240

Bank crisis, 78

Bank failures, 168–170

Bank liquidity, 107–110

"Bank money," and natural-market interest rate disparity, 132, and recovery, 214

Bankers' banking, credit creation, 17

Banking policy, disturbing to saving, 77, and stable price level, 191–193

Banks, commercial, 25, member and non-member credit expansion, 29–33, purchase of government securities, 33, entanglement with depression, 167

Beveridge, W. H., 221, 232, 242, 245

Bickerdike, C. F., 75

Booms, 81, instability of, 112

Bradford, F. A., 79, 161

Brand, R. H., 243

Burgess, W. Randolph, 98, 181

Burns, A. R., 123

Business activity, swings, 128, origin of cycle, 173

Business cycle, theories of, 37–39, 57–58, 147, 151, 170–174

Capital funds and market rate of interest, 134

Capital goods, 73–76, oscillation, 120–122, indications of activity in, 122–126, shaken confidence in, 162, lower prices and wage rates, 236–240

Capital saving, absolute, 75, banking policy, 76–77, expansion and contraction, 79

Cassel, Gustav, 2, 3, 39, 51, 53, 63, 102, 121, 123, 128, 197

Catchings, W., 60, 206

Central banking, 25, relation to gold, 43, 46, explanation of cycle, 117–118, intensity of cycle, 139–140

Chapman, J. M., 82, 95

"Cheap credit," 113

Clark, J. M., 1, 3, 12, 117, 121, 126, 134, 138, 157, 177

Clay, Henry, 171

Cole, G. D. H., 116

"Coming boom," 211

Commercial loans, 105

Commons, J. R., 178, 193, 196

Conclusion, 244

Construction, pre-depression, 124–125, financing, 236

Consumption goods, 73–76, production of, 126–127

Corporate earnings and stock prices, 155–158

Cost reduction, 220–222

Credit control, rediscount rate and open market operations, 182–184, suggested guide, 202, means of, 210

Credit creation, purchase of investments, 17, 85, 133, "slack," 22–23, member bank expansion, 32

Credit expansion, relation to misapplication of capital, 67–68, factors underlying, 79–81, indirection of, 111, cessation of, 142–146

Credit growth, stabilized rate, 203–204, equilibration of investment and saving by, 207

Currency management, 181–182

Currie, Lauchlin, 189

Cycle theory and control policy, 195

Davenport, H. J., 63, 69
Debt level, 244
Deflation, 167
Demand loans, 167
Deposit expansion, 15–16
Deposits, time, 29, increase of, 47, 49, 82, 95–96, interest payments on, 100
Depression, causes, ultimate, 4, 35, immediate, 4, 35, 142, inevitability of, 35, popular and erroneous explanations of, 37–40, effects of stable price level, 177–178
Distribution of national dividend, 233–234
Dollar management, 179–181
Durbin, E. F. M., 116

Eade, W. F., 195
"Easy money," international effects, 197
Economic dislocation, by World War, 11–12, technological advances, 66, inherent forces, 119, frictions, 135
Economic equilibrium, 171, cost-price relationship, 219
Edie, L. D., 88, 181

Federal Reserve Board, cognizance of time deposit developments, 100–101, price level management, 176–177
Federal Reserve policy, war conditioning, 36, expansion of 'twenties, 102, stock market, 159, price stabilization, 196
Federal Reserve System, creation, 11, provisions of act, 27, notes, 28, time deposits, 29, operation of, 31, rising reserve ratio, 101–102
Fisher, A. G. B., 201, 204
Fisher, Irving, 39, 117
"Forced saving," 208
Forecasters' error, 149–150
Forecasting, 146
Foreign loans, 197
Foster, W. T., 60, 206
Fraser, H. F., 116, 190
"Freezing" prices, 201
Friday, David, 20, 21

Gold, value of money, 21, reserve function of, 28, crisis explanation, 37–38, Warren-Pearson contentions (analysis, 40–43, fallacy, 44), in central banks, 42–44, production and monetary stock of, 43–45, economizing by Federal Reserve System, 45, maldistribution, 51–53, reserves, 83–84, 87, reserves and liquidity, 110
Gold bullion standard, 49
Gold exchange standard, 48
Goldschmidt, R. W., 82
Gold standard, relation to prices, 38, conditions requisite to, 53–55, breakdown, 54
Gold Standard Act, 39
Governmental finance, borrowing, 15, bond sales to banks, 33, 214–216
Graham, F. D., 221
Gregory, T. E., 1, 38, 129, 204, 218, 234, 240

Haberler, G., 115, 116
Hamlin, C. S., 89
Hansen, A. H., 60, 75, 115, 116, 135
Hardy, C. O., 40, 52, 93, 129, 196
Harris, S. E., 179
Hartzell, Elmer, 98
Harwood, E. C., 79, 116, 195
Hawtrey, R. G., 21, 49, 115, 144, 206
Hayek, F. A., 17, 115, 116, 132, 139, 142, 146, 160, 177, 178, 184, 187, 191, 196, 202, 204
Hobson, J. A., 60
Hollander, Jacob, 16
"Homeless" funds, 54
Hull, G. H., 121

Income, impact of capital goods collapse, 164
Index numbers, 237
Industrial efficiency and falling prices, 206
Industry, 172
Inflation, defined, 13, extent of, 20, 82, forces underlying, 20, cause of, 23, investment credit, 81, initiating source, 84, facilitating factors, 91–92, effect of rediscounting, 95, nature of, 103, effects on bank liquidity, 107, measures of extent, 190, "relative," 193
Interest rates, oscillation of market and natural rates, 129–132, tend-

ency to equilibrate, 142, restoration of equilibrium, 232–234
Inventory inflation, 189
Investment, relation to bank credit expansion, 135, margins, 143, deflation, 160
Investment and saving disparity, 128
Iron and steel production, 123, "the barometer of trade," 122–124

Jay, Pierre, 179
Jevons, W. S., 121
Jordan, David F., 236

Kaldor, Nicholas, 65
Kemmerer, E. W., 13
Keynes, J. M., 34, 39, 115, 116, 117, 122, 124, 130, 131, 133, 134, 145, 162, 179, 203, 218
Key to employment and recovery, 234
Kitchin, D. A., 192
Kitchin, Joseph, 39
Knight, F. H., 63, 120, 129

Labor, income expenditure, 138, money wages and real wages, 223–226
Lauderdale, 60
Laughlin, J. L., 108, 109
Lawrence, J. S., 180
Leffingwell, R. C., 16
Lenin, 34
Lippmann, Walter, 237
Liquidity of banks, 107, liquidity and shiftability contrasted, 108, banking system, 109, influence of gold decline, 110
Loans and investments, 1914–1920, 31–33, 1921–1929, 103–105, 1928–1932, 169

McAdoo, William G., 19
Machlup, Fritz, 108
Maldistribution of income, 73
Malthus, 60, 133
Marshall, Alfred, 62, 63, 74, 129, 130, 191, 204, 206
Marx, Karl, 60
Maxwell, Arthur, 54
May, G. O., 166
Mill, John Stuart, 59
Miller, A. C., 86, 89, 90, 104, 180, 183, 184
Mises, Ludwig von, 55, 115, 116, 139

Mitchell, W. C., 21
Mlynarski, F., 48
Moulton, H. G., 64, 116

National Bank Act, reserve requirements, 29
National income, 165
Natural rate of interest, 129–130, 144
"Neutral money," 202
New Deal, 239
New Era, 159
Norris, G. W., 179, 180

Ohlin, Bertil, 198
Open market operations, defined, 26, significance, 88, relation to other policies of control, 89–90, relation to rediscount rate, 93, growth of time deposits, 95–99, effects, chronologically developed, 99
Opportunity profits, 144
Overinvestment, 68
Overproduction, defined, 61, apparent, 63, vs. ill-assorted production, 59
Oversaving, 74–75

Paish, George, 182
Palyi, Melchior, 45, 55
Pearson, F. A., 39, 40, 41, 42, 43, 44, 46, 47, 50
Phillips, C. A., 15, 17, 106
Pigou, A. C., 13, 16, 35, 122, 127, 223, 232
Price, war time rise, 22, 33, abnormality of post-war, 34, decline, 55, "key-log" of production, 61, stabilization, 147 (motivation of, 184)
Price level, post-war behavior, 175, fullness of post-war recession, 184, impact of technical progress, 186, artificial support, 193, collapse of, 200–201, objections to fall of, 204, relation to wage rates, 231, "natural" or forced rise, 241, relation to debt level, 244
Production, relation to demand, 62, structure of, 132, effect of stock market collapse, 160, and bank credit, 188, durable goods, 234
Purchasing power and equilibrium, 219, relation to wage rates, 225

Recovery program, 211–216, management aspects of, 212–214, "royal road," 216, "saving versus spending," 218

Rediscount rate, 92–94, member bank borrowing, 93

Reed, H. L., 183

Reserve banking, inherently inflationistic, 24–28

Reserves, surplus, 15–16, excess (dissemination through system, 25, and disruption of interest rates, 139), economized, 22, requirements reduced, 23–24, 92, legal, 24, reserve-deposit ratio, 27, exhaustion of, 47

Riefler, W. W., 133

Robbins, Lionel, 8, 37, 72, 116, 246

Roberts, G. E., 43, 171

Robertson, D. H., 5, 116, 117, 121, 145, 179, 186, 187, 192, 206, 242

Robey, R. W., 243

Rogers, J. H., 39

Roosevelt, F. D., 39

Röpke, W., 177

Say, 62, 70

"Second Industrial Revolution," 65

Security valuation and production activity, 161–162

"Shiftability," 108

Sismondi, 60

Slichter, Sumner, 71, 72, 224, 228

Snyder, Carl, 63, 64, 191, 197, 198, 204, 208

Spahr, W. E., 40

Sprague, O. M. W., 14, 16, 171, 218

Stamp, Josiah, 12, 14, 36, 117, 205

Standard of living and recovery, 220–222

Steiner, W. H., 133

Stock market, delay of crash, 150, boom and profits, 153, stimulation of boom, 153, effect on methods of financing, 158

Technical progress, 186

Technocracy, 63

Theories of business cycle, monetary, 37–39, underconsumption, 57 (variants of, 58), past cycle theories, 140–141, structural, 147, equilibrium, 151, 170–174

Thornton, Henry, 142

Tout, H., 75, 115, 116, 135

Underconsumption contention, 69, partial validity, 69, refutation, 70–73, recovery program acceptance, 215

Unemployment, 151, technological, 64, 65

Viner, Jacob, 225, 229

Wage rates and purchasing power, 222–226

Wage rates, depression and recovery, 229–232

Warburg, P. M., 106

War finance, banking relationship, 14, taxation, 14, effect on currency management, 199–200

Warren, G. F., 39, 40, 41, 42, 43, 44, 46, 47

Wells, D. A., 60, 61

Wholesale prices, 194

Wicksell, Knut, 115, 134, 202

Williams, John H., 102, 188

Willis, H. P., 82, 95

"Windfall profits," 203

Withers, Hartley, 14, 16, 17, 54

World War, financial dislocations, 11–12

Young, Allyn, 62, 141

Young, R. A., 54, 82

Mɪsᴇs Iɴsᴛɪᴛᴜᴛᴇ, founded in 1982, is a teaching and research center for the study of Austrian economics, libertarian and classical liberal political theory, and peaceful international relations. In support of the school of thought represented by Ludwig von Mises, Murray N. Rothbard, Henry Hazlitt, and F.A. Hayek, we publish books and journals, sponsor student and professional conferences, and provide online education. Mises.org is a vast resource of free material for anyone in the world interested in these ideas. For we seek a radical shift in the intellectual climate, away from statism and toward a private property order.

For more information, see Mises.org, write us at info@mises.org, or phone us at 1.800.OF.MISES.

Mises Institute
518 West Magnolia Avenue
Auburn, Alabama 36832

www.ingramcontent.com/pod-product-compliance
Lightning Source LLC
Chambersburg PA
CBHW060543200326
41521CB00007B/468